Campaign Finance Reform
and the Future of the Democratic Party

Campaign Finance Reform
and the
Future
of the
Democratic Party

Jerrold E. Schneider

ROUTLEDGE
New York and London

Published in 2002 by
Routledge
29 West 35th Street
New York, NY 10001

Published in Great Britain by
Routledge
11 New Fetter Lane
London EC4P 4EE

Copyright © 2002 by Routledge

Routledge is an imprint of the Taylor & Francis Group.

Printed in the United States of America on acid-free paper.

All rights reserved. No part of this book may be reprinted or reproduced or utilized in any form or by any electronic, mechanical, or other means, now known or hereafter invented, including photocopying and recording, or in any information storage or retrieval system without permission in writing from the publisher.

10 9 8 7 6 5 4 3 2 1

Library of Congress Cataloging-in-Publication Data

Schneider, Jerrold E.
   Campaign finance reform and the future of the Democratic Party / by Jerrold E. Schneider.
     p. cm.
   Includes bibliographical references and index.
   ISBN 0-415-93320-X — ISBN 0-415-93321-8
     1. Campaign funds — United States. 2. Campaign funds — Law and legislation — United States. 3. Democratic Party (U.S.) I. Title.
JK1991. S36 2002
324.2736—dc21   2001058883

To Katharine with love and gratitude

Contents

Acknowledgments ix

Chapter 1
INTRODUCTION 1

Chapter 2
WOULD CAMPAIGN REFORM WORK? 13

Chapter 3
THE DECLINE OF THE DEMOCRATIC PARTY 35

Chapter 4
WOULD CAMPAIGN REFORM YIELD ENOUGH MONEY
TO REFLOAT THE DEMOCRATS? 49

Chapter 5
ARE WEAK PARTIES INEVITABLE? 69

Chapter 6
NINE PARTY-UNIFYING FORCES 79

Chapter 7
ARE THE DEMOCRATS BIG SPENDERS OR BIG INVESTORS?
INEQUALITY AND PRODUCTIVITY 97

Chapter 8
PUBLIC SECTOR INVESTMENT 119

Chapter 9
CONCLUSIONS 139

Epilogue
IS CAMPAIGN REFORM POLITICALLY FEASIBLE? 147

Appendix
TWO PROMINENT CAMPAIGN REFORM PLANS 155

Notes 161

References 201

Name Index 209

Subject Index 213

Acknowledgments

I AM GRATEFUL TO THE SEVENTY DEMOCRATIC MEMBERS OF CONGRESS WHO granted interviews for this study, along with the many senior congressional staff who gave generously of their time. The insights gleaned from these interviews were crucial in guiding the development of the argument presented here. I also wish to thank then Congressman now Senator Tom Carper (D-Delaware) and his aid Jeff Bullock, a former student, for assistance. Of course none bear responsibility for the conclusions drawn here.

Though a good deal of time has since passed, three years at the Brookings Institution as a Research Fellow and Guest Scholar had a large influence on this study. I am especially indebted to James L. Sundquist, and several Brookings economists whose work influenced chapters seven and eight, notably Arthur M. Okun and Barry P. Bosworth. The approach to campaign finance reform used in this study flows from Okun's insights.

Among my colleagues in the Political Science Department at University of Delaware, I particularly wish to thank Marian Palley, Henry T. Reynolds, Leslie Goldstein, and James Soles. Among Delaware economists, my two sometime collaborators Kenneth Koford and Jeffrey Miller provided extraordinary stimulation and colleagueship. Laurence Seidman taught me key economic arguments, which affected my own argument.

Last but not least, Paul D. Stolley, M.D., contributed a great deal to this study at many levels, as did Theodore Kleinman Esq. John Schneider and Liese Schneider were a constant source of inspiration, and some solid criticism. Most of all, my wife Katharine shared my values and helped in so many ways that they cannot be enumerated.

Chapter 1

Introduction

Q. *Why stake your Presidential bid on a seemingly quixotic call for a campaign finance overhaul?*
A. Bill Bradley: It's the most important reform we could enact, as important as any in the twentieth century, with the exception of the expansion of voting rights in the 1960s. Money fundamentally distorts our democracy today. We live in a system of one person, one vote. But we all know some people have a lot more clout [due to campaign spending].

Q. *You really think reform has a shot?*
A. Bill Bradley: Once people realize that they're paying higher taxes because of the way we finance our political campaigns, we'll find broader support. For every $500,000 soft-dollar contribution, they need to . . . see if someone got a loophole or a regulatory ruling that cost the rest of us.[1]

THIS STUDY EXAMINES FOUR RELATED ISSUES. FIRST, IS IT POSSIBLE TO CONstruct a campaign finance law effective enough to prevent campaign contributors from buying legislation, enable legislators to more faithfully represent ordinary citizens, end the disproportionate influence of money in politics, and not crumble into loopholes? Second, is it possible to construct specific mechanisms for putting enough pressure on Congress to force it to enact an effective campaign finance law? Third, would an effective campaign finance law incentivize Democratic lawmakers to shift resources from vast federal waste to popular programs, and thereby reverse the decline in the Democrats' voter base? Fourth, would reallocating wasted resources to popular programs enable the United States to achieve key national economic goals—faster growth in productivity and a reversal in the growth of inequality?

The interaction among these four issues reflect recent changes in American politics and in the Democratic Party. Some time ago, the author was exposed to an insider's view of changes in the Democratic Party. The late Wes Barthelmas was a former senior aid to Senator Robert F. Kennedy. In 1973, at the suggestion of Democratic Party leaders, he went to work for a new young senator, Joe Biden of

Delaware, to help him learn the Senate's folkways. Barthelmas was known as a savvy player, and so when I had lunch with him in 1976, I was curious about his views of how and why Democrats in Congress were changing. What he said stayed with me for a long time, and I now know it was wrong. The reasoning in this book carried me beyond his views.

He said a new breed of young Democrats who were different from older northern Democrats had come to Congress in the 1970s. Sometimes called "Atari Democrats," they were more probusiness, less supportive of unions, and less likely to stand up for major new federal programs. They were also more adept at using television than older politicians. Older northern Democrats in Congress like Hubert Humphrey and Tip O'Neill found a philosophical gulf had grown up between themselves and such Atari Democrats as Paul Tsongas, Tim Wirth, and Gary Hart. Barthelmas believed generational differences accounted for the gap between the Atari Democrats and older liberals. These younger Democrats, he said, had not lived through the Depression and World War II as adults. In his view, they had only known prosperity and so, paraphrasing, they lent themselves less to the solidaristic culture born of those older hardships and more to a culture of personal careers.

I came to see this explanation as inadequate. What troubled me about Barthelmas's view was it ignored all the younger activists and their constituents who were born into the same generation as the Atari Democrats, but were committed to progressive politics. Young progressives were found in unions, in the environmental movement, in the civil rights movement, in the women's movement, in the civil liberties community, in the antiwar movement, in progressive religious groups, among consumer advocates, in education reform, and among health reformers. In the intellectual community progressive leadership was provided by such mainstream economists as the Nobel Laureates Robert M. Solow, James Tobin, and Joseph Stiglitz as well as Arthur M. Okun and Lester Thurow.

A more parsimonious theory better explains the rise of the Atari Democrats in Congress during the 1970s. The Atari insurgency occurred at roughly the same time as the emergence of television and TV-centered election campaigns. Money has always been the mothers' milk of politics. Yet, once Democratic legislators began chasing money to pay for TV ads, they needed much more money than in the past.[2] The Atari Democrats needed to supply large quids pro quo to a growing number of large campaign contributors. These quids pro quo included tax expenditures, business subsidies, weakened regulations, and wasteful federal projects. Federal waste is estimated in chapter four at more than $1 trillion a year in a $10 trillion plus economy. So, campaign contributions now cause the misallocation of national resources on a grand scale. No one quid pro quo meant to satisfy a contributor reduces the capacity of the government to fund national priorities. But cumulative losses from many quids pro quo remove the funds needed for national goals.

As more public money went to service the demands of campaign contributors, the Democrats' agenda contracted accordingly.[3] Inadvertently, the Democrats found themselves retreating from their traditional economic agenda and from their philosophy that government should play a large role in the economy by supplying public goods. Thus, the growing pressure to raise money to buy TV ads weakened the Democratic Party and moved it to the right. Public money used to meet contributors' demands became money unavailable to meet voters' needs.[4] Not surprisingly, the decline of the Democrats' voter base proceeded in tandem.[5] After the 2000 election, the Democratic Party was the minority party at every level of government in the United States. This story, linking the decline of the Democratic Party to the effects of the present campaign finance system, accounts for the Democrats' decline more plausibly than Barthelmas's explanation.

If contributors preempted monies needed for national priorities, and the Democratic Party thereby lost money needed to appeal to its voter base, would effective campaign finance reform reverse the process and lead to a massive reallocation of resources from federal waste to national priorities?[6] Widespread skepticism surrounds the view that even a best possible campaign finance law would reduce the influence of money in politics. Many knowledgeable observers believe that soon after the enactment of a reform law, K Street's lobbyists would create new loopholes in the tax, expenditure, and regulatory systems of the U.S. government. Even more in doubt are the chances of persuading Congress to enact a truly effective campaign reform law. Skepticism among knowledgeable observers on these two points is wide and deep.

The actual prospects for effective campaign reform can only be illuminated by a broad theory that can capture the likely outcome of conflicts between reform forces and opposing status quo forces. Such a theory, the Strong Parties theory, is presented below and is contrasted with Pluralism, the theory of American politics long dominant among political scientists. These two theories generate quite different answers to the question of how a best possible campaign reform law would affect, and be affected by, the dynamics of the American party system.[7] These two theories generate different answers to the question of whether effective reform would trigger a major reallocation of resources. Even more fundamentally, the two theories also generate different answers to the question of whether privately financed election campaigns distort democracy in the United States, and whether reform would increase democracy.[8]

The Pluralist Theory

Pluralism provides four major arguments that conclude reform efforts are bound to fail, cannot lead to a major reallocation of resources from waste to national priorities, and cannot reduce undemocratic influences of wealth in politics.[9]

The first Pluralist argument is that, reform or no reform, well-informed interest groups are bound to prevail in Congress, and parties and poorly informed voters are bound to be relatively weak. If so, then interest group dominance ensures the allocation of national resources will be skewed toward influential interest groups at the expense of national priorities, reform or no reform. In this view, enacting reform would accomplish little, since campaign contributions are not the only tools that enable interest groups to influence legislators. The same large resources that allow wealthier interest groups to make large campaign contributions also enable these groups to exert influence through other mechanisms. Grassroots lobbying is one such mechanism. Issue advertising is another. Bombarding Congress and the media with information is a third. The influence of media advertisers and media owners over what the public does *not* learn about its interests is a fourth mechanism.[10] So public financing of campaigns might make some difference, but probably not much.

A second Pluralist argument concludes private financing of campaigns is not anti-democratic, and so reform would not increase democracy. Pluralists and non-Pluralists agree interest groups are a vital mechanism for democratic representation. Interest groups mobilize like-minded citizens to lobby legislators, advancing preferences more intense and more complex than elections can reflect. But what distinguishes the Pluralists' story about the role of interest groups is their claim that many interest group contributions go to support those legislators who would have voted with a contributing group anyway, whether or not a contribution of money was made.[11]

A third Pluralist argument is that enacting campaign reform would change very little because congresspersons are not inclined to change the status quo, and lack incentives to reallocate resources to popular policies. Roughly 90 percent of members of the House of Representatives who run for reelection are reelected. With little competition and secure seats, they have little cause to innovate or engage in conflict with influential interests over resource allocations. According to this view, their ability to get themselves reelected makes them independent of their party's leaders *and relatively uninterested in a party program.* Members' independence from their party's leaders weakens their party's ability to pursue a national agenda. After reform, legislators would continue to concentrate on satisfying an assumedly *inelastic* configuration of local interests. If so, campaign reform would have only marginal effects on policy outcomes at best.

A fourth Pluralist argument asserts political parties are divided by cross-cutting cleavages on different issues. These cleavages are said to flow from an American society fragmented by cross-cutting ethnic, racial, religious, cultural, regional, and economic currents. These cross-currents preclude both majoritarian preferences and a majoritarian party, in this view. Therefore, parties are intrinsically too weak to provide much representation beyond what interest groups provide, especially to the unmobilized. A single cross-cutting cleavage weakens a party, and many cross-cutting cleavages make the party system inevitably weak. In such a context, Pluralists argue the representation that parties can provide to ordinary voters will always be weak, interest groups' influences will be much stronger, and the effects of campaign finance reform will therefore be minimal.

The Strong Parties Theory

The above four Pluralist arguments are refuted by the Strong Parties theory put forward in this study. This theory suggests campaign reform *would* greatly enhance the democratic character of the political system, and would lead to a major reallocation of resources from federal waste to national priorities. The Strong Parties theory sees strong parties as the normal centerpiece of the political system, and private financing of elections as weakening otherwise strong parties, especially the Democratic Party.

Pluralism's critics emphasize that the current interest group system poorly represents both ordinary citizens and the national interest, and overrepresents wealthy contributors. It should be obvious, therefore, why democracy requires strong parties. In a democracy, a strong party is the only instrument able to provide true representation to uninfluential people, the vast majority. Only a political party independent of wealthy interest groups can balance the power of wealthy interest groups. Only such a political party can provide representation to those citizens, the vast majority, who do not buy extra helpings of representation with campaign contributions and other exertions of wealth.

American parties would be stronger after campaign reform for several reasons. With regard to the first Pluralist argument, it is true interest group influence on legislatures is built on more than just their campaign contributions. But strong publicly financed parties would balance all of the influences of wealth on politics, by drawing strength from the party-unifying forces described below. Publicly financed candidates and parties would have a much greater incentive to represent voters' preferences if they did not depend on contributions from those interest groups whose demands fit poorly with the interests of the party's voter base.

The second Pluralist argument, again, is that many interest group campaign contributions go to legislators who would have supported a contributing group's demand, whether or not a contribution was made. Therefore private financing of campaigns does not undermine democracy.[12] Strong Party theory, on the other hand, assumes campaign contributions do buy legislative behavior. No one has measured directly how much such contributions influence legislative behavior, and it would be difficult to measure such influences since they involve counterfactual claims about what legislators would have done differently had they not accepted contributions. But if contributions are not needed for effective representation, and if they might be the cause of conflicts of interest, which at least sometimes they surely are, why not eliminate them? Supreme Court decisions arrayed below establish that democracy requires the elimination of certain conflicts of interest, and the maximization of democratic representation. Public financing of campaigns could only augment democracy by removing any incentive for legislators to be responsive to corrupting contributors, while increasing their incentive to be responsive to voters, including voters stirred up by interest groups. Most fundamentally of all, Pluralists ignore the effects on democracy that may occur when some interest groups are able to make large contributions to elected representatives, while others and the citizenry at large cannot afford to purchase influence over or access to their representatives. It is impossible to suppose contributors give generously so that they may have no effect in changing legislative outcomes from what they would be otherwise.

With regard to the third Pluralist argument, congresspersons' ties to local interests weaken parties far less than Pluralists claim, because most members of the House are even more strongly attached to their local party voters. Members of Congress represent partisan congressional districts whose lines have been drawn to disproportionately include voters who belong to the member's party. A member cannot take the support of his party's base voters for granted, given how volatile the electorate has become. If a member loses support among the partisan voters in his district or state, the chances of his attracting a strong opponent from the other party or from a primary opponent go up exponentially. So, partisan districts make legislators into strong partisans. Members' partisan voters back home are the bedrock of their political capital. Moreover, campaign contributors aside, many local interest groups that influence legislators are partisan interest groups operating in partisan coalitions.

Local partisan pressures are spliced with partisan coalitions in Congress. When these partisan congresspersons arrive in Congress, eight other party-unifying forces bind them to their party in Congress. To pass legislation constituents demand, party leaders must create a majority coalition to enact that legislation. To create coalitions, legislators must minimize the transaction costs—time, energy, money, and information—they expend in forging them. Party leaders reduce transaction costs of coalition formation far more easily than anyone else. This function is so fundamental it makes political parties necessary. Other party-unifying forces include members' need for party messages, ideologically compatible interest group allies, party ideology, and the economic needs and incomes of a party's base voters, when they are different from the economic needs and incomes of the other party's voters.

These party-unifying forces cause members' partisanship to be far greater than Pluralist accounts allow, which interviews for this study with 70 Democratic members of the House in 1991 to 1992 confirmed. Party-unifying forces make parties strong instruments of representation, and strong mechanisms for winning elections and passing legislation, insofar as they are not cross-pressured by contributors. These partisan forces would overwhelm that subset of local interest group influences that are orthogonal to partisanship, and drive legislators to support strong party programs, if effective campaign reform became law.

Ninety percent incumbency return rates notwithstanding, Democrats in Congress have three incentives for partisanship. The first incentive is their desire to regain effective party control of Congress, following the defeats of 1994, 1996, 1998, and 2000. Members see major benefits in being in the majority party in Congress. Being in the majority helps them respond to constituencies' demands, bring attention to the party's agenda, and advance their programmatic goals and careers through majority control of committees. Members routinely report their intense dislike of being in the minority party. The congressional Democrats' second incentive for partisanship is their need to reverse the decades-long decline in the Democratic Party's voter base. Their third incentive is the desire to enact good public policy for the country in keeping with their political philosophy. After reform, these three incentives would lead them to reallocate resources to popular economic programs.

Despite party-unifying forces and partisan incentives, the Democrats have been unable to reverse the trend decline in their partisan voter base. For several decades, the money "has just not been there" to pay for popular programs, illusory budget surpluses, symbolic reassurances, and token programs to the contrary notwithstanding.[13] Howsoever strong the nine party-unifying forces make them, they are enormously weakened by the diversion of vast resources to campaign contributors. Campaign reform would enable Democratic legislators to shift monies now spent on contributors to popular programs, reverse the decline in their voter base with an effective party message,[14] and regain effective control of Congress.

The fourth Pluralist argument has been subjected to direct empirical testing. Strong Party theorists deny that cross-cutting cleavages routinely weaken congressional parties. Some of the literature on congressional coalitions shows partisan/ideological coalitions in Congress are quite stable across issues and across time.[15] The Pluralists' cross-cutting–cleavages explanation also does not fit with the evidence that each major party is supported by a remarkably stable coalition of interest groups—the Republicans by business interests and Christian fundamentalists, and the Democrats by labor unions, education associations, environmentalists, and minorities. Nor does Pluralism fit with the stability of opinion among a majority of primarily working- and middle-class voters, who prefer that government provide a stable list of public goods, from expanded health insurance to quality education and environmental safety.[16] Strong Party theorists see a stable coalition of wealthy interests defending an allocation of resources that maintains high levels of luxury consumption and "competitive consumption" by the well-off. This allocation of resources detracts from both public and private investment that would both increase productivity and decrease inequality.[17] Overall, Pluralists have never explained the stability of interest group coalitions on one or the other side of the issue of whether to expand investment in public goods. They have not reconciled these various stable relationships with their claim that cross-cutting cleavages weaken parties and ever-shifting coalitions across parties dominate the passage of legislation. The stability of voter coalitions, congressional party coalitions, and interest group alliances with party coalitions all indicate that parties in the United States are fundamentally strong.

In sum, the Strong Party theory fits the facts better than Pluralist theory. If so, then campaign finance reform is less likely to be overwhelmed by powerful interest groups, and effective campaign reform can be achieved.

The viewpoint that political parties are potentially strong is far from new. Two generations ago some leading scholars believed that interest groups need not inevitably dominate parties and voters. These scholars believed that effective parties are indeed possible. They claimed that parties can be strong by uniting a majority of voters behind popular measures and themes, and in so doing, would curtail the influence of powerful interests. This view was advanced in such political science classics as E. E. Schattschneider's *The Semisovereign People*,[18] V. O. Key Jr.'s *Politics, Parties, and Pressure Groups*,[19] Grant McConnell's *Private Power and American Democracy*,[20] and the *1950 Report of the Committee on Parties* of the American Political Science Association.[21] However, all of these academic landmarks were written before the birth of TV forced candidates to raise a great deal of money to purchase television advertising. Such studies were bound to seem less plausible once candidates' hyperactive money chase began in earnest in response to the need to buy television advertising to win campaigns for political office.

Five Anomalies

This study examines how campaign finance would affect American politics as viewed through the prism of the Pluralist and Strong Parties theories. These theories, and any other theory of change and stability in American politics, must pass one key test: they must account for the following five anomalies. It is argued here that a Strong Parties theory tied to campaign finance reform accounts for the following five anomalies, and no other theory does.

Before listing these anomalies, the centrality of anomalies in science should be highlighted. Why did Einstein's Theory of Relativity displace Newtonian physics? Because Einstein's theory could explain everything Newton's theory could, but could also explain a range of phenomena Newton could not explain—phenomena that were anomalous under Newton's theory.[22] The progress of science is closely tied to the identification and explanation of anomalies.

The first anomaly is why the American political system is unresponsive to many perennial preferences of majorities of Americans. Ever since President Harry S. Truman proposed universal health insurance in 1948, majorities of Americans have expressed their preference for such a system. Every other advanced nation provides universal health insurance. What accounts for the anomaly that Americans prefer, but do not have, the universal health insurance every other advanced country enjoys? The same reasoning applies to other issues, notably a high-quality national education system, extensive job training subsidies, and high-quality paid child care. Current theories provide no convincing explanation of why the American political system is unrepresentative of most voters' preferences on these and other issues.

Some scholars claim the "individualism" of the American political culture weakens Americans' demand for health insurance and other government programs.[23] Yet, this theory ignores America's equally strong values of pragmatism and humanitarianism. Everyone needs health insurance and everyone wants health insurance that cannot be taken away or reduced in scope. The health insurance plan every congressperson enjoys under a law passed by Congress provides all the insurance most Americans want. How is it possible congressional "individualists" could vote themselves what they deny a large portion of the American people, including many American children?

A second anomaly extends the first. Nothing can make all Americans better off than greater productivity of the economy. Grasping the magnitude of the benefits accruing to the American nation from policies raising the level of U.S. productivity is vital to any sound understanding of American politics.[24] Surely responsible political leaders could propose policies raising the level of productivity, if not the long-term rate of growth in productivity. Yet, they do not. Policies increasing productivity include those that would increase public and private investment in human capital, knowledge capital, and physical capital. Anti-government views to the contrary notwithstanding, efficient public investments complement private investments. Public highways complement private automobiles, and public investments in workers' education and training complement private investments in the equipment those workers run. The second anomaly, then, is that underinvestment in both the public and private sectors exists even though everyone, especially the wealthy, would be better off if more such investment was painlessly financed from federal waste and increased savings. Everyone, that is, except campaign contributors.

A third anomaly is that Democratic officeholders have failed to legislate programs to meet voters' needs for health insurance, education, job training, and other things. Yet, the Democrats would have profited politically from delivering those programs, and might have reversed the decline in their voter base. Instead, the

Democrats have mainly provided symbolic reassurances and token programs. A typical example is found in the official Gore-Lieberman 2000 election proposal of a mere $17 billion a year total for all new education spending, including tax incentives.[25] In the 2000 campaign, Al Gore identified improving education as a top priority, reflecting opinion polls. Yet, the list of education programs presented in chapter eight shows $17 billion a year would be a grossly inadequate budget for upgrading American education.[26] Similarly, many millions of low- and moderate-income retirees were denied coverage under the Gore-Lieberman prescription drug plan, apparently for no other reason than the money "just isn't there" to cover the costs of providing coverage.[27] Democratic members of Congress and Democratic presidential candidates put a high value on regaining effective control of Congress and winning the White House, and on reversing the long-term decline in their voter base. Yet, they do not do supply the policy proposals most likely to make them popular. Their failure to propose such policies is an anomaly, until one examines the ways in which legislators are cross-pressured between voters and campaign contributors who preempt the needed funds.[28]

A fourth anomaly points to how the Democratic Party has built a very strong organization for competing in elections. It also enjoys a strong congressional party organization for shaping and enacting legislation. How is it possible for a party to be so strong organizationally yet so weak in its ability to retain and attract loyal voters? Why has voter loyalty declined so dramatically during the very same period that Democratic Party's election organization and congressional party cohesion and leadership became so much stronger than they had been in the past? This anomaly requires an explanation. Yet, no convincing explanation has been offered.

A fifth anomaly points to divisions within the Democratic Party's voter base, especially along racial lines, that might have been overwhelmed by shared economic concerns. Potentially, party economic policies would deliver far more to dissident party elements, particularly white working-class males, than realized social issue preferences ever could. As shown in chapters seven and eight, public investment and social insurance programs would benefit blacks and whites, men and women, old and young. Yet, messages emphasizing division, and exploiting so-called wedge issues often crowd out economic issues. The most egregious example of the use of a race as a wedge issue was the infamous Willie Horton ad of the 1988 presidential campaign. The anomaly is, how can divisive political efforts succeed so often in the United States when it would be so overwhelmingly profitable for most Americans to unite behind economic policies making everyone better off except campaign contributors?

One possible explanation of this anomaly is that divisive social issues are more salient because progressive economic policy options are less salient. The latter are less salient because the Democrats did not propose them, but might have. The

Democrats' failure to propose popular policies reflected their disbursement to campaign contributors of the money needed for those policies. As a result, the Democrats were unable to use economic issues to distract voters from divisive social issues. The dynamics of relative issue saliencies (changing the subject) often determine election outcomes.

These five anomalies challenge theories of change in the American political system. Pluralist theory cannot explain these anomalies. The Strong Parties theory developed here does explain these five anomalies. If campaign contributors have preempted the large amounts of money needed by the Democrats to fund popular programs, perhaps the decline in the Democrats' voter base can be explained accordingly. If reform of campaign financing would enable the Democrats to recapture funds now wasted on contributors' demands, and reallocate them to popular programs, then perhaps enough money could be recovered to satisfy the needs of disaffected voters, strengthen the economy, reverse the decline of the Democratic Party, capitalize on strong party organization, and override divisions within the party's ranks. If so, then the five anomalies would dissolve.

Campaign reform could reverse the Democrats' decline, but only if a campaign reform law was loophole-free, and only if Congress could be pressured into enacting a truly effective campaign reform law—two highly uncertain assumptions. The next chapter examines the elements of a truly effective campaign reform law. The Epilogue examines the political feasibility of enacting such a campaign reform into law. All in all, campaign finance reform is theoretically interesting. It is the core of the Strong Parties theory, which allows this study to offer a new interpretation of the dynamics of the American political system.

Chapter 2

Would Campaign Reform Work?

THIS CHAPTER CONSIDERS REMEDIES FOR THE DISPROPORTIONATE AND COR-rupting influence of money in politics. Before turning to these remedies, doubts about the severity of the corruption problem should be addressed. Perhaps the influence of money in politics is overblown. Perhaps campaign contributions from wealthy interests have smaller effects than many believe. If so, the gains from achieving effective campaign reform could be much smaller than reformers hope. Three arguments arrive at the conclusion that the influence of money in politics is exaggerated.

Is Corruption Overblown?

The first argument is that many contributions are "small;" many contributors are not rich, and legislators do not sell the Republic for $100 or $200 contributions, or even for a $10,000 contribution. If so, then perhaps the influence of money in politics is overblown, because the influence of any individual contribution is relatively small.

The evidence contradicts this argument. A tiny fraction of the electorate provides most of the money contributed in election campaigns. In the 1996 election cycle,

> less than one-fourth of 1 percent of the American people made a campaign contribution of $200 or more to a federal candidate. Only 4 percent made any contribution of any size to any candidate for office—federal, state, or local. On average, only 20 percent of the money came from individuals giving contributions of less than $200 per candidate. That means that an astonishing 80 percent of political money came from the tiny group of donors who gave $200 or more.[1]

Even granting no one $10,000 contribution is necessarily corrupting, such contributions are often bundled together and the bundle is what is contributed to a politician. Quids pro quo are given in return for the bundle, not for each part of the bundle. Moreover, contributors have common characteristics, interests, and networks noticeably different from those of ordinary Americans. Ordinary Americans do not lobby for tax expenditures. Nor do most Americans belong to a well-organized interest group that successfully lobbies Congress for some of the $1 trillion per year in federal waste specified in chapter four.

Contributors' unusual propensity to contribute reflects a highly unequal distribution of wealth. Ninety-four percent of financial wealth in the United States is owned by the top 20 percent of the wealth distribution, excluding housing, autos, and consumer durables. Put another way, the bottom 80 percent of Americans only own 6 percent of the financial wealth in the United States.[2] Campaign contributors are mostly found at the top of this highly skewed distribution of wealth. In addition, most organizations that make contributions are wealthy business interests. If politicians in both major parties depend heavily on a tiny group of wealthy contributors to raise the money they need to win elections, why would it be surprising that both parties are much less representative of most American voters than if effective campaign reform became law?[3]

A second argument also leads to the conclusion that campaign contributors' influence is overblown. This argument raises more doubts about the benefits of campaign reform than any other. The claim is that legislators ordinarily take the same policy positions *they would have taken anyway* if they had not accepted campaign contributions. Take away that PAC dollar and congressperson X would have cast the same vote anyway, this argument claims.[4] Any representative from that district or state would be anxious to please the same constituents and local interest groups *whether or not* they made campaign contributions.

This argument has a major flaw. There is no way of telling whether it is true or false. The only way to know would be to pass campaign reform and see whether or not congressperson X still voted the same way as she did before reform. However, it is not necessary to wait for reform to be enacted before judging this issue. It is desirable to err on the side of making sure the democratic integrity of the political system is not being sold off because of conflicts of interest and the perversion of legislators' incentives. Why, in other words, should the burden of proof fall on those who see campaign contributions as likely to be significantly corrupting? The Supreme Court has asserted a preference to err on the side of upholding a democratic system. In the *Austin* decision, the Court ruled that proof of a specific quid pro quo is *not* necessary to establish that a given action is corrupt. In *Buckley v. Valeo* (1976), the Court said there is a "legitimate government interest" in acting so as to avoid even the appearance of corruption, lest "the integrity of our system of representative democracy be undermined."[5]

A second and more powerful version of the same argument can be stated as follows. All pork is divided into two parts: contributor waste and constituency waste. Contributor waste is public money spent only because campaign contributors demand quids pro quo. Constituency waste, on the other hand, is public money spent to satisfy the demands of those constituents whom any representative from that district would be bound to mollify, campaign contributions or not. Campaign reform would not reduce the incentive of a legislator to spend public funds on wasteful pork barrel legislation his constituents demand. Those who are skeptical about the benefits of campaign reform argue implicitly that most federal waste is this kind of constituency waste, and contributor waste is much smaller. Therefore, government waste is as inevitable as it is inevitably large, reform or no reform.

A counter-argument, however, seems more convincing. It is useful to distinguish inelastic constituency waste from elastic constituency waste. It is false that any legislator from a given district would support all the same constituency waste any other possible legislator from that district would support, campaign reform or no campaign reform. More likely, any congressperson supports the demands of some of her constituents over others. For example, suppose, under pressure from contributors, a legislator supported a bill funding a particular road project in her district. Perhaps her support for the road project was affected by campaign contributions from certain contractors who stood to benefit from building that road. Suppose some jobs and some commerce might also flow from building the road. But the important question is whether, after reform, other roads or other projects or other programs, those not backed by campaign contributions, might be supported by that district's congressperson instead? These projects, perhaps no longer a road, might be even more popular, more economically efficient, and might provide even more jobs, commerce, and/or votes than contributors' favorite wasteful projects provided. When congresspersons deliver pork, certain district interests gain thereby whose preferences *are often quite different from the manifest or latent preferences of most voters in that district.* If so, then campaign reform would eliminate massive amounts of wasteful government spending now labeled as inelastic constituency waste. After reform, the district projects that receive funding might be very different projects or programs than those contributors had favored. They might also be much less economically wasteful projects.

Even in a district dominated by a single large industry—for example, wheat growers—to say the interests of a large wheat company coincide with the interests of its employees and the people in related service industries in that congressional district stretches credulity. Workers in that district without health insurance might benefit from reallocating funds from inefficient wheat subsidies over to universal health insurance. The number of jobs could very well be unaffected by such a reallocation. Simply to assume that the preference hierarchies of all voters in any particular congressional districts are the same, as this argument implies, is a heroic assumption. If so, then legislators operating under campaign reform might better represent voters whose demands for district projects might be much less wasteful than contributors' preferred projects had been prior to reform.

To the extent inelastic constituency waste is greater than contributor waste, to that extent campaign finance reform would fail to bring about the reallocation of wasted funds to national priorities. But there are no extant studies that show *how much* current government spending is contributor waste, and *how much* is inelastic constituency waste. Yet, again, the reasoning in *Buckley* and *Austin* justifies a preference to err on the side of giving reform the opportunity to eliminate waste.

A third argument supports the conclusion that the corrupting influences of campaign contributions are overblown.

> The argument of a Congress for sale ignores, first, the other influences at work on the Congress: home districts, party, the president, the values of the MC. Second, it ignores the countervailing effect of interested money on both (or all) sides of a policy dispute.[6]

If this claim is correct, then these different influences actively offset and neutralize the corrupting influence of campaign contributions. So private funding of political campaigns may be a minor problem, and reform, therefore, would only have minor benefits at best. What arguments run counter to this claim?

First, if members' personal values offset the effects of private contributions, how is it members seldom turn down contributions that do not fit with their personal beliefs? If they were so principled, they would risk losing contributions they rely on for winning elections. Such scruples would keep candidates out on the trail chasing money for their campaigns for even longer periods than they now spend, which they find exhausting. By all indications, members' behavior is dominated by the need to raise money for the next election. The case of the Keating Five, for example, surfaced in 1990. It provides a counter-example to the claim that the personal values of honorable legislators transcend mere campaign contributions. This case showed even such honored legislators as senators John Glenn and John McCain were not above subordinating their personal values to the need to raise contributions, as their public apologies show.[7] So it is difficult to understand the assertion in the above quote that members' personal values offset the effects of corrupting private contributions.

Second, the claim that home district influences offset the influence of private contributors is similarly flawed. This claim assumes ordinary voters have the same access to information about policy problems and options that powerful interest groups have. Yet, information asymmetries as between interest groups and voters weaken voters' ability to influence their legislators. The leadership (information) legislators might have provided to voters, which might have mobilized them, is blocked by campaign contributions that coopt those legislators, and by media gatekeeping. Given relatively inert voters who lack leaders to rally around, it is no mystery why legislators are more responsive to campaign contributors than to ordinary citizens. Thus, it is difficult to understand the assertion in the above quote that pressures from voters on their representatives offset the pressures coming from contributors.

Third, what of the claim in the quotation above that competing forces are equally able to raise enough money to get their views across to voters, and pressure legislators accordingly? The Children's Defense Fund cannot begin to match the oil or small business lobbies in the ability to buy access to the media or to legislators. Haynes Johnson and David Broder show forces opposed to the Clinton health plan spent massive amounts of money to run the Harry and Louise ads nationally during 1994, while the forces on the other side were totally outspent.[8] So it is difficult to believe opposing sides on most issues are equal in advertising and lobbying resources.

Fourth, the above quotation also claims the influence of parties regularly offsets the influence of contributors. On the contrary, this study shows payoffs to contributors remove so much money from the table, parties cannot deliver the programs voters want and national goals require. Similarly, presidents raise money from interest groups and acquiesce in the existing allocation of resources more than they change it.

Though the relative magnitudes of different influences acting on Congress have not been established empirically, the American people think the influence of campaign contributors is powerfully undemocratic. According to many studies, distrust of the political system in the United States has been growing steadily and dramatically for decades.[9] Distrust has been growing since the time when politicians began to chase campaign contributions to pay for TV advertising.[10] Ninety-two percent of Americans believe special interest contributions buy votes of members of Congress, and 88 percent believe people who make large contributions get special favors from politicians.[11] So the doubts about the need for reform arrayed earlier in this section are nowhere near shared by most Americans.

Two Tests of the Effectiveness of a Reform Bill

Many experts believe corrupt politics is inevitable and reform efforts will fail. Skeptics argue even the most effective campaign reform package might not change anything because, as they see it, money seeking influence will always find a way around any reform.[12] As Senator Bill Bradley put it, "Money in politics is like ants in the kitchen. You have to close every hole or they will find a way in."[13] If so, then any effective reform legislation must prevent loopholes from being created. But if a reform plan only deserves support when it is free of loopholes, there must be a way to identify a loophole-free reform plan.[14]

Two tests of effectiveness can identify a loophole-free campaign reform bill. The first test is whether a reform proposal eliminates the corruption of officeholders. The Supreme Court has defined corruption as "the real or imagined coercive influence of large financial contributions on candidates' positions and on their actions if elected to office."[15] Corruption flows from the creation of political debts resulting from campaign contributions.

The second test of an effective reform bill is whether it shrinks the inequality in different leaders' opportunities to communicate their views to voters. Democracy requires that different policy viewpoints be heard in election campaigns. Democracy requires that no one viewpoint, in effect, "shout down" other reasonable views because some advocates can afford to purchase the tools of campaigning, especially broadcast time, while their adversaries cannot. If some leaders' access to money enables them to bombard voters with their message, while other leaders lack money enough to buy advertising, then voters may be denied the opportunity of learning what policies and candidates would serve their interests. Then bad ideas may drive out good ideas. A democratic nation is supposed to be a happier and more productive nation because it relies on persuasion and forswears political manipulation and coercion.

It is argued here that members of Congress would more faithfully represent voters' preferences, and would legislate public policies more likely to meet national priorities, if they adopted three specific reform measures: (1) voluntary full public financing of election campaigns of candidates and parties; (2) public financing of matching funds given to candidates to reply to privately funded political advertisements, notably "attack ads" and "issue advertising directly affecting an election"; and (3) expanded public broadcasting. Some influential reformers prefer a fourth option, expenditure limits. Expenditure limits could substitute for public matching funds that balance attack ads. Yet, it is argued here expenditure limits threaten free speech, are unacceptable to the Supreme Court, and are unlikely to be ratified as a Constitutional Amendment. These four options are examined next.

Reform Option 1. Voluntary Full Public Financing of Campaigns

The Supreme Court in *Buckley v. Valeo* (1976) affirmed the constitutionality of public financing of election campaigns, provided candidates participate voluntarily.[16] So, no legal barrier blocks full public financing of campaigns. Public financing of campaigns would make it unnecessary for officeholders to incur any political debt in order to finance their campaigns, and so would escape corruption from that source. Raising campaign contributions requires large amounts of time and energy candidates would prefer to spend on other activities. Raising money often directly compromises a legislator, as the Keating Five found when forced to apologize publicly. Given the desirability of avoiding these difficulties, legislators are likely to accept public funding of their campaigns if public financing were already enacted into law and especially if their challengers accepted public funding. Ninety-five percent of legislators in Minnesota chose voluntary public financing when it became available.[17]

Once candidates' campaigns are publicly funded, two changes are likely: First, elected candidates would give up representing contributors as such, and would more faithfully represent voters' preferences. Second, a wider range of candidates would choose to run for office. Currently, many potential candidates cannot raise enough money from private sources to compete. Others decline to run because they find the money chase morally repugnant.[18] A wider range of candidates would offer voters a wider range of policy options from which voters might choose.

Only two problems stand in the way of public financing of campaigns. First, it may not be possible to enact public financing into law over the opposition of opponents in Congress. Winning 218 votes in the House, 60 votes in the Senate, and the support of the president will be difficult. This problem is discussed in the Epilogue at the end of this study.

A second problem is that, even if publicly financed, candidates might still lack enough money to respond to attack ads paid for by opponents, and might therefore lack an equal chance of winning their race. Moreover, candidates who benefit from public financing, but who also benefit from election advertising purchased by wealthy interests, might deliver corrupt legislative quids pro quo to those interests. The Supreme Court has denied the existence of this problem. It ruled in *Buckley* that candidates do not become indebted to contributors whose contributions are spent on a candidate's behalf independently from any direction by that candidate. The Court ruled such independent expenditures create no political debts.[19] Others argue persuasively that officeholders know who makes an independent expenditure. Contributors who fund independent expenditures have ample opportunity and more than adequate incentives to seek gratitude from the candidates they back, and are likely to inform the candidate of their contribution. Candidates are unlikely to take the risk of offending independent expenders whose support will be needed for the next campaign. Hence, independent expenditures do corrupt officials now, and could corrupt publicly financed candidates, thereby undermining any system of public financing of elections.

Only two possible remedies might solve the problem of corruption caused by independent expenditures. The first is to impose an expenditure limit on how much money may be spent on an independent expenditure. Yet, this remedy poses serious dangers to First Amendment protection of speech, which dangers are discussed below.

The second remedy is to provide public matching funds to finance candidates' responses to privately financed political advertising aimed at defeating them. This remedy would greatly reduce candidates' incentive to acquiesce to pressures from independent expenders, and would level the playing field between candidates with unequal backing from wealthy interests. Without such a matching mechanism, the likelihood that public financing of campaigns would reduce the disproportionate influences of money in politics would be substantially diminished.

Reform Option 2. Matching Privately Funded Campaign Communications

If publicly funded candidates were not given additional monies to match privately financed advertising,[20] they could be buried in an avalanche of attack ads, or they might be intimidated or corrupted by those who can afford large-scale attack advertising. Hence, effective campaign finance reform requires both public financing of candidates' campaigns and public financing of candidates' responses to privately funded attack ads that benefit their opponent.

House Democratic Leader Richard Gephardt expressed the problem as follows:

> And so, short of changing the Constitution and free speech, which I don't think is likely and probably not a great idea, you're in a new world. And even if you could get voluntary limits on what you could spend, which is what the '89 bill had, I don't think candidates and members are going to vote for legislation anymore that ties their hands even in the face of lots of money being spent by third parties—whether it's the National Rifle Association or the Christian Coalition or labor or business or whoever—*that wouldn't allow them to go ahead and try to respond to those ads.* [italics added][21]

Using public funds to match private contributions fits neatly with *Buckley*. It asserted that the First Amendment aims to secure the "widest possible dissemination of information from diverse and antagonistic sources" to guarantee free exchange of ideas, so as to promote "political and social changes desired by the people."[22] The remedy acceptable to the Court for an imbalance in communications is not to limit speech, but to expand it. Using public funds to match privately funded political communications could only expand the flow of political information. Matching would ensure greater competition among ideas seeking attention. Thus, matching fits neatly within the spirit of the Supreme Court's decisions.

This rationale for matching draws added support from the decision in *Austin v. Michigan State Chamber of Commerce* (1990). As already mentioned, the Supreme Court in *Austin* ruled it is not necessary to prove a quid pro quo in order to establish officeholders were corrupt. The Court asserted a "legitimate government interest" in avoiding even the appearance of corruption, lest "the integrity of our system of representative democracy be undermined." However, the decision went further. The Court expanded the notion of corruption beyond "quid pro quo corruption" to what Justice Scalia termed "new corruption":

> [A] different form of corruption in the political arena: *the corrosive and distorting effects of immense aggregations of wealth* that is accumulated with the help of the corporate form and that has little or no correlation to the public's support for the corporation's political ideas.[23] [italics added]

The Court can be interpreted as saying this new corruption requires measures that would eliminate, reduce, or balance it. So far, at least, this doctrine from the *Austin* decision has had little influence on other Court decisions, because equalizing campaign expenditures to neutralize corruption has been taken as requiring expenditure limits. But if separated from expenditure limits, *Austin* provides a legal rationale supporting the use of public matching funds to balance private campaign advertising, including advertising paid for by drawing on "*immense aggregations of wealth.*"

Matching not only fits comfortably with First Amendment speech rights. It is also justified by the Fourteenth Amendment's guarantee of the "equal protection of the laws." Equal protection lies at the center of democracy, because it is concerned with the fairness of the political process to all citizens. In the past, the Supreme Court has applied the equal protection clause to election law in cases concerning white primaries, malapportionment, poll taxes, and candidate filing fees, among others. The equal protection clause is difficult to reconcile with private campaign financing that denies less wealthy voters and candidates the opportunity to participate in the democratic process as the equal of wealthy interests.[24] Only campaign finance reform with matching can meet an equal protection standard.

In support of using matching to equalize election resources, it is crucial to note two Supreme Court decisions, *Buckley v. Valeo* and *Regan v. Taxation* (1983).[25] Both decisions put forward the pivotal doctrine that "a government decision to subsidize some speech but not other speech is not subject to strict scrutiny because it places no burden on the right of the unsubsidized speaker to exercise fundamental rights." A decision by the 8th Circuit Court of Appeals in 1994 in *Day v. Holahan* claimed public matching funds create a chilling effect on independent expenditures. This ruling directly contradicts the *Buckley* and *Regan* decisions that matching does not burden speech. But the *Day* decision did not directly address the reasoning in *Buckley* and *Regan* that matching does not impose a burden on speech. This omission leaves the reasoning in *Day* vulnerable to attack.[26] So the constitutionality of matching is on firm ground.

Under a matching scheme, public funds would match private expenditures on issue advocacy that affects elections, and would match express advocacy as well, whether paid for by opposing candidates or by opposing independent expenders.[27] Issue advocacy expenditures are protected by First Amendment guarantees of free speech and assembly, and so no limit may be applied to them regarding the amount that may be legally spent. In theory, issue advocacy expenditures are supposed to be spent on issues rather than parties or candidates, and soft money is supposed to be spent on party building. But in practice, all of these sorts of funds are spent to elect candidates, and so should be subject to election law. Issue advocacy that *does* directly affect an election must be distinguished from issue advocacy that *does not*. An advertisement could be judged to have "directly affected an election" if it used words or pictures to express one of the following three messages:

> (A) a candidate is less worthy of election than another candidate; or (B) issue position x should be rejected and candidate c supports x; or (C) x should be rejected [and polling shows some significant portion of the voters know the position taken on x by the candidate attacked or supported by the ad].[28]

Express advocacy is political speech expressly urging the defeat or election of specific candidates. Express advocacy, unlike issue advocacy, is subject to contribution limits, disclosure requirements, and restrictions as to sources of funding. Corporations and unions may not make direct contributions for the purposes of express advocacy. The Supreme Court in *Buckley* has ruled only those communications using one of eight specific phrases could be subject to the rules applicable to express advocacy: "vote for," "elect," "support," "cast your ballot for," "Smith for Congress," "vote against," "defeat," and "reject."[29] However, reformers, following the decision in *Furgatch*,[30] claim many political ads do not use those eight terms, and yet nonetheless unmistakably imply them. When a candidate's photograph is shown with phrases like "Congressman Jones is bad for America" shortly before an election, a normal voter will understand the message as urging the candidate's defeat. Nevertheless, guessing what implications an audience might draw from a particular ad is an uncertain matter. Therefore, building tests of what is or is not express advocacy on the basis of what inferences an audience may draw would be unconstitutionally vague. Such vagueness, they implied, might allow tests to be used that illegitimately inhibit free speech. Ornstein, Mann, and Malbin propose Congress pass, and the Supreme Court accept, an expanded list of instances expressly advocating the defeat or election of a candidate, including use of a candidate's photo or name (see the Appendix). Should that happen, some of the money now spent on unregulated issue advocacy ads would become subject to limits applying to express advocacy.

Public financing of campaigns is embodied in state election laws in Maine, Massachusetts, and Arizona.[31] Matching as described here is an extension of reforms embodied in these state laws. Specifically, those laws match expenditures by advantaged candidates only. The proposal here would also match expenditures by groups who are independent of candidates but who take sides in an election. A partial matching remedy is found in the Clean Money Option developed by The Working Group on Electoral Democracy.[32] The McCain-Feingold bill would raise voluntary spending limits on candidates' expenditures when their opponents benefit from large independent expenditures. So, McCain-Feingold accepts the principle of equalizing competing candidates' resources, even while it would tolerate a far larger imbalance between competing candidates' resources than would a full public financing scheme with matching.[33]

The matching approach has one weakness. Matching may be costly, and the public may be reluctant to pay for public funding of candidates' responses to attack ads. Voters often respond negatively to campaign ads, especially negative ones, and may resist paying for still more political ads. Would the public support the costs of public financing with matching if reform opponents ran ads saying reform was "food stamps for politicians" and promising reform would require massive new taxes?[34]

This weakness can be overcome if the public understands no new taxes are required to fund campaign reform. Instead, public financing of campaigns could be supported with funds from "takebacks" of government waste. Takebacks drawn from egregious waste would be popular (see chapter four, where $1 trillion per year in waste is listed). One example of waste that could be held up to public attention is the mortgage interest deduction on million-dollar homes and vacation homes. At a ten percent interest rate on a million-dollar mortgage, wealthy taxpayers in the 39.6 percent tax bracket receive a subsidy from other taxpayers of $39,600 each year for the life of the mortgage.[35] Voters are unlikely to support this subsidy.[36] Similarly, public subsidies going to profitable multibillion dollar corporations, many listed below, will not seem legitimate to voters, and would be accepted as the kind of takeback that could pay for public financing of elections.

Reform Option 3. Expenditure Limits versus Matching Funds

Using public matching funds to balance privately funded attack ads has a rival: expenditure limits. Both the matching funds approach and the expenditure limits approach aim to reduce the advantage of wealthy interests in election campaigns. Advocates of expenditure limits and advocates of matching do not appear to have different interests. Their disagreement seems to be purely intellectual, which suggests that reconciling the two sides to this dispute would strengthen the campaign reform movement considerably.

A group at the Brennan Center of the NYU Law School advocates expenditure limits as the best way to reduce the disproportionate influence of money in politics. Yet, the *Buckley* decision forbade expenditure limits.[37] *Buckley* denied independent expenditures create political debts. Yet, as already discussed, independent expenditures are corrupting because candidates probably know who made them, and feel indebted to these contributors as much as if they had contributed directly to their campaigns. So, according to the Brennan group, and contrary to *Buckley*, expenditure limits deserve judicial support. Therefore, the Brennan group concludes, the Court might be persuaded to allow expenditure limits at some point in the future.

Yet, the Supreme Court is unlikely to reverse itself because of a bedrock doctrine in *Buckley* that colors every discussion of expenditure limits. That doctrine states, "The concept that government may restrict the speech of some elements in our society in order to enhance the relative voice of others is wholly foreign to the First Amendment."[38] The Court is unlikely to overturn this doctrine, even to achieve "a legitimate government interest," such as reducing corruption or restoring public confidence in democracy.

Expenditure limits could undermine democracy. These limits may be set too low to allow the public to become aware of its choices, foreclosing effective challenges to the status quo. Challenging the status quo requires a volume of communications large enough to inform the electorate and create pressure on Congress for change. Future politicians could lower expenditure limits below the threshold necessary for the mobilization of their opponents.

Because the Supreme Court is unlikely to accept expenditure limits,[39] some reformers believe it necessary to bypass the Court by means of a constitutional amendment making expenditure limits constitutional.[40] The Constitution requires first, a proposal to the states enacted by a two-thirds vote of both Houses of Congress, and second, ratification by three-quarters of the states. Ratification of such an amendment is unlikely, since supporters of the status quo and defenders of the First Amendment would mount formidable opposition. The failures of past efforts to adopt constitutional amendments are not reassuring as to the political feasibility of this approach: amendments to achieve term limits, equal rights for women, a ban on flag burning, and a balanced budget all failed. By comparison, legislating public financing of campaigns would only require 60 votes in the Senate, 218 votes in the House, and an acquiescent president—barriers routinely overcome.

So an expenditure limits approach is likely to prove both less politically feasible and less legally feasible than a matching approach. A matching approach, on the other hand, would satisfy both equal protection concerns and First Amendment concerns, while balancing the political influence of wealthy interests. Matching would not require overturning *Buckley*, nor would it require a constitutional amendment. The Court would allow such a legislative remedy, since, by its own reasoning, matching encourages more speech and, unlike expenditure limits,

Reform Option 4. Expanding Public Broadcasting

If public broadcasting were expanded, it could leverage the democratic effects of publicly financing campaigns. Expanding public broadcasting could give citizens greater access to competing views relevant to voters' choices.[41] Done right, the clash of different well-informed views is the backbone of democracy.[42] Many commentators believe the commercial media starve the public of the kind of information and argument that informs understanding. An expansion of public media would compensate for the limits of commercial media, which tailor program content to maximize audience size and advertising revenue. Paid political ads and the contributions that pay for them are so important in part because coverage of candidates and issues by the commercial media is so thin. Distinguished media observers such as Max Frankel, a former editor of the *New York Times*, see commercial media as unable to bear the responsibility of educating the electorate ("the news as entertainment").[43]

It is often claimed viewers are not interested in knowing more about public affairs, notwithstanding the impact on their lives. Yet, if public media had programming budgets as large as used by commercial media, they would be better able to make complicated issues clear and interesting, not least with links to human interest stories. Moreover, public media are freer than commercial media to lose some audience share in return for the opportunity to inform the citizenry, especially the opinion-leading segment of the public. Public broadcasting can afford to target the people who listen in and tell their coworkers at the 10 A.M. coffee break what they heard. In addition, if public media could dispense with corporate funding, they would be more likely to broadcast controversial political views.

Yet, perhaps it is print media rather than broadcast media who are responsible for helping citizens comprehend important issues. But it is commonly understood broadcast media are much easier to use, and so are bound to be used much more. In addition, tastes for the more complicated analyses of public affairs found in the elite press have to be developed through socially induced experiences with them. Not everyone will immediately profit by picking up the *New York Times* or the *Wall Street Journal*. And coverage in the regional press is usually seen as homogeneous and light.

Beyond broadcast and print media, those who are concerned about overly narrow information channels have begun to see the Internet as a vehicle for democratizing information. Yet the Internet may narrow users' interests more than help them focus on what is important. Searching on the Internet requires a prior conceptual framework telling the user what is important to search for and what sources are authoritative and reliable. It is not clear how citizens develop such frameworks sufficient to guide them in selecting information about their interests.[44] Moreover, many who search the net seek out congenial ideas, not views that challenge their existing biases. Furthermore, millions of websites compete for attention, and there is a growing disparity between those who can afford to advertise their website and those who cannot. Large inequities also exist among groups in ability to fund the new research and expensive presentation effects increasingly found on the web.

In such a context, public broadcast media seem the channels most likely to both present voters with information they can recognize as addressing their interests, and expose them to debates that challenge and develop their current beliefs. The technological underpinnings of communication are changing rapidly. The one constant is that a concern for democracy deserves to be the centerpiece of national policies that shape communications policy. The expansion of public broadcast media seems to offer the best possibility of balancing whatever biases of omission result from gatekeeping by commercial media.

Present political conditions in Congress make highly unlikely a large expansion of public broadcasting. However, enactment of effective campaign finance reform legislation would propel an expansion of public media. Campaign finance reform and an expansion of public media would both promote democratization and revive the party system as an instrument of representation.

Nine Additional Elements of an Effective Reform Bill

In addition to public financing of campaigns and public matching funds for candidates to respond to attack ads, nine additional elements might be included in an effective reform package.

First, candidates' and parties' acceptance of public funds should be voluntary. The *Buckley* decision requires candidates be free to refuse public funding. Even if *Buckley* had not required it, such a requirement would still be desirable. At some future time, candidates could be forced by new federal legislation to agree to some onerous condition in order to receive public funds. For example, public funding of campaigns could be reduced to a level too low to allow challengers who lack the resources of incumbents to communicate effectively with voters. By making public funding voluntary, any candidate who wishes to opt out can do so without fear of the law.

Second, while public financing would destroy the incentive to sell legislation to raise funds for campaigning, it would not prevent legislators from taking bribes for other reasons, such as the desire to live more luxuriously or build up wealth. Specific corrupt practices should be banned specifically in a new law, and such bans would be effective if backed by severe legal penalties and vigorous enforcement. Examples of such corrupt practices include contributions to officeholders' legal defense funds, jobs for relatives, and advantageous bank loans.

Third, the Federal Election Commission is often criticized for weak enforcement of campaign laws. FEC enforcement is routinely underfunded and given too little statutory authority to effectively administer these laws. The agency's capacities for gathering information, investigating complaints, and prosecuting violations are quite weak. The FEC needs to be made independent of politicians in both parties who now routinely block effective enforcement. Effective reform would supply to a refurbished FEC what is needed to reverse all of these problems. In particular, it should make sure enforcement was administered by independent neutrally competent civil servants who would enjoy long terms of office, and who would receive adequate funding and statutory authority to fulfill their mission.[45] Publicly financed incumbent members of Congress would lack any incentive to interfere with setting up an FEC with the characteristics just described.

Fourth, candidates who use their own personal fortunes in their own election campaigns can be denied an advantage by supplying their opponents with equal public financing of their campaigns.

Fifth, the current rules allow presidential candidates and their surrogate committees to accept both public and private financing, the latter creating political debts negating the whole point of public financing. The same rules described in this chapter should apply to congressional and presidential candidates alike.

Sixth, Political Action Committees both contribute money to candidates and buy independently expended political advertisements. After reform, direct PAC contributions to publicly funded candidates' campaigns would be illegal. However, PAC expenditures on independently expended express advocacy and issue advertising would continue to enjoy protection under the First Amendment. Where found to directly affect an election, PAC expenditures on issue advocacy and express advocacy could be matched by public funds given to candidates so they may respond. While many PACs are sponsored by large businesses and labor unions, other PACs provide a vehicle for bringing many small donors together behind an effort to persuade their fellow citizens of a particular viewpoint. No barrier exists to providing public matching funds to candidates and parties to respond to PAC ads. So under an effective campaign reform plan, PAC spending would not present a problem for democracy, and would actually enhance democracy if tied to low contribution limits.

Seventh, the issue of out-of-state money given directly to candidates should disappear as a problem under public financing. Candidates who choose to take public financing would not be permitted under the law to take private money from either in-state or out-of-state sources. Out-of-state money that supported independent expenditures or privately financed opponents would be matched. But out-of-state money spent on issue advocacy should not be prohibited, because dominant political forces in a particular state may inhibit the full discussion of issues voters care about. Banning out-of-state money would interfere with First Amendment rights of speech and association.[46]

Eighth, soft money should be banned.[47] Soft money contributions are made to parties for party-building activities, such as voter registration, voter turnout, generic party ads, redistricting efforts, and voter education. Such contributions do not fall under federal election law restrictions that apply to hard money. In reality, soft money regularly shows up in coordinated campaigns for candidates in which local, state, and national parties cooperate and commingle their funds. Soft money contributions are allowed to be unlimited in magnitude and the source is allowed to go undisclosed. Very large soft money contributions are commonplace. As such, soft money creates large opportunities for corruption. The total of all soft money contributions is estimated to have been more than $262.1 million in the 1996 election cycle.[48] Corporate and labor contributions to candidates are ordinarily prohibited by hard money regulations, but are tolerated when given as soft money. The McCain-Feingold bill would subsume any contribution affecting a federal election under existing federal regulations limiting contributions. In that way, McCain-Feingold abolishes soft money.[49] Any reform scheme is bound to do the same.

Even with soft money banned, a hidden soft money channel might remain. Soft money could continue to be raised by artfully commingling regulated federal accounts with state and local soft money funds. Such commingling would amount to a large loophole, which could be closed only if vigorous federal scrutiny and enforcement by a reformed FEC making sure such funds were appropriately segregated.

Ninth, contribution limits should be written into law wherever they are not operative now, and uniformly applied to *all* categories of funding that affect elections. Contribution limits would serve as an important backup to public financing of campaigns plus matching. The disproportionate influence of large contributors on campaign advertising can be greatly reduced, though not eliminated, by contribution limits. Such influence can be reduced further if contribution limits on independent expenditures are combined with a strict separation of issue advertisements that affect an election campaign, and thus may be regulated, from those that do not and should not be regulated.

The public supports low contribution limits. According to Derek Cressman of the U.S. Public Interest Research Group (PIRG) in testimony before the Senate Rules Committee,

> A 1994 poll by the Mellman group found that 77% of the public supported reducing individual contribution limits. The public has demonstrated their support for contribution limits much lower than the current federal limits. . . . Over the past six years, at least eleven states, Arizona, Alaska, Arkansas, Cali-

fornia, Colorado, Maine, Massachusetts, Missouri, Montana, Oregon, and Vermont, have moved to lower their contribution limits, with all but three of those states doing so through a direct vote of the citizens. . . . Many of these initiatives called for contribution limits as low as $100 for most races.[50]

On January 24, 2000, the Supreme Court ruled low contribution limits are acceptable. In *Nixon v. Shrink Missouri Government PAC*, the Court upheld contribution limits of $275 for state legislative races and $1,075 for statewide races. The Court stated contribution limits could be as low as Congress and the states saw fit, so long as political association was not interfered with and a candidate's voice could be heard.[51] A line must be drawn between contribution limits that are low enough and limits that are too low, which only the courts and new legislation can decide. Yet, *Nixon v. Shrink Missouri Government PAC* shows the courts are willing to see low contribution limits, as defined by legislatures.

However, the benefits of contribution limits are reduced to the extent large contributors are able to spread their contributions around among different campaigns. The benefits of contribution limits also are undermined when such contributions are politically coordinated. An example of such a coordinated effort can be seen in George W. Bush's Pioneer system in the 2000 presidential campaign. A large group of individuals close to the Bush campaign, so-called pioneers, were each assigned the task of raising $100,000 in $1,000 contributions, the contribution limit.[52] This is a common practice. Regarding bundled contributions going to Governor Bush's presidential campaign, Ellen S. Miller notes,

> And company executives regularly "bundle" hard money contributions. . . . It's telling that his fundraising operation has given its top money men individual tracking codes for donors to write on their checks. An internal memo written by the head of the electric power industry's main lobbying group explains to potential donors why these codes are important, with capitalization used in the original document for emphasis: "IT DOES ENSURE THAT OUR INDUSTRY IS CREDITED, AND THAT YOUR PROGRESS IS LISTED AMONG THE OTHER BUSINESS/INDUSTRY SECTORS." If there's no quid pro quo connected to contributions, why else should Bush keep track of which industries are favoring him and by how much?[53]

Thus small contributions become large contributions when leveraged by such networking and bundling. But if low enough and widely applied so that contributors cannot shift money from those channels requiring contribution limits to others that do not, contribution limits might prove highly effective if used in conjunction with public financing of campaigns and public matching funds to balance attack ads.

Still another problem with contribution limits is they would not limit the impact of expenditures by large organizations who have the capacity to spend a lot of money to raise a lot of money through small contributions from a large membership base. The National Rifle Association (NRA) has much more money than do gun-control groups. Other examples of such organizations include the National Federation of Independent Business, the Chamber of Commerce, the National Education Association, the American Association of Retired Persons (AARP), the Veterans of Foreign Wars, the Christian Coalition, the National Association of Realtors, and unions. Even with low contribution limits, the funds raised by these organizations may enable them to advertise their views so as to overwhelm the competing views of other groups who lack the capacity to raise equal amounts of money. However, publicly funded candidates and parties using public matching funds would balance such groups somewhat. If so, then the democratic character of elections might be protected from this source of imbalance.

One other disadvantage of contribution limits is frequently mentioned. Absent public financing of campaigns, contribution limits give incumbents an advantage over challengers who need to raise more money than incumbents do to overcome incumbents' edge.[54] However, public financing would equalize most campaign funds between challengers and incumbents, and could make additional funds available to challengers to balance incumbents' office allowances and free mailings.[55]

It is sometimes said people should be free to contribute money as one means of participating in politics, wealthy individuals and groups included. But that contradicts the fundamental democratic principal that wealthy people not be allowed to buy votes, whether of voters or of legislators, so as to buy more political representation. Other kinds of participation are intrinsically more democratic than contributions, because there is a more equal opportunity to employ them: discussing and debating, sending a letter to the editor, going door-to-door to rouse one's neighbors, participating in a congressperson's town meeting, and casting a vote in an election. If it is desirable to accept the contribution of some limited amount of money as one kind of democratic participation, what is the argument against limiting contributions to a maximum of $50 per person, rather than $500 or $5,000 or $50,000? If the goal is increased participation, many more people can afford to "participate" in politics by giving $50 than can "participate" by giving $500.

There does not seem to be a reasonable case for allowing any small contribution above $50. Contributors who give $50 to support an issue ad can feel as strongly as those who would contribute $500. A very low $50 limit on contributions would not prevent legislators from obtaining the funds they need to present their ideas to the voters, if they can obtain public funding of campaigns and public matching funds to respond to attack ads. At the same time, voters' abilities to freely associate so as to propagate their ideas about issues and elections would *not* be unduly restricted by a $50 contribution limit. Voters associating together in PACs to propagate their views would merely have to find enough $50 contributors to pay for broadcasting their views. *Finding enough small contributors is no more onerous a problem than finding enough voters to back a candidate in an election.* Moreover, many public forums exist for the free expression of ideas, and candidates would be free to express the views of any groups they believe have reached reasonable conclusions. In addition, public matching funds would balance ads attacking candidates. Thus, low contribution limits on activities directly affecting an election plus public financing of campaigns plus matching would allow full expression of competing viewpoints, but without the shouting down effect of letting more wealthy interests own the microphone while other interests are left without one.

In summary, any effective reform proposal would include the nine reforms surveyed in this section, along with the three main reform proposals analyzed earlier in this chapter.

Public Funding of Parties

A tenth provision, public funding of parties, might be added to an optimal reform plan. Justice Clarence Thomas claims not to be able to understand how a party can corrupt its own candidates, since its best purpose is to influence the party's candidates in office.[56] But if a party is corrupted by money it takes in and associated political debts, it has an incentive to try to corrupt its officeholders so as to raise more money in the future. Then party officials will ask its legislators to alter legislation in their committees to benefit its contributors.

The problem of party corruption can also be solved by offering parties voluntary public funding on the condition they refuse all private funding. A publicly funded party would be provided with additional matching funds if needed to stay competitive with a privately funded party that raised more money.

If direct public funding of parties were not saleable to the American public, a scaled-down version may be more saleable. It could provide public funding for voter registration drives, advertising of party views on issues, candidate presentations, and other functions. Minor parties could be funded in the same way, but would receive only partial funding based on the percent of the vote won in a previous election or the number of signatures on petitions.

Okun's Principle: Anchor of the Three Main Remedies

The three main remedies for corruption presented above—public financing of campaigns, public funds to match private funding of attack ads, and enhanced public media to complement private media—all share a common property: they all depend on public funding and so embody a fundamental principle, called Okun's Principle of Countervailing Resources.[57] Arthur M. Okun, a former chairman of the White House Council of Economic Advisors, claimed the political equality required in a capitalist democracy can only be achieved by institutionalizing countervailing public resources to balance the anti-democratic influences of private wealth in politics.[58] Both democracy and free markets are desirable. The main question is, how can the wealth accumulated in the marketplace be prevented from corrupting the democratic process? How can wealthy interests be prevented from taking away from ordinary voters the representation a genuinely democratic political order guarantees? The only available way to reconcile market-generated wealth and true democracy is to adopt Okun's countervailing public resources approach.

Conclusion

This chapter arrays the elements likely to be included in an effective campaign finance reform law aimed at eliminating the undue influence of money in politics. Any effective campaign finance reform law would include full public financing of campaigns, provision of public matching funds to candidates for countering attack ads, low uniformly applicable contribution limits, and expansion of public broadcast media. The campaign reform package put forward here meets two criteria of effective reform: that reform end the corruption of officeholders, and that reform equalize political communications capabilities among candidates and major parties. Overall, democratic representation of voters in the United States would not be improved by any reform measure less effective than the package described above, because loopholes are opportunities.

Effective reform would guarantee that democratic rights are available equally to the non-wealthy and the wealthy, and that wealthy interests not monopolize the power to determine the direction of the society and the economy. Most Americans oppose the disproportionate influence of wealth in politics.

Karl Marx tried to remove the undue influence of wealth in politics by proposing the abolition of private property. James Madison hoped that different wealthy interests would balance one and another, and not collude. But they do collude by forming durable coalitions and by coopting legislators.[59] Looking beyond Marx and Madison, Okun's approach alone provides a means of reconciling capitalism and democracy, and the measures outlined in this chapter are at least necessary if not sufficient to achieve any effective reform embodying Okun's principle.

No one would dare campaign for public office by claiming the rich deserve extra votes or extra representation. Democracy requires equality before the law as a bulwark of human dignity.[60] Equality before the law strictly entails equality in influencing the enactment of the laws, since all citizens must obey them. Campaign contributions that buy influence over what laws are passed are incompatible with the "use of reason operating through accountable institutions."[61]

Chapter 3

The Decline of the Democratic Party

ONE MAJOR CONSEQUENCE OF CAMPAIGN FINANCE REFORM WOULD BE THE strengthening of the Democratic Party. As this chapter shows, the Democrats' voter base has declined dramatically, as have their seat totals in Congress and in state governments. Campaign reform would give Democratic lawmakers the opportunity to recapture an enormous amount of money now wasted servicing campaign contributors, as the next chapter shows. Once this money was recaptured, the congressional Democrats would have a strong partisan incentive, as described in chapter six, to reallocate these funds to popular programs so as to refloat their party. But the story starts with the decline of the Democratic Party.

Judging from indicators surveyed here, the Democratic Party has suffered a sharp secular decline in its voter base. As a result, the Democrats did poorly in the last four elections. First, in the 1994 election, the Democrats lost the House of Representatives for the first time in 40 years, and the Senate at the same time. Second, the Democrats regained almost no ground in 1996 and 1998.[1] Then in 2000, the Republicans achieved simultaneous control of the White House, the Senate, and the House for the first time since 1954, and also controlled a majority of governorships.[2]

It is surprising, therefore, that Democratic politicians have not proposed popular policies to win back lost voters. Why did the Democrats fail to enact popular programs when they controlled Congress and the presidency in 1993, and 1994? In the early 1990s, 70 to 90 percent of the public said there was a crisis in the American health care system.[3] In 1993, the Democrats took control of both the executive and legislative branches, and promptly announced their intention to enact universal health insurance. When they failed to deliver on this promise, voters viewed the 103rd Congress as a failure and the stunning defeat of the Democrats in 1994 was the direct consequence.[4] Mysteriously, since 1994, they have not offered proposals for universal health insurance and other popular but expensive programs. By failing to offer what voters want, normally entrepreneurial Democratic politicians seemed to have neglected their own self-interest. The reason is clear: the funds needed for popular programs go instead to campaign contributors.

Seven Indicators of the Democrats' Decline

The following seven indicators show the extent and duration of the decline in voters' loyalty to the Democrats: (1) the decline in Democratic Party identification; (2) increased volatility among the Democratic voters; (3) new voter registration tilting toward the Republicans; (4) weaker ideological and partisan intensity among Democratic voters than among Republican voters; (5) the realignment of the South into the Republican camp with no offset elsewhere in the country; (6) the potential for future seat losses due to redistricting around the 2000 Census; and (7) recent seat losses in Congress.

1. THE TREND IN DEMOCRATIC PARTY IDENTIFICATION. The term *party identification* refers to responses to survey questions asking voters if they identify with one of the parties, or if they are independent of them. Party identification is an indicator of a disposition to vote consistently for a party's candidates across different offices and across time.[5] The literature acknowledges the importance of partisan identification. For example, the authors of *The Personal Vote* wrote, "Even in the United States the single most important variable affecting the congressional vote remains the voter's partisan identification."[6]

The two best measures of U.S. party identification come from the University of Michigan's American National Election Studies (NES) and the Gallup Poll. For the period 1968 through 1982, NES data show the average number of Democratic identifiers led Republican identifiers by 20.75 percent.[7] In 1984, after the Reagan presidency was resurrected by a solid recovery from the worst recession since the 1930s, the Democrats' advantage in party identifiers dropped nearly 11 points. From 1984 through 1998, the Democratic lead in the NES data averaged 8.5 percent,[8] a nearly 60 percent drop. Gallup in-person interview data[9] for the same period shows almost the same results.[10]

Other Gallup data, however, show a much more dramatic loss of Democratic advantage over Republicans in the number of party identifiers. When Gallup used telephone interview data, the results showed that between 1978 and 1991, the Democrats dropped virtually *all* of a 24 percent point margin of voters calling themselves Democrats over voters calling themselves Republicans.[11] Since 1991, the Democrats recovered 8 of the 24 points.[12] Telephone data consistently show lower numbers of respondents reporting Democratic identification, and higher numbers reporting Independent identification, than do the in-person interview data.[13] It is possible people feel more comfortable in acknowledging that their party identification has changed in the more impersonal telephone interviews. If so, telephone interviews are more valid.[14] Gallup has now dropped in-person data for telephone interview data.

The 24 percent drop in the Democrats' advantage from 1978 to 1991 should have been a warning to the congressional Democrats that an upcoming election might deny them the control of Congress they enjoyed for so long. They should have inferred from the magnitude of this decline that their political capital had been greatly reduced.[15] Had they done so, they might have been more inclined to deliver some program that met the strong preferences of their base voters. The interviews for this study revealed many congressional Democrats understood this problem. It is all the more puzzling, therefore, that they failed to enact popular programs to remedy their problem with their base voters.

Various surveys put the number of the two parties' loyal partisans at rough parity all through the 1990s.[16] One might think the Democrats' problems are smaller than they seem if the Republicans have the same problems. On the contrary, even with parity in party identifiers, Republicans still have an advantage. In the United States (though not in Europe), the higher the income and education level, the higher the voter turnout. This disparity in voter turnout among different income classes widened in recent years.[17] So parity in voter identification should not provide the Democrats with grounds for complacency.

Differences in turnout rates between the two parties are not the only reason why parity in voter identification should not comfort the Democrats. The Democrats lack a message as intense and as focused as the Republicans have. The Republican message promises tax cuts, spending cuts, regulatory ease, support for school prayer, and opposition to abortion. These promises successfully target the intense concerns of many Republican voters. As the interviews for this study revealed, congressional Democrats have all but concluded they cannot find much money for the expensive programs their base voters want most—universal health insurance, education, job training, child care, long-term care, and others. For that reason, the Democrats' message has been less focused, less intense, and less successful than the party needs it to be. The Democrats' weaker message is reflected in their weaker turnout rate. The Republican base, being more satisfied with their party, is more intensely partisan than the Democratic base. Even though it has shrunk as much as the Democratic base, it turns out to vote more. Commenting on the 1994 election, Walter Dean Burnham notes, "The whole election was marked by very asymmetrical energizing and consolidation of the Republican, but not the Democratic, base."[18]

Furthermore, breaking out party identifiers by age shows Democratic Party identifiers more heavily clustered among cohorts who lived through the New Deal, Fair Deal, and Great Society periods. Time alone, then, is likely to disadvantage the Democrats, as older more loyal Democratic voters depart the electorate.[19]

2. INCREASED VOTER VOLATILITY. The literature has shown a decline across several decades in voters' disposition to vote consistently for the same party.[20] Voters

have increasingly split their votes, voting for one party for one office and the other party for other offices, and voting for different parties across elections. This growing volatility is the best indicator of the deterioration in voters' partisanship. Key indicators of voters' detachment from political parties, so-called dealignment,[21] include growing ticket-splitting between votes for President, House, Senate, and gubernatorial races, and growing neutrality of attitudes toward both parties. These indicators point to an increasingly less partisan electorate.[22] Moreover, party decomposition was evident in elections for open seats as well as incumbents' races, and in non-southern seats as well as southern ones.[23] The decline in partisan linkage is quite steep over the period from 1946 to 1988. Jacobson notes, "Wherever one looks, the association between election results for different offices with overlapping constituencies has diminished, often to insignificance."[24]

Moreover, Gary Jacobson notes, House elections have become increasingly detached from each other. Inter-election vote swings in the party vote have become more variable across districts in the same election, and district-level results show less consistency from one election to the next.[25] The same pattern holds for the 1994 election. The variation from one district to another was not significantly less in 1994 than in the period 1982 to 1988. All this fits neatly with the data on declining party identification. The party identification data reviewed in the previous section, if anything, underestimate party decomposition when compared with the data on voter volatility in voting for different offices and in different elections.[26]

But the above evidence of party decomposition is subject to misinterpretation. Jacobson notes,

> On a district-by-district, state-by-state basis, the link between the outcomes of state legislative and House elections has become remarkably weak. In the aggregate, however, these sets of elections continue to move together with considerable precision. . . . At the highest level of aggregation, House and state legislative elections continue to track one another quite closely. . . . Dissociation between individual elections does not, then, necessarily mean a decoupling of aggregate electoral results across offices; *it does not preclude strong and consistent national electoral change across a range of offices in response to national conditions.* (italics added)[27]

That is just what happened in the 1994 Republican surge. Democrats lost ground across the board in both the House and Senate, in the number of governors, and in the number of state legislatures they controlled. The Republican Party in 1994 offered the nation a clear anti-government message, which worked in no small part because the Democrats' base was softened up prior to 1994 by the failure of congressional Democrats to achieve an effective message/program of their own.

3. NEW VOTER REGISTRATION. Between 1988 and 1994, there was a large surge in new Republican voter registration relative to new Democratic voter registration in the 28 states that gather such aggregate state data. New voter registration favoring the Republicans occurred most of all in the South, but also was evident to a lesser extent in such large diverse states as California (14 percent), Pennsylvania (16 percent), Maryland (40 percent), and Oregon (23 percent). Then over the election cycles of 1994, 1996, and 1998, the distance between the two parties' registration levels stopped growing. Little change occurred in the proportion of voters registered as Democrat or Republican.[28] Yet the new lower level of Democratic voter registration is associated with the Democrats' minority status in Congress. The increases in Republican registration since 1988 suggest a long-run Republican realignment might be taking hold.[29]

4. THE DEMOCRATIC DISADVANTAGE IN IDEOLOGICAL AND PARTISAN INTENSITY AMONG PARTY VOTERS. Even more troubling for the Democrats are polling results from the Tarrance group, a prominent Republican polling firm working with Lake Research, a prominent Democratic polling firm. These polls show Democratic voters are much less focused ideologically than Republican voters. The July 12, 1999, Battleground 12 poll found 86 percent of Republican voters identified themselves as conservative, 6 percent as moderate, and 8 percent as liberal. Yet, only 49 percent of Democrats identified themselves as liberals, while 40 percent identified themselves as conservatives, and 11 percent as moderates. In Battleground 11 polled a year earlier, they found similar results.[30]

Other polls show other differences in Democratic and Republican voters' support for their party. In April 1995 Lake/Tarrance reported 67 percent of Republicans had a positive image of the GOP, while only 43 percent of Democrats had a positive image of their party.[31] So, support for the Democratic Party among its own partisans is soft compared with Republican voters' more intense support for their party. A reasonable interpretation of these polls is the Democrats' agenda/message does not have anywhere near the coherence, intensity, or clarity enjoyed by the Republicans' anti-government agenda.

5. REALIGNMENT IN THE SOUTH. The 1994 election results saw the Republicans capture a majority of southern House seats, a majority of southern Senate seats, and a majority of southern gubernatorial seats for the first time since the Reconstruction.[32] The realignment in the South may expand if, as Democratic incumbents retire, their seats are also picked up by the Republicans, and if redistricting gives more seats to the Republicans. However, some experts believe the Republicans may have already captured as many southern seats as they are likely to win. Either way, regaining effective control of Congress will require that the Democrats offset recent

Republican gains in the conservative South by picking up seats elsewhere. But winning enough seats elsewhere to offset Democratic losses in the South does not appear imminent.

6. EFFECTS OF REDISTRICTING ON THE DEMOCRATIC PARTY IN CONGRESS. Every ten years, after the Census Bureau has tabulated population movements among the states, Congressional district boundaries are redrawn accordingly. Some states gain and other states lose seats in the House of Representatives. Trends in regional economic growth make it likely that the more conservative, less Democratic, parts of the country will gain seats in Congress after the 2000 census.[33]

How many seats will be lost by the Democrats is unclear.[34] Despite population movements to conservative areas prior to the 1990 Census, the Republicans gained fewer seats than predicted. Democratic-controlled state legislatures were able to draw district lines more to their party's advantage than anticipated. Election Data Services has estimated that in 2003 Arizona and Texas will each gain two seats. California, Colorado, Florida, Georgia, Montana, and Nevada will gain one. New York and Pennsylvania will lose two each, and Connecticut, Illinois, Mississippi, Ohio, Oklahoma, and Wisconsin will each lose one.[35] In these 16 states, Democratic state legislatures and governors will control the redistricting of 68 congressional seats, including California's 52 seats. Republicans will control the redistricting of 43 seats. All the rest will be subject to either partisan contention or bipartisan deals.[36]

If partisan redistricting conflicts cannot be settled by state governments, federal judges may play a large role in redistricting. Since 1981, a large part of the federal bench has been filled by Republican judges appointed by Ronald Reagan and George H. W. Bush. Since 1995, appointees to the federal bench have been controlled by Senate Judiciary Committee Chairman Orrin Hatch (R-Utah) who tolerated a large number of vacancies on the bench rather than compromise with the Clinton administration on nominees' ideologies. So, conservative Republican federal judges may play a key role in drawing new district lines.[37] At stake is nothing less than the 10 or 20 House seats that may determine which party controls the House.

Republicans fear the loss of as many as five congressional seats in California, where Democrats control both the legislature and the executive. But overall, with population moving toward such conservative states as Texas, Florida, and Arizona, and away from traditionally Democrat states in the Northeast and Midwest, the redistricting picture joins other indicators in pointing to the potential of further losses of Democratic House seats.[30]

7. SEATS IN CONGRESS. The decline in Democratic Party identifiers was accompanied, with a significant lag, by an unprecedented decline in Democratic seat totals in the House in the 1990s. In the decades following World War II, Democratic

domination of the House showed remarkable stability. From 1954 through 1993, the Democrats never won less than 53.3 percent of House seats, and won 64.9 percent in 1964.[39] The Democrats lost a large number of seats only during a recession or major inflation under a sitting Democratic president (1980), or in rebound elections, which reversed unusual gains in a previous election (1960, 1966). Hence, incumbent congressional Democrats had little fear of large preventible party seat losses, until 1994 demonstrated their vulnerability.

Incumbent return rates of all members of the House seeking reelection between 1954 and 1993 averaged 92.8 percent,[40] and have been above 90 percent since 1994. The lowest rate was 87.7 percent in 1974. Clearly members had to work hard to achieve such rates. But they were unlikely to rethink the fundamentals of their approach to the voters with incumbency return rates so high. These rates obtained despite the sharp decline in voters' party identification, and despite growing ticket-splitting, as outlined above. So the Democrats' vulnerability, and the vulnerability of their party's control of Congress, at least until 1994, was seen as largely detached from national conditions and the fate of presidents of their own party.

The 1994 election, on the other hand, was fundamentally different from other elections. In 1994, the Democrats suffered large net seat losses—52 seats in the House and 8 seats in the Senate. They lost control of both the Senate and the House. Combining the results of the 1992 and 1994 elections, the Democrats lost a startling 63 seats net in the House and the same 8 net in the Senate. These losses were not attributable to economic conditions or any scandal or foreign policy disaster.[41] So the Democrats' disastrous losses in the 1994 election are better seen as resulting from Democratic voters' sense that Democratic politicians were failing to deliver what they needed.[42]

The 1994 election was a resounding repudiation of the Democratic Party more than anything else. Every single Republican incumbent was reelected to the House, the Senate, and to governorships. Thirty-five Republican challengers beat incumbent House Democrats, three Republican challengers beat Democratic senators, and five Republicans beat Democratic governors. Republicans won more open seats at every level. This repudiation of the Democrats was the only large seat loss in the postwar period when there was no recession, no major increase in inflation, and no Republican rebound from a previous election.[43] The 1996 and 1998 results hardly changed the House seat balance from 1994 election results.[44]

The next largest Democratic seat losses since 1946 occurred in the 1980 election. With historically high inflation, growing unemployment, and an energy crisis, the Democrats lost 34 House seats net, but lost 12 Senate seats, most by a hair. Combining the 1978 and 1980 results, the Democrats lost 49 House seats net and 15 Senate seats. Leaving 1980 aside, to find larger Democratic losses it is necessary to go back to 1946 when the party lost 56 seats in the House and 13 seats in the

Senate. So the Democrats' seat losses in 1992 and 1994 combined were of historic proportions.

From the 1994 election through the 2000 election, the Republican party was the majority party in the Senate, in the House, and in sitting governors, and held even with the Democrats in the number of state Houses and state Senates they controlled. And then in the 2000 election, the Republicans also took control of the White House, after intervention by the Supreme Court, despite an exceptionally strong economy under a Democratic president. So, the Democratic Party's continuing decline reveals a major message problem, notwithstanding the incumbency advantages of their members of Congress.

Some analysts believe congressional candidates do not need a national message to get themselves elected. Yet, Burnham has noted the tendency of political scientists to overemphasize the individualized congressional candidate campaigns as reflected in "the personal vote":

> 1994 is a very big event indeed. Conventional political science wisdom will in many respects have to be discarded and textbooks will have to be rewritten. Those who have stressed partisan dealignment will now have to consider how this abrupt emergence of something remarkably like an old-fashioned partisan election fits their models. And those who have placed their bets on the argument that critical realignments don't occur in modern, candidate-driven elections will have to reconsider their positions.[45]

Even before the 1996, 1998, and 2000 elections reestablished the seat balances established in 1994, Burnham categorized the 1994 election as "a critical realignment." The above trends indicate the chances are small the political balance will shift back toward the Democrats in the short or intermediate run.

Why Did the Democrats Get Weaker?

Some analysts believe the Democrats have become weaker because their national policy positions have been unpopular, notably their tastes for bigger government, higher taxes, and programs for minorities. These analysts conclude that because these policies have been unpopular, Democratic congresspersons learned to depend instead on increased use of incumbency advantages to dispense benefits to parochial local interests.[46]

The facts contradict this view. Stanley Greenberg's polls show the Democrats' support for those limited social insurance and public investment measures they did campaign on was popular.[47] Moreover, if the Democrats' national positions were so unpopular, how could the Republicans fail for decades to win more open seats (in which no incumbent was running) than Democrats did? From 1968 to 1998, Republicans only won 82 open seats in the House, while Democrats won 95.[48] The Democrats' party image, howsoever weakened, must have helped their open seat candidates win, since non-incumbent candidates could not access incumbency advantages. Moreover, had Democratic congresspersons cast unpopular votes in Congress, they could not have hidden behind incumbency advantages. Primary opponents or clever staff at the Republican National Committee would have made these unpopular votes the subject of attack ads.[49] And so, the Democratic Party's ties to its base voters, though weakened, must have continued to benefit from the image of its traditional economic program commitments, even if those commitments had become weaker.

The decline of the Democrats' voter base occurred despite changes that strengthened their congressional party in the same period. The departure of many southern Democrats from Congress increased party cohesion, as reflected in increased party unity scores.[50] At the same time, Democratic congressional leaders became better organized in using polling, focus groups, media, and fund-raising. Yet, this high-tech campaigning—finding out what voters wanted to hear and then telling them just that—did not prevent a dramatic weakening in the congressional Democrats' seat totals anyway.[51]

Only one explanation seems to account for how the Democratic Party became weaker despite the changes just mentioned. Because of the introduction of television in the 1960s, and because of the high costs of buying ads on TV, members' need to raise money grew dramatically. So, the party's legislators had no choice but to satisfy contributors, whose demands preempted the funds needed for programs that might have been used to court voters. The party's ties to voters weakened accordingly over time.[52]

Three Views of the Post-1994 Party Balance

The trends discussed above can be interpreted in three ways. The first interpretation, the story of the complacent Democrat, argues the Democrats have lost less ground than the above trends suggest, and can win back control of Congress by fine-tuning the machinery so as to gain a few more votes here and there.

The second interpretation, the story of the pessimistic Democrat, argues the Democrats do need to change their message/program if they are to win back a majority of voters. However, in this view, money enough to fund popular programs and support a new message *just isn't there*, and so the decline in the Democrats' voter base is unlikely to be reversed. This interpretation is rooted in the Pluralist paradigm described in chapter five.

The third interpretation, that of the optimistic reformer, agrees the Democrats need to strengthen their message, but argues the money *is there* to fund programs that would support a more effective message. Effective campaign finance reform, by releasing Democratic legislators from the grip of campaign contributors, would allow them to massively reallocate funds from waste to popular programs. The optimistic reformer's interpretation draws on the outline of federal waste in chapter four, and on the Strong Parties theory described in chapter six.

What evidence supports these three views? The evidence supporting the complacent Democrat's interpretation of past trends is substantial. First, the Democratic Party's strengths in fund-raising, polling, focus groups, media projection, and coordinated campaigns, make the party highly competitive. Second, many of the congressional seats the Democrats lost in recent years were held by conservative southern Democrats. Their departure from Congress strengthened party cohesion and effectiveness. Third, after the 2000 election, the Democrats were only seven seats shy of controlling the House, and only one seat shy of controlling the Senate. Normal fluctuations in seat balances might give the Democrats control of the House in the near future. Fourth, of the 33 senators up for reelection in 2002, 20 are Republicans and only 13 are Democrats, and so the Democrats will have an advantage in their efforts to regain control of the Senate.[53] However, retirements in 2002 may well subtract substantially from Democratic seat totals in the House. Fifth, most congressional districts are dominated by one party or the other, and incumbency return rates above 90 percent imply most Democratic congresspersons will continue to hold their seats. Sixth, after several years of Republican control of the White House, voters will blame the Democrats less and the Republicans more.

Other evidence, however, undermines the optimism of the complacent Democrat. The 2000 election was the fourth in a row in which the Democrats failed to win enough seats to regain control of Congress. Moreover, even if the Democrats regained control of both houses of Congress, much of the Democratic agenda would be buried in a Senate controlled by the conservative coalition of Republicans and conservative Democrats. The Democratic mainstream would need a Senate with at least 60 seats controlled by progressive Democrats to vote cloture on a filibuster, so votes on major party initiatives could take place on the Senate floor. In the House, given deviations from party voting, passage of a popular Democratic agenda would require a Democratic seat total significantly larger than a strict majority of 218 votes, though some moderate Republicans might be supportive on some votes. So, to achieve *effective* control of Congress, the Democrats would need more seats than just a numerical majority, and at present that many seats are not within reach.

The complacent Democrat's interpretation is also undermined by a number of other considerations. There is no indication the long-term trend decline in voters' loyalty to the Democrats has come to an end. Democratic voters' turnout decline and ticket-splitting is likely to continue as long as the Democratic Party fails to address their concerns aggressively. The continuing replacement of older Democratic voters by younger, less loyal voters may also continue to weaken Democratic partisanship. Moreover, growing cynicism about the role of money in politics can only disproportionately weaken voters' loyalty to Democratic politicians. In addition, the Republicans will most likely gain seats in Congress from redistricting, further reducing the Democrats' chances of regaining effective control of Congress.

Furthermore, in the 2000 election, the Democrats were advantaged by very high job approval ratings of a sitting Democratic president,[54] low unemployment, low inflation, and a booming stock market. Yet, surprisingly, they still failed to win control of the White House—an unfavorable omen.[55] Nor did the Democrats gain significant ground in the 1998 congressional elections, despite the backlash against the Republicans' unpopular effort to impeach President Clinton, and despite the unusually successful effort by the AFL-CIO, other unions, the NAACP, and other minority organizations to increase Democratic turnout, an effort larger yet in 2000.[56] The Democrats just held even plus one seat in each chamber in the congressional election of 1998. So, the long-term decline in the Democrats' base outlined above, and the message problem it reflects, may continue to put Democratic seat totals in Congress at risk.

In the short run, elections can be won by strong party organizations adept at fund-raising and media manipulation.[57] Yet, sooner or later a price must be paid for running campaigns lacking broad and intense appeal to the party's base. An abundance of polling data show most voters want major new economic programs, and are dissatisfied with existing policies.[58] The Republicans' relatively clear and intense message unites them with their base more than the Democrats' message unites them with their base. The pessimistic Democrat and the optimistic reformer both interpret recent trends as showing the Democrats need a more powerful message to reverse the decline in their voter base and regain effective control of Congress.

Supporting this theory is an analysis by Ruy Teixeira, who points to a number of polls that explain the evolving relationship between the Democrats' message and their declining voter base. He drew in part on *Washington Post* reporter Dale Russakoff's interviews in September 2000 with white working- and middle-class voters in the Lehigh Valley, a swing area of Pennsylvania. These voters are insecure about their ability to cope with the future, about paying for college, the health care of aging parents, and retirement. They fear the globalizing economy, and are concerned about child care and the extent of coverage provided by HMOs. Candidate Al Gore's promise to use government programs to meet health, education, and retirement needs was very attractive to these voters. So were Gore's populist attacks on such corporate interests as big oil, tobacco and pharmaceutical companies, and HMOs. Yet, the voters were still not convinced by Gore's appeal. Bush was able to persuade voters he too was concerned with Gore's issues. Bush's efforts to preempt Democratic issues worked to a considerable extent. Teixeira notes,

> But while the voters seem be on Gore's turf, their bond with the vice president was tenuous. Russakoff has found a considerable lack of clarity in what Gore proposed to do about these problems and an uneasy sense that politicians might be substituting easy answers for truly workable solutions. . . . Where voters became confused about the real differences between Gore and Bush on policy . . . the tie frequently went to Bush. . . . The move away from Gore over this period was driven primarily by non-college voters, particularly younger women among whom Gore had made some of his larger gains after the convention. . . . Voters also lack a Democratic vision for the new global economy [that would help them] fix the key differences between the parties in their minds. . . .[59]

Thus, the Democrats have failed to address voters' discontents with an appealing message, such as one promising universal health insurance and effective education. They have failed to distinguish their policies from Republican rhetoric promising similar things in broad terms. The lack of convincing specifics in the Democrats' message is reflected in the findings that the Democratic voters show considerably less intense loyalty to their party than Republican voters do, as shown in the Tarrance/Lake Battleground polls presented earlier in this chapter. These same polls also showed greater ideological intensity among Republican voters. Both findings fit neatly with the Teixeira/Russakoff results.

The Democrats' opportunities were anticipated by the Democrats' most determined opponent. According to Haynes Johnson and David Broder:

> To Gingrich, defeating health care reform was essential to making himself the first Republican Speaker of the House of Representatives in forty years. . . . Had *any* part of the Clinton plan passed Congress in *any* form, Gingrich and his closest conservative allies believed, their dreams for forging a militantly conservative future would "have been cooked," as a key Gingrich strategist explained. It would have been the final nail in the coffin of the American marketplace resulting in a social-welfare state like Britain and Canada, creating greater public dependency on government and a government run plan, and a stronger allegiance of voters to majority Democrats, who provided them with their benefits.[61]

Analyses of Democratic losses that year emphasize the huge impact of the Democrats' failure to deliver on their promise to legislate "health security."[62] Why did Democratic leaders, themselves skillful political entrepreneurs, fail to unite their party behind the sort of policy proposals that would have provided the popularity they wanted to achieve? The answer proposed here is that the Democrats are severely cross-pressured between their base voters and their contributors, who preempt the funds needed for popular programs.

Contrary to the views of the complacent Democrat, tweaking the election machinery a bit here and there for a few more votes is unlikely to reverse the long-term decline in the Democrats' base, or restore the Democratic Party to effective control over American political institutions. Like the pessimistic Democrat, the optimistic reformer believes the Democrats will have to change their message if they are to reverse their decline. The optimistic reformer's interpretation, however, is anchored in the view that once campaign finance reform released members of Congress from the grip of campaign contributors, the funds needed for popular programs could be taken from federal funds that are now wasted. Thus, assuming reformers can bring enough pressure to bear on Congress to force enactment of effective campaign finance reform, campaign reform holds the key to the dynamics of the party system. The next chapter shows where the Democrats would find that money, and how much money they could find, once effective campaign finance reform freed them to do so.

Chapter 4

Would Campaign Reform Yield Enough Money to Refloat the Democrats?

THE PREVIOUS CHAPTER ARGUED THE DEMOCRATIC PARTY IS IN DECLINE, NEEDS a new message to win back its voter base, and needs to legislate costly new programs to support such a message. But many observers believe the money to pay for such programs can only be found by legislating politically unpopular tax increases. So, Democratic politicians believe "the money is just not there" to fund new government investments in education, job training, health care, child care, and other priorities. But perhaps the money is "there." Campaign finance reform would change the incentives of members of Congress, making them much more willing to recapture wasted federal funds and reallocate them to new popular programs. Yet, only if the amount of wasted money is quite large can it support a party program and critical national priorities. This chapter examines the magnitude of federal waste to see if it is large enough to support major new programs.

Some prominent observers believe the magnitude of federal waste is very large. According to Derek Bok, president emeritus of Harvard University,

> For years, pundits have criticized voters for wanting to keep all their [government] benefits without being willing to raise taxes. Yet a careful look at the record suggests that it might be possible to have our cake and eat it too if only we could find a way to keep so many morsels from falling off the table. Had we designed our health care system more wisely, targeted our spending more precisely to accord with genuine needs, developed more cost-effective methods of regulation, and cut back on farm subsidies and other unjustifiable benefits, we could have saved enough not only to keep from running deficits but to provide universal medical coverage, create better programs for long term health care, build more affordable housing, and attend to many other needs in which we lag behind other leading industrial democracies.[1]

Much waste is hidden from the public. This year was not the first year Washington's K Street lobbyists persuaded Congress to write their clients' requests into law. Decade after decade, windfalls won by campaign contributors and their lobbyists have been stacked on top of gains they had won in previous years.[2] Decade after decade, lobbyists have persuaded legislators to implant their clients' demands in the tax, expenditure, and regulatory systems of the federal government. The cumulative effect is that every year systemic corruption causes the nation to lose more and more money that might have been used for national priorities. Members of Congress of both parties are afraid to challenge those who may withhold campaign contributions, launch attack ads, or fund challengers. Hence the status quo and the perception that waste is inevitable and nothing can be done about it. Understandably, most analyses stop there.

A Note on Projected Federal Budget Surpluses

An argument might be made that present and future federal budget surpluses will be so large that other potential sources of funds would not be needed to support national priorities. That is not the case. It is necessary to present projected surplus figures accompanied by corresponding projections of expenditures. Consider the budget surplus for on-budget (non-social security) discretionary spending at the rate of inflation for spending levels under current law. Those figures are $86 billion for 2001 and $135 billion for 2010. However, no allowance is made in these figures for additional funding that will be needed to pay for increased Medicare and other outlays for a growing elderly population. Large tax cuts and increases in military spending, proposed by the presidential candidates during the 2000 election campaign, would also shrink these surpluses, as would spending needed for a growing population, for environmental challenges including global warming, for education and job training, and for faster federal debt reduction. Surplus projections also make no allowance for the next recession, since its timing, depth, and duration are unknowable in advance. Yet, any recession will reduce revenues and therefore reduce the surplus as well. Moreover, estimates of surpluses need to take account of spending demands that surplus projections themselves stimulate, especially after a decade of fiscal restraint, and especially after the expiration of the spending caps in 2001. Robert D. Reischauer notes,

> To maintain current real per capita discretionary spending would require 19 percent more discretionary spending in 2009 than the budget projections assume will be provided.[3]

Hence, it is necessary to look beyond projected federal budget surpluses to find the funds with which to support national priorities.

Finding the Money: (1) Reducing Direct Government Waste

The enumeration of federal waste below shows that eliminating it would provide enough money to finance large-scale increases in public and private investment and social insurance. Federal government waste is much greater than ordinarily understood. There are two major categories of government waste. The first category includes *direct waste*—what government does. It subsidizes where it should not, commits tax expenditures where it should not, leaves massive amounts of tax revenue uncollected, permits rent seeking, manages federal programs inefficiently or ineffectively, and makes grants to the states and to private agents who act on inappropriate incentives, and fails to conduct adequate oversight.

The second waste category is *indirect waste*, which is based on government's failure to act. A prime example of indirect waste is the waste that arises from children being left untaught, causing opportunity costs never added up for the voters. How much more productive would those children have been had they been better educated, and how much more productive would the economy have been as a result? Such waste entails quantifiable losses to the nation, even if there is no "opportunity costs budget." This study does not attempt to quantify total indirect waste. But indirect waste buttresses the case for campaign reform at least as much as direct waste does.

What follows examines five kinds of direct federal waste: individual tax expenditures, business tax and non-tax subsidies, rent seeking, uncollected revenue from taxes on legal activities, and federal program waste. Much of this, and possibly all of it, could be recaptured and reallocated to national priorities if effective campaign reform became law.

Waste I: Individual Tax Expenditures

Tax expenditures are a large part of total direct waste. The 1974 Congressional Budget and Impoundment Control Act defined tax expenditures as "revenue losses attributable to provisions of the federal tax laws which allow a special exclusion, exemption, or deduction from gross income or which provide a special credit, a preferential rate of tax, or a deferral of tax liability."[4] The domain of tax expenditures, divided between individual and corporate taxes, is vast. Joseph A. Pechman estimated tax expenditures, good and bad, equaled a full 34 percent of all federal outlays, even after the dramatic reductions of the Tax Reform Act of 1986.[5] The Congressional Budget Office has estimated that tax expenditures equaled 34 percent of all federal outlays in fiscal year 1998, or about $601 billion.[6] If even half this much—$300 billion—could be shifted to more productive uses, the productivity gains for the nation would be large. Pechman also pointed out the distributional effects of tax expenditures are less progressive than direct expenditures. Moreover, tax expenditures are virtual entitlements. Once in the tax code they are likely to remain unchallenged for long periods, because they are not subjected to scrutiny each year in the annual appropriations process of the Congress.

Surprisingly, in a period when federal spending has been cut back sharply, tax expenditures are actually increasing dramatically. Discretionary programs—all programs except entitlements and debt interest—are capped. After inflation, discretionary programs are expected to decline 13 percent from 1995 to 2001, and are expected to decline 26 percent as a share of the economy by 2001. In contrast, tax expenditures will increase $175 billion by 2002.[7]

Some tax expenditures fund worthwhile programs. The exclusion from both income and payroll taxes of employer-financed health insurance is both popular and justifiable. One estimate finds that ending this exclusion would lead to a decline in demand for health insurance of between 11 and 38 percent, and the uninsured would rise by 5.5 million people.[8] Reformers would also leave some other tax expenditures intact, notably exclusion of taxes on social security income for less well-off taxpayers, workman's compensation, and the earned income tax credit.

But many other tax expenditures do not efficiently serve national goals, including some in the categories of personal tax expenditures and corporate tax expenditures. What follows examines both.

A. THE HOME MORTGAGE DEDUCTION is capped at a million dollars per home, and extends to second homes.[9] In addition, interest payments up to $100,000 on home equity loans are deductible. Suppose a wealthy individual purchases a home with a million-dollar mortgage at ten percent interest a year. His interest payments would equal $100,000 per year, which is deductible. At the highest federal income tax rate of 39.6 percent, his deduction would be worth $39,600 dollars per year to him. Someone with a $150,000 mortgage paying ten percent interest who is in the 15 percent tax bracket, only gets a deduction of $2,250 per year. Moreover, only 27 million tax returns deduct home mortgage interest out of 64 million homes, and renters miss all benefits. Most of the benefits of the deduction go to the wealthiest citizens.

Mortgage interest overall will amount to $285 billion in 1998 to 2002, or $57 billion a year over five years. The amount of revenue that can be recaptured from altering the deduction depends on political decisions as to whether deductions should be denied to the top ten percent of family incomes, the top quarter, the top half, limited to houses less expensive than the median-priced house in the state, or some other limit. If the National Association of Realtors and the home-building industry could no longer distribute campaign contributions on Capitol Hill, Congress might at least establish the principle that the richer the family, the smaller the subsidy. Reducing the ceiling on the price of a house eligible to receive a deduction from $1 million to $300,000, and phasing out the deductibility of interest on home equity loans would net $32 billion a year in revenue that could be applied elsewhere.[10]

One common critique of housing subsidies is they lead to excessive aggregate investment in housing relative to other investments that would increase productivity more. Leaving aside subsidies for lower-income households, concern for productivity growth is a sufficient reason for reallocating housing subsidies to other more productive uses.

B. THE DEDUCTIBILITY OF PROPERTY TAXES ON OWNER-OCCUPIED HOUSING was worth $17 billion in Fiscal Year 1997 and $95 billion in 1998 to 2002. Owners of capital largely bear the burden of the property tax, and therefore it is a progressive tax.[11] Consequently, the benefits of its deductibility are enjoyed disproportionately by the well-off.

C. THE STEP-UP BASIS OF CAPITAL GAINS AT DEATH also benefits the wealthy most because they have the bulk of the capital gains. It was worth $31 billion in 1997, and will be worth $173 billion from 1998 to 2002. This tax provision might have some positive saving incentive effects, tied to the desire of a parent to leave money to their children, the so-called bequest motive. But since little is known about the bequest motive,[12] this provision depends on unproven assertions regarding the benefits to all from a tax advantage enjoyed primarily by the well-off. Other saving and investment options have positive effects that are far better established.

D. DEDUCTIBILITY OF STATE AND LOCAL TAXES reduces revenues to the federal government by about $44 billion per year.

E. THE EXCLUSION OF INTEREST ON STATE AND LOCAL BONDS costs the Treasury an additional $20 billion per year in lost revenue, for a total loss in revenue of $64 billion a year.[13] Once again, the more affluent a taxpayer, the larger his deduction. A substantial portion of the bond interest exclusion is a windfall for very wealthy individuals. This deduction and exclusion are quite controversial on both efficiency and equity grounds.[14] The rationale for allowing the deduction of state and local taxes supposedly is that it subsidizes public expenditures in the states and municipalities. In fact it encourages state and local governments to lower the effective rate on otherwise progressive income and property taxes. The deduction also reduces the revenue available to the federal government, requiring either reduced services or increases in other taxes. A deduction or exclusion under a progressive tax is more valuable to a taxpayer the higher his income. A far more efficient and more equitable alternative to the deductibility of state and local taxes would be to have the federal government substitute direct subsidies to state and local governments.[15]

F. OTHER CONTROVERSIAL TAX EXPENDITURES ENJOYED BY INDIVIDUALS INCLUDE lower tax rates on capital gains than on other income and deferral of income from controlled foreign corporations. The amounts of lost revenue associated with each are, respectively, $8 billion in 1998 and $45 billion 1998 to 2002, and $2 billion and $14 billion, for a total of $10 billion in 1998. In addition, agriculture, timber, iron ore, and coal enjoy their own special preferential capital gains treatments, which are not calculated here.

Almost two-thirds of total reported capital gains go to those whose incomes exceed $200,000 per year.[16] One authoritative study of capital gains tax treatment shows the efficiency arguments for the tax preferences are weak. This study argues these tax preferences do not improve saving, investment, and growth.[17] If this and similar studies are correct, capital gains tax preferences should be removed from the tax code, and the recovered funds reallocated to national priorities.

So far only the largest individual tax expenditures have been listed. The White House Office of Management and Budget list, from which these numbers were taken, contain many other smaller tax expenditures, which when added together take significant amounts of money away from national priorities.[18] Let us arbitrarily add another $20 billion a year in lost federal revenue for these, though this is surely a considerable understatement.

Waste II: Business Tax and Non-Tax Subsidies

Business tax subsidies are more complex than individual ones. They take a wider variety of forms, including low-interest loans, loan guarantees, grants, below-market insurance rates, trade restrictions, provision of public goods and services at below-market rates, federal purchases of privately produced goods and services at above-market rates, exemptions from laws, as well as tax deductions, exemptions, credits, and allowances. The rationales for these different subsidies are accordingly complex and varied. These complexities in turn interact with specific problems in defining a tax expenditure, in determining the coverage of a tax expenditure, in selecting a tax benchmark, and in choosing a method of calculating tax expenditures.[19] No attempt is made here to examine the justifications of any of the following business subsidies. Rather, what follows will point to some that have been questioned by responsible analysts, and lists some of the amounts involved. Absent a convincing defense, such tax breaks should be cut.[20]

One catalogue of business subsidies, by Robert J. Shapiro, then of the centrist Progressive Policy Institute of the Democratic Leadership Council, came up with

$131 billion in savings over five years from cutting questionable federal subsidies for business, or nearly $26 billion a year.[21] Two-thirds of the subsidies go to three industry groups: agribusiness, transportation companies, and energy and other natural resource companies. In addition, Shapiro found business tax expenditures of $102 billion over five years, or $20 billion a year. His total list of unjustified business tax expenditures and subsidies costs the taxpayers $46 billion per year. Trade protection is responsible for directly transferring an additional $32 billion a year to 21 protected industries from consumers and other businesses,[22] for a total of $78 billion per year.

The libertarian-conservative CATO Institute, headed by William Niskanen, has identified four industries enjoying $65 billion a year in unjustified federal aid: agriculture, exports, high technology, and energy. Large recipients within these four industries included such companies as the Archer-Daniel Midland Corporation, Rockwell International, Westinghouse, B. F. Goodrich, McDonnell Douglas, and AT&T. The issue arises whether such highly profitable companies are appropriate recipients of federal aid, given other needs that go unfunded.

The progressive Citizens for Tax Justice (CTJ) has identified a large number of corporate tax expenditures and subsidies that are unjustified from their viewpoint. The biggest corporate tax expenditure by far is for accelerated depreciation of machinery and equipment worth $23 billion in 1998 and $259 billion over the next seven years. This tax preference allows many large corporations to reduce their corporate tax liability by half the 35 percent statutory rate. This tax preference is supposed to encourage corporations to make investments they might not find economic without the tax break.[23] The issue is whether they would have made those investments anyway. CTJ estimates accelerated depreciation is worth $13,000 per year to people making $200,000 per year, and less than $70 per year to families earning under $50,000 per year.

CTJ estimates of other corporate tax expenditures, those over $1 billion per year, include (with Fiscal Year 1998 estimated revenue losses) accelerated depreciation of buildings other than rental housing ($3 billion), the graduated corporation income tax rate ($5 billion), exclusion of interest on public purpose state and local debt ($6 billion), a tax credit for corporations receiving income from doing business in U.S. possessions ($3 billion), exclusion of income earned abroad by U.S. citizens ($2 billion), exclusion of income of foreign sales corporations ($2 billion), and deferral of income from controlled foreign corporations ($2 billion). The total of all corporate tax expenditures over $1 billion a year cost $58 billion in fiscal year 1998 in lost revenues, and roughly half again as much revenue is lost to tax expenditures below the $1 billion threshold, or roughly another $25 billion. Together they total $83 billion a year in lost revenues.

Transfer pricing is sometimes used as a form of tax avoidance, when multinational corporations identify as foreign income what is actually domestic income, sales, assets, and so on. Transfer pricing is said to cost the Treasury between $15 billion and $20 billion per year.[24]

Other corporate tax breaks identified by CTJ include tax breaks for the insurance industry, worth $22 billion a year over seven years, including preferences for interest on life insurance savings, preferences for small property and casualty companies, the deduction of unpaid property loss reserves of property and casualty companies, special treatment of life insurance company reserves, preferences for insurance companies owned by tax-exempt organizations, and for Blue Cross and Blue Shield. CTJ identifies $21 billion in tax preferences over six years going to energy companies for exploration and development costs, percentage depletion, oil and gas exception to passive loss limitation, and so on. Timber, agriculture, and mineral extraction industries receive an additional $10 billion over six years. And there are others.[25]

$6 billion in deductions are made a year in business meals and entertainment.[26] These exemptions are widely used for non-business purposes, and there is no adequate rationale to support a subsidy to the restaurant or entertainment industries, who routinely testify in favor of this deduction.

Waste III: Rent Seeking

Another major area of federal waste includes benefits obtained by purchasing government protection from competition and from government regulation.[27] Exchanges of government benefits in return for campaign contributions is rent seeking.[28] William J. Baumol characterizes rent seeking as a source of wasted resources that might have been devoted to increasing productivity, especially lost entrepreneurial energies. Baumol discusses such rent-seeking activities as unjustified lawsuits, manipulation of certain kinds of government regulatory oversight of prices and investments of firms under agency supervision, and financial market devices such as golden parachutes, greenmail, poison pills, and risk arbitrage. He notes,

> Battalions of business persons, lawyers, and economists were diverted from productive contribution in pursuit of available rent . . . it seems to be widely agreed that it takes its most extreme form in the United States . . .

He counsels changes in law and in government regulations to stop rent seeking, as have been used extensively in other advanced countries.[29]

The ability of securities firms to block an efficient national saving plan (see below) may be the single most expensive example of rent seeking. The rent involved would be the foregone national productivity gains that would have occurred had national saving increased and fueled more investment.

Baumol does not try to come up with a dollar figure for the amount of waste due to rent seeking. But it's clear from his and other accounts it is quite large. I take the liberty here of arbitrarily adding $100 billion a year to the list of wasted resources, which the discussion of saving policy later in this chapter shows is probably understated.

Waste IV: Uncollected Revenue

Still another source of massive waste, perhaps the largest of all, is uncollected tax revenues from tax cheats, which could be recouped if increased funds for IRS agents were appropriated by Congress. The Internal Revenue Service has conservatively estimated that in 1992, $119 billion in taxes owed to the government were uncollected. Roughly three-quarters of this is unpaid individual income taxes, and one-quarter is from corporate income taxes.

But in a study based on IRS data, Slemrod and Bakija arrive at a much larger estimate of uncollected revenue. They find about $750 billion per year in unreported income and illegitimate deductions.[30] These figures do not include such illegal sources of income as drug profits. In addition, tax evasion lowers the costs of many services and goods paid for under the table. Those lower costs act to divert resources to those services and goods whose prices are lower because of the tax avoidance. These lower costs pull resources toward less economic uses than would be utilized absent tax evasion.[31] In addition, they add a large increase in revenue from the added deterrent effect from increased auditing. Combining direct and indirect gains from more vigorous enforcement of the tax laws could yield huge resources that could be devoted to national priorities.

This uncollected revenue could be recovered efficiently if congressional appropriations for more IRS agents were forthcoming.[32] The official IRS estimate is for every extra dollar the IRS spent on auditing returns, it would gain an additional $4 to $7 of additional revenue directly from the audited returns.[33] If Congress invested in enough additional agents and if it fully utilized information technologies to follow an individual's income and expenditure trails, one could guess arbitrarily but very conservatively that the IRS could easily recover $250 billion from the $750 billion a year in funds now lost to tax evasion, given the lower estimate of $4 returned for every dollar spent on an additional IRS agent. This $250 billion figure is probably too low.

It is difficult to understand why Congress has failed to give the IRS the added funding needed to collect taxes now evaded. Congresspersons are eager to find enough revenue to satisfy different constituencies, all clamoring for federal funds. Budget surpluses make life easier for Congress compared with tough choices imposed on them by deficits. Yet, anomalously, not a single account has surfaced to explain why the Congress has failed to fund the IRS enough to enable them to capture the additional revenue owed under existing tax laws.

Waste V: Direct Federal Government Program Waste

The Congressional Budget Office offers annual analyses of spending and revenue options, and their presentation offers many items that might qualify as waste.[34] However, not everyone would agree on which items are wasteful. Some of CBO's candidates for cuts come from conservatives, others from liberals. Let's assume half of the proposals identify true waste, and half are ideologically driven. To gain some sense of the magnitude of true federal program waste, we can total all of the CBO items and divide by half.

In the list of possible program cuts that CBO offers, entitlement programs and options for raising revenue are not included, nor are interest payments on the national debt. CBO's list of discretionary outlays that could be cut, and their costs during Fiscal Year 1998 to 2002 were added, and divided by five years, for a total of $92 billion in outlays per year.[35] Dividing by half, we arrive at $46 billion, as a very rough estimate of federal government program waste. In a budget with nearly $2 trillion in outlays, a mere $46 billion in waste does not seem surprising.

This number, however, is undoubtedly too low. CBO fails to consider many other wasteful projects noted by others. Yale economist William Nordhaus has offered his own view of egregious waste:

> The problem is not that government has a pro-consumption bias but that government investment projects are often inefficient and poorly targeted and have a low social benefit-cost ratio.
>
> Examples of misdirected investments are as plentiful as the stars. Why are we building attack submarines to combat a former adversary that has become a third-world economy? Why are we funding $10 billion in energy, defense, and Superfund environmental cleanups with no perceptible health benefits? Does it make sense to eliminate the R&D tax credit, a subsidy that has proven effective in stimulating high yield, private-sector investment activity? Is it really effective for the Export-Import Bank and other agencies to spend $1.3 billion on "combating foreign subsidies"? Does the nation need a massive agricultural extension service while we are paying farmers not to produce? How long should we continue to invest $1 billion per year in new veterans hospitals? Why must we invest medical dollars disproportionately in the last months of life rather than the first few years of life? Why do we continue to give away federal lands and airport slots? The list could go on and on.[36]

Hence, $50 billion a year in federal program waste is, then, undoubtedly too low a figure.

Total Direct Government Waste: A Preliminary Tally

The numbers attached to all of the above categories of direct federal government waste add up as follows:

(1) There are, conservatively, $250 billion a year in questionable individual tax expenditures, heavily benefiting the top strata of the income distribution.
(2) There are, conservatively, $150 billion a year in questionable corporate tax expenditures and subsidies, which mostly benefit the top strata of the income distribution.
(3) There are, conservatively, at least $250 billion a year in uncollected tax revenue that could be recovered, which is only a small part of a total estimated $750 billion in uncollected tax revenue, not counting taxable income from illegal activities.
(4) There is at least $100 billion a year lost to the government due to rents from purchased government protections from competition and from government regulation.
(5) There is at least $50 billion a year in waste from direct government programs, cutting in half CBO's estimates of options for program reductions.
(6) An additional $200 billion a year could be raised after a more thorough analysis of these same categories.

On the last point, a House Democratic Caucus Task Force on Government Waste cited relatively smaller items totaling $60 billion to $85 billion per year that were not included in the above categories.[37] In addition, the income tax has been compromised by various legislated leakages—deductions, exemptions, credits, and allowances—not all of which were listed above. These income tax leakages totaled $1.270 trillion in 1993.[38] Scrutiny of the process by which interest groups exert influence in the Congress and the Executive Branch suggests digging deeper will reveal much more waste.[39]

The total waste indicated above in these six categories is, then, at least $1 trillion a year. This figure may seem too high. After all, total federal outlays for the year 2000 were estimated to be $1.739 billion.[40] Could waste be 57 percent of the federal budget? But that is the wrong baseline. The correct baseline is the budget plus off-budget categories, including tax expenditures, rent seeking, and uncollected revenues on legal activities. Avoidable interest on the national debt would be an additional waste item, and a large one, on top of the estimate provided here. Elimination of the federal debt, if achieved rapidly, could contribute substantially to waste reduction. None of this includes indirect waste that might be specified in an opportunities cost budget, if there were such a thing.

Much of this waste is the direct result of campaign contributors' demands for quids pro quo. Hence, effective campaign finance reform can be expected to eliminate most of this waste, freeing up these wasted funds so they may be spent on national priorities.

Finding the Money: (2) Increasing the National Saving Rate

A higher national saving rate creates a larger national pool of capital. The larger the pool of capital, the lower the interest rates, which increases the affordability of borrowing for investment, both private and public. Both businesses and government benefit from lower interest rates when they borrow to finance investments. For example, when interest rates are lower, a local government can float a school bond issue at a lower cost to taxpayers, making it possible to build more schools. When interest rates are pushed down by increases in the saving rate, new investments, public and private, drive up national productivity and national income.[41] Hence, a government that fails to adopt policies to increase the saving rate wastes the opportunity to have a permanently higher national income—an enormous waste.

Many economists claim the U.S. saving rate is unacceptably low compared with rates in earlier decades, and compared with other nations' rates.[42] This claim supports those who argue for new government policies that aim at stimulating more saving. Other economists, however, argue the saving rate is mismeasured, and if properly measured would not seem low.[43] Whether or not the U.S. saving rate is mismeasured, and whether or not the rate is low compared to the past, these disputes need not be resolved. To have a clear and justifiable policy direction, one need only assume that at full employment, more saving is always better than less saving. Even if the saving rate were not lower than in the past, a higher saving rate would still be highly desirable, since by shifting resources from consumption to investment, productivity and living standards would rise from any previous level.

Some economists doubt any government policy could cause an increase in personal saving, since people often consume what they wish to consume and only save what is left over. Yet I will assume, following James Tobin and others, that if other countries can manage to have considerably higher saving rates than the United States has had over the last several decades, then the United States could also use public policy to achieve a higher saving rate.[44] Even those economists who claim government policy cannot increase personal saving nevertheless agree government policy can decrease government dissaving by decreasing federal deficits and federal debt.

The virtues of a tight fiscal policy are well known. The potential gains from a universal voluntary saving plan are not. A government saving policy could encourage individuals to save more. It is the thesis of this study that enacting campaign finance reform would transform the congressional Democratic Party, who would then cut federal waste and increase national saving. Waste reduction and increased saving would make abundant funds available for increasing investment, productivity, and national living standards.

A National Saving Plan

A national saving plan aimed at raising voluntary personal saving would borrow features from 401(k) plans and the college professors' pension plan, TIAA-CREF. A national saving plan is so desirable it is difficult to understand why it does not exist already. The only possible beneficiary of efforts to block the creation of an efficient national saving plan is the securities industry. Currently they can charge high fees and commissions on their customers' transactions, and persuade their customers to buy and sell securities frequently ("churning") even though much of this trading is not justified by market outcomes. Competition within the industry fails to drive out these inefficiencies, because customers lack the technical knowledge needed to recognize and exploit more efficient opportunities when they are offered. However, inefficient practices could be reduced if an efficient government-sponsored saving plan, run by experts with appropriate incentives, competed regularly with inefficient private firms. The risk/return ratios achieved by a government plan could be compared regularly by Morningstar and other private scorekeepers with risk/return ratios achieved by private plans. Such an arrangement would maximize competition and offer the individual saver more choices. TIAA-CREF is highly efficient, and could be a model for a national plan.

The only reason an efficient government plan has not been enacted into law is that the securities industry uses its campaign contributions on Capitol Hill to block an efficient plan. If so, then campaign finance reform could put an end to the ability of the securities industry to block the creation of an efficient national saving plan that would increase national saving.

The potential market for a national saving plan is indicated by Americans' inadequate provision for retirement, for which the only remedy is increased savings. Despite living longer than their parents, most Americans have not made provision for the larger medical bills and larger income needs over their lifetime that living longer entails. A large fraction of American families reach retirement age with almost no personal financial assets other than the equity they have in their houses and social security accumulations. In 1991, the median value of the future social security benefits of retired families with heads 65 to 70 was about $100,000, the median value of housing was about $50,000, and the median value of future employer-provided pension benefits was about $16,000.[45] The median level of all financial assets of households aged 60 to 64 was only $50,419 in 1991. Whether or not these assets are adequate even for the wealthier half of retirees is the subject of dispute.[46] Almost 20 percent of families in this age cohort had no financial assets at all.

What these findings indicate is there exists a wide range of potential savers who would have an incentive to save more if government created a better vehicle for saving than is now available in the marketplace. Seventy-six percent of respondents in a Public Agenda survey said they should be saving more for retirement.[47]

While a voluntary national saving plan may simulate saving behavior, such a plan raises three concerns: First, such a plan must actually succeed in getting people to save more than they did in the past. Second, a plan should not provide a windfall to the affluent, by allowing them to transfer savings from taxable vehicles to tax-sheltered vehicles without increasing saving proportionately. This issue is called the issue of "shuffled saving." Third, the effects of such plans should have a neutral effect on federal budget deficits.

Economists do not actually know why people save. They have identified nine different reasons people have for saving. One could, for example, have a strong motive to save so as to make bequests to one's children. One could also save to take precautions against unemployment, against growing older, because one wanted to be financially independent, to have more money to spend later, to grow a business, to accumulate more durable goods, to grow wealthier and derive interest income from the added wealth, or because of a purely miserly motive. If one were to try to anticipate how much different policies would increase the saving rate, one would not only have to ascertain the interaction of a new policy with all nine of these saving motivations, but also combinations of and hierarchies among all nine as well. Economists freely admit they do not know how much weight to give to any of these motives for saving as determinants of actual saving behavior. Therefore, framing policies predicated on getting individuals to save more has a weak analytical foundation. Comparing policy options is accordingly more difficult.[48]

This gap in economists' knowledge makes policy calculations more dependent on evaluations of recent policy experiments, as limited as they are. The two main plans enacted into law in recent years are tax-sheltered Individual Retirement Accounts (IRAs) and 401(k) plans. Roth IRAs are too recent to evaluate yet. Unfortunately, economists disagree about the net effects of IRAs. Some economists say IRAs have had little or no effect in increasing saving, while others say they have had large and significant effects in increasing saving. Bernheim's review concludes, "the literature on the relation between Individual Retirement Accounts and personal saving is inconclusive."[49] How much saving is "shuffled," and how effective these policies are in stimulating new saving are unresolved technical issues.[50] What does seem well-established is most IRA participants have been well-off older savers.

401(k) plans, however, are much more promising than IRAs as a means of raising the national saving rate. What is most striking is 401(k)s have elicited a far higher than expected participation rate among numerous low-income and younger workers who are traditional non-savers. Bernheim finds "the available evidence on 401(k) plans allow one to conclude with moderate confidence that, all else equal, eligibility for such a plan significantly stimulates personal saving."[51] Only some employers provide 401(k) plans. Among workers whose companies do offer the plan, the participation rate has been 55 percent for those earning $15,000 to $20,000, and 83 percent among workers earning more than $50,000 in 1993. Among younger workers, participation rates were 55 percent among eligible workers 21 to 30, and 67 percent for those 31 to 40. For those from 41 to 65, the rate was 70 percent. However, the research literature has not sorted out whether the 401(k) enrollees are more eager savers than individuals who are not enrolled in these saving plans. So, it is not known whether more universal plans would encounter less eager savers, and so increase national saving less. Nor does the literature sort out various offsets, such as whether savers who increase their 401(k) savings do so in part by borrowing more money through home equity loans, thereby decreasing the saving they had accumulated in the form of home equity.[52]

Annual contributions to 401(k) are now approaching $100 billion a year, from a base of zero in the early 1980s, and contributions to 401(k) plans now exceed contributions to traditional pensions, including both defined contribution and defined benefit plans. They mostly represent new saving. Individuals are freer to add or withdraw assets from 401(k) plans than from many other saving vehicles, especially defined benefit pensions. Only 50 percent of employees nationwide are eligible for a 401(k) plan, and about 70 percent of these contribute.[53] Many issues remain however.[54]

Hopes that a national 401(k)-type saving plan would increase saving are also supported by findings that even the poor save. According to one analysis,

> [A] substantial proportion of low-income households save a great deal. Within income deciles, very little of the dispersion in wealth can be explained by household attributes that may have limited resources available for saving.[55]

Still another reason for optimism regarding future participation rates in a national saving plan is that, thanks to increased productivity, the United States is richer than it was and is bound to become richer yet. A richer society devotes less of its income to necessities, and more to either saving or luxuries. Hence, it seems reasonable that Americans' growing incomes could lead to a higher saving rate, because a higher income creates a greater opportunity to save more. Therefore, a national saving plan may be that much more likely to raise aggregate saving and investment.

A government saving plan is the vehicle most likely to exploit opportunities to increase personal saving. A government saving plan would enjoy economies of scale, and would increase savers' returns over what is available through private brokerage accounts. That is because a government plan would have the incentive to reduce brokerage houses' inefficiencies—inflated fees and commissions and excessive trading—and would reduce information asymmetries by "socializing" information in ways familiar to participants in TIAA-CREF. Lower transaction costs would allow increased returns. These higher returns over time would attract more savers and increase saving.

Consider the provisions a national saving plan would be likely to have if it were to succeed in increasing saving:

- An efficient plan would be universal. Automatic enrollment would encourage maximum participation.[56] If enrollment were not automatic, then advertising would be intensive, on the scale of commercial ads, to maximize participation.[57]
- A universal plan would spread the plan's costs over the widest possible pool of participants, thereby increasing the affordability of various investor information and analysis services.
- A fair plan would be voluntary. Participants could leave the plan at any time if they find they have more important needs for their money.
- To create efficient incentives and lower costs, the plan's managers would not collect fees on individual transactions, but would be compensated according to their fund's performance against measures of comparable industry funds.
- The usual set of investment options would be offered: funds of funds, index funds, different varieties of stock and bond funds, foreign funds, real estate funds, and so on. Participants would be offered options appropriate for limiting age and income-related risks. These options would lower risks related to picking individual securities and market timing.
- Participants would be informed at regular intervals what income in constant dollars they should expect at retirement for a given schedule of contributions and asset allocations. Such information should increase participation.
- Participants would be assured neither an employer nor the government could manipulate the saver's assets, unlike some employer-based pension plans.

Currently what is known does not allow clear projections about how much any given national saving plan would increase the number of savers and the amount of saving. Yet, lack of clear evidence about the future ought not to lead to agnosticism. A universal plan that either included automatic enrollment or was heavily publicized and clearly explained could not but increase saving to some significant degree. The costs and risks of proceeding to enact a universal saving plan are almost nil, while the potential benefits are enormous, both to the country and to individuals who would want to save more. Such a public program would supply a classic public good—something people cannot readily do for themselves, something business cannot supply enough of—which would make many individuals and the nation better off.

Again, a national saving plan would expand the pool of national savings. A larger pool of savings would allow both the government and private investors to borrow at lower interest rates. Lower interest rates would drive up private and public investment. More investment would drive up national income. The failure to achieve a national saving plan wastes a massive amount of potential national income that could be devoted to national priorities.

Finding the Money: (3) Efficient Taxes to Raise Investment

As a last resort, a modest increase in progressive taxes or a higher level of taxation could also fund increases in public investment, after funds derived from waste reduction and increased savings have been exhausted.

But voters often reject higher taxes, which rejection legislators anticipate. Presidential nominee Walter Mondale promised to raise taxes to reduce the federal budget deficit in his acceptance speech to the 1984 Democratic Convention. The popular reaction was so bad that ever since then, Democratic politicians have said this episode made them gunshy about ever advocating higher taxes, except when a modest burden is imposed on the very well off alone. But Mondale said he wanted to raise taxes to reduce the deficit, and then failed to explain why deficits were bad. He did not explain why some deficits were too big, and others were not, or why running deficits in a recession is good and the Reagan structural deficits were bad. Most of all, Mondale did not explain that financing deficits required cutting popular programs, or increasing taxes, or giving up on national investments. Mondale could have said "To pay the interest on the debt, do we cut program X or increase tax Y?" But he did not.

Perhaps Mondale was wise. Perhaps he believed, as some political scientists claim, the voters want to have their cake and eat it too. Some poll data showed many voters did not want their taxes raised or their government benefits cut, despite deficits. Some analysts think the voters are unreasonable. Yet, voters believe there is a lot of government waste, and the evidence in this chapter supports their belief. Voters understand that a lot of waste could be cut out long before it was necessary either to cut benefits or raise taxes.

Suppose political leaders believed national priorities required raising additional tax revenues. How much would raising taxes hurt economic growth? Slemrod shows the economics literature leaves unresolved the question "How much has government taxing and spending increased or decreased economic growth?" He concludes,

> This review of the existing cross-country literature suggests that there is no persuasive evidence that the extent of government has either a positive or a negative impact on either the level or the growth rate of per capita income....[58]

William G. Gale notes, "but more government could, in fact, raise or reduce economic activity, especially over selected ranges or types of government spending."[59]

Another main issue is whether voters would tolerate higher taxes if they bought highly valued benefits, such as universal health insurance, if they thought the money would not be wasted, and if they believed the tax code was no longer riddled with loopholes. In general, it is probably tautological to say that it would be surprising if voters did not support higher taxes if they believed what they get in return was worth the tax.

As to greater progressivity in the tax code, three-quarters of respondents in a 1993 Gallup Poll said "upper income people" pay "too little" in taxes. The voters believe the well-off should be taxed more than less well-off people.[60] In most of the twentieth century, tax rates have been higher for the affluent. Progressivity is the norm, not only in the United States, but in every advanced country.[61] William Nordhaus cites "ensuring a fair distribution of income" as one of the three main roles economists take government to be responsible for, along with stabilizing the economy (aggregate demand policies) and promoting productivity (aggregate supply policies).[62] Other prominent studies conclude that "the evidence that tax rates matter for growth is disturbingly fragile."[63] In a recent review, Harvard economist David Cutler describes competing views of progressivity as follows:

> As first shown in James Mirrless (1971), optimal tax schedules generally have flat marginal tax rates. Progressivity is achieved not through high marginal tax rates at the top of the income distribution, but through a large exemption at the bottom of the income distribution. The preference for low marginal tax rates, coupled with the desire to avoid intertemporal distortions, leads to a policy prescription for low tax rates on a broad tax base.... Optimal tax structures will differ, however, if income differences are a result of random outcomes for otherwise similar people or a result of inherited advantages and disadvantages.....
>
> Haveman takes a more skeptical view of the spirit of income tax design. Haveman lists 12 reasons why he considers the correct shape of the income tax

"highly speculative" and "genuinely ambiguous," ranging from the difficulty of determining individual and social welfare functions to issues of administration and compliance. And even Arnott, in offering a forceful defense of optimal tax theory, notes that the quantitative and qualitative features of the model *are sufficiently fragile to make drawing policy conclusions about the optimal tax structure very speculative.*

At one level it is not surprising that a question as complicated as the design of optimal income taxation remains so murky. This problem, after all, has been at the heart of academic and policy debate for well over a century. At another level, it is disheartening that a problem with such a long lineage as design of income taxation yields so few results that the developers of the theory would apply to policy. [italics added][64]

Thus, this literature cannot presently determine with any scientific rigor whether any overall policy mix that taxes more or taxes more progressively actually increases or decreases economic growth by any given amount. The economics literature, then, leaves the door open to the possibility that at least some mildly progressive tax policies, especially those that fund public investments efficiently, could promote growth. Thus, policymakers have warrant to believe that there is nothing at all conclusive in the literature requiring that they reject policies that modestly increase progressivity in the tax system in order to gain revenue for major public investments.

But again, it cannot be emphasized enough that increased taxes on anyone might be wholly unnecessary to fund national priorities. Combining waste reduction with increased saving might make it unnecessary to raise taxes to achieve national priorities.

Conclusion

By every indication, the American people want better health insurance, education, job training, child care, elderly care, and environmental systems among other things. They would rally to any political party that met these needs efficiently. But both parties have been saying no. The Republicans claim such governmental activities are economically inefficient, and would hurt long-term growth in the economy by robbing investment. The Democrats believe that the money is just not there. But reducing government waste would provide a huge potential source of funding for both public and private investment. At least $1 trillion a year could be extracted from federal government waste, on budget and off, if and only if effective campaign reform were accomplished. In addition, reform would allow a national saving plan that could increase the saving rate and thereby increase the supply of capital for investment. An increased pool of saving would lower interest rates, allowing increases in both public and private investment, which would increase productivity while reducing inequality.

Both waste reduction and a national saving plan are now blocked by campaign contributors, who by influencing members of Congress have a powerful effect on the allocation of scarce resources in the United States. What this chapter has established is that the amount of money lost to waste and unrealized saving is huge. This amount of money is large enough to fund popular programs that would be good for the economy while refloating the Democratic Party.

Chapter 5

Are Weak Parties Inevitable?

[T]he Democrats routinely stock the Democratic Senatorial Campaign Committee with Finance Committee Members in order to mine their fundraising potential.
—Senator Mitch McConnell (R-Kentucky)[1]

PREVIOUS CHAPTERS ARGUED THAT THE DEMOCRATIC PARTY HAS DECLINED A great deal over several decades, that only a new message based on popular programs would reverse that decline, and that the Democrats' failure to propose popular programs is due to their inability to raise the funds such programs require. This lack of funds results from wasting large amounts of money meeting the demands of campaign contributors. Effective campaign reform would free congresspersons to reallocate wasted funds to public investments. The next chapter shows that, after reform, powerful partisan incentives would give Democratic legislators the will to reallocate wasted funds to national needs.

But, perhaps, even after reform, powerful interest groups would continue to dominate congressional resource allocation. If so, the money needed to support popular programs would be unavailable, reform or no reform. Whether reform would fail to change resource allocation because powerful interest groups would dominate political parties is the subject of this chapter and the next. A number of different arguments, some mentioned in the introduction, conclude campaign reform would not lead to a reallocation of wasted funds to national priorities.

The first such argument, following Pluralist theory, is that interest groups are usually strong, while parties and voters are relatively weak. That is because, as Pluralists see it, a multiplicity of highly organized interest groups have a clear conception of their interests, enjoy a high degree of mobilization among their supporters, are armed with a great deal of information and money, and so can influence legislators more than ordinary voters or parties can. As a result, Pluralists see parties as relatively weak representational links between voters and their government, reform or no reform.[2]

Moreover, according to this theory, campaign reform would not change the relationship among interest groups, parties, and voters. That is because campaign contributions are only one of several tools by which interest groups influence legislators. Other tools include broadcasting issue ads, lobbying the grassroots, informing legislative committees and executive branch agencies, and taking legal action. As Pluralists see it, these different tools, whose uses are legitimate in any democratic order, enable interest groups to dominate legislators and their parties, whether or not campaign contributions are also used to influence legislators. Hence, campaign reform can only have marginal consequences.

A second Pluralist story emphasizes the fragmentation of American society as a source of party weakness. In the United States a large variety of cross-cutting ethnic, racial, religious, cultural, regional, and economic groups, all participants in an individualistic culture, make competing claims on the political system. Pluralists doubt that strong political parties could emerge from such a pluralistic society to unite voters and legislators behind national goals in a sustainable way, reform or no reform. Majoritarian preferences are few and far between, and so cannot sustain a majoritarian party, according to Pluralists.

A third story about the relative strength of interest groups and the resulting weakness of parties emphasizes the considerable degree of political independence that members of Congress have from their party leaders, both in Congress and back home. Members of Congress can afford to say no to their party's leaders. Their independence weakens parties. Members' independence is based on the "personal vote"—the accumulation of votes a candidate earns through personal service—as opposed to the "party vote," which is harvested from the legislative accomplishments and image of the member's party.[3] The personal vote draws from a number of sources. Members (1) assemble their own campaign organizations; (2) raise their own funds, building war chests of campaign money large enough to scare off challengers; (3) cater to a large variety of local interest groups; (4) perform constituency service; (5) deliver federally funded district and state projects; (6) use congressional office allowances and staff for campaigning; (7) engage in endless self-advertising; and (8) use the free mailing (franking privilege) given to incumbents. Member independence is also advanced by (9) self-recruitment through primaries rather than recruitment by party leaders and by (10) building knowledge of their own districts and states greater than most potential opponents can construct. Members' independence from party leaders weakens a party's ability to pursue a national agenda.

The best evidence that members' personal vote makes them independent of their party is the incumbent return rate. Even when voters blame their party and its presidents for recessions, inflation, or foreign policy failures, incumbent members get reelected around 90 percent of the time, and have for many decades. Moreover, members routinely run ahead of the presidential candidate of their party in their own districts.[4] Their independence would make a party program difficult to achieve even if campaign reform became law. And so, the consequences of campaign reform would be diminished proportionately.

Morris Fiorina has argued members of Congress are even more independent from their party than they used to be. He claims the growth in federal programs since the New Deal and Great Society increased members' opportunities for intervening directly with federal bureaucracies on behalf of constituents.[5] According to this theory, this expansion in constituency service brought in more political IOUs from constituents, decreasing members' need to stand up for particular policies, and so decreasing their attachment to their party and its agenda. Fiorina's story is meant to show why parties have become weaker than they were.

If the above stories are correct, then campaign reform would change congressional parties and public policy very little. Powerful interest groups would continue to dominate parties and the allocation of resources for their own benefit. So the misallocation of resources to benefit interest groups is simply inevitable, campaign reform or no reform.

Arguments Contrary to the Weak Parties Theory

Several arguments counter the theory that parties inevitably represent most voters poorly, while being dominated by interest groups. The first argument is that members' party vote might vary significantly relative to their personal vote under varying conditions. If campaign reform changes the incentives of Democratic legislators, who then reallocate funds from waste to popular programs, then the Democrats' party vote might grow larger relative to their personal vote, thereby decreasing their responsiveness to unworthy interest group demands. Pluralists tend to see the constraints on parties as inelastic, and so underestimate potential variation in the strength of parties.

A second argument is that voter partisanship in congressional districts has been underestimated as a source of party strength. The lines of most congressional districts have been drawn to include voters who mostly belong to the sitting member's party. No doubt, the personal vote explanation and the partisan district explanation both account in part for high incumbency return rates. But strongly partisan congressional districts seem inconsistent with the claim that legislators are relatively independent from party influences.

A third argument that counters the Weak Parties theory is that, far from weakening parties, interest groups and parties are often mutually supportive. Some interest groups' alliance with a party is ideologically "natural." Officeholders seeking support from influential groups tend to form alliances only with groups that are ideologically compatible with their existing support base. The ties between the

Democratic Party and unions, environmentalists, minorities, and women's groups, and between the Republican Party and business groups, are ideologically natural, durable, and strengthen the party ally. Other interests, like those of Charles Keating of the Lincoln Savings and Loan,[6] are tied to parties solely as a function of their campaign contributions. Groups whose influence with a party is based primarily on their campaign contributions tend to weaken that party. An interest group weakens a party to the degree that the party spends the public's money to help it, instead of meeting the needs of the party's voter base.[7] Comparing the actual dollar amount of campaign contributions given by a party's naturally allied interest groups with that given by unnaturally allied interests would require major new research into a counterfactual—whether a given group would give equivalent support after campaign reform.

A fourth argument that counters the Weak Parties theory is that members of Congress do not give government benefits to any and all parochial district constituencies. Nor do they favor any local constituent over every national and party priority. Congress often distributes money by formula. These formulae embody criteria for allocating resources among various localities and states.[8] These formulae impose the priorities of party and nation on members' legislative efforts, and reduce the extent to which constituency influences and member independence weaken the allocative discretion of party coalitions.[9] Louis Fisher of the Congressional Research Service has disputed Fiorina's theory, noting that it

> is largely contradicted by the legislative record. Recent decades have witnessed the growth of mechanical, automatic formulas *that sharply circumscribe the opportunity* of members to intervene in agency decisions. What we have is a system run on permanent authorizations, permanent appropriations, entitlements, indexing . . . and assorted "uncontrollables." [italics added][10]

These allocative formulae indicate that the common good often constrains narrow interests. It is true many instances of appropriations, tax expenditures, regulatory relief measures, and rent seeking are not covered by legislative formulae, and so are more responsive to lobbying by contributors and constituents. Yet Fisher's point allows that members' dependence on constituency service may be less than assumed, and would be smaller yet after the reform of campaign finance.

Moreover, Congress's fiscal policy record shows Congress regularly puts the common good ahead of narrow interests. According to Paul E. Peterson, Congress ran a prudent fiscal policy at least from 1946 through 1980. Except for the Reagan era, Congress almost always balanced tax revenues and spending outlays. What deficits there were in those years reflected wars and recessions. After applying an inflation adjustment, and separating out capital expenditures from the national debt, most postwar budgets actually ran a surplus. Even without these two adjustments, between 1950 and 1981, the national debt as a percent of Gross National Product in constant dollars declined steadily, except during recessions and wars. Fiscal profligacy in Congress, then, was exceptional, not usual, prior to 1981.[11] The structural deficits of 1981 to 1990 were an aberration. The Bush and Clinton deficit reduction bills of 1990 and 1993 returned policy to the path of fiscal responsibility.

The lesson of this history is that Congress has successfully subordinated interest group demands to national priorities for long periods of time. It follows that parties may be far less susceptible to being fragmented by members' attachments to parochial district constituencies than Pluralists claim. Hence, it is reasonable to suppose that, after campaign reform, members of Congress would be even more likely to subordinate interest groups' demands to national goals than at present, which would allow parties to offer leadership to the nation.

A fifth argument that Pluralists advance is that social pluralism causes political pluralism. Supposedly political parties are inevitably weak because a pluralistic society causes instablity in party coalitions. In this view, party coalitions are made up, at least partially, of ever-shifting elements of ethnic, racial, religious, cultural, regional, and economic groups, and so parties seldom represent the interests of majorities of citizens in a sustained way. According to Pluralists, majoritarian preferences are few and far between, and so cannot sustain a strong majority party.

Yet, the main social groups that supported the Anti-Federalists, the economically less advantaged, were also the mainstay of Jacksonian Democrats in the first half of the nineteenth century, and also provided Democrats their core support for most of the twentieth century. Similarly, Federalists, Whigs, and Republicans drew their main support from the economically advantaged across this same time period. The continuities across centuries in the social bases of American party coalitions is remarkable:

> The Jeffersonian platform of suspicion of business, of anti-monopoly, and of opposition to government favors to the special interests has become a seemingly inexhaustible reservoir of ideals and rhetoric upon which numerous radical and democratic groups have drawn. Jacksonian Democracy, Greenbackism, Populism, the Progressive Movement, the New and Fair Deals, and Kennedy's New Frontier are only the best known of such beneficiaries of the Jeffersonian economic tradition. . . . Certainly . . . the Jeffersonians placed a larger measure of trust in the "Great Beast" of the people, as Hamilton is supposed to have described them, than did the . . . Federalists.[12]

Throughout American history, populist sentiments opposing the political power of wealthy interests have played a prominent role in structuring conflict between the parties. The antiquity of this populist theme is indicated by such slogans from American electoral history as "robber barons, " "trusts," and "malefactors of great wealth," as it is by the symbolism of the Democrats' annual Jefferson-Jackson Day dinners. Such symbols suggest ordinary Americans, *despite diverse social backgrounds*, have often come together behind a political party that advances common economic interests. Older ethnic and religious cleavages, on the other hand, once seemingly cast in concrete, were substantially diminished by the Depression, two world wars, the New Deal, the Fair Deal, the Great Society, and by economic growth.[13]

What makes strong parties almost inevitable, however, is that no matter how many narrow interests press their individual advantage, they always need allies with whom to form coalitions strong enough to capture political institutions. These interests need to find common ground with others so as to control Congress and the presidency. Every interest group needs reliable long-term allies with whom to form cohesive legislative majorities operating across issues and across time to minimize the transaction costs of forming coalitions.[14]

A sixth problem associated with Pluralist theory is that the recent behavior of Republicans does not fit the theory that parties are weak because interest groups are strong. The Democrats moved away from their voter base and became weaker after 1966 because funds needed for Democratic programs were diverted to contributors. But the Republicans did not move away from their base in the same period, though they did become much more a southern party and much less a northeastern and midwestern party. Nonetheless, the Republican Party has displayed impressive cohesion on economic issues, and has provided intensely loyal representation to upper-income groups across the nation. Republicans have continually marched in lockstep in support of upwardly redistributive tax cuts for affluent voters. Their greatest successes were in the tax legislation passed in 1981, 1986, and 2001. They also achieved large cuts in government spending, which put downward pressures on the need for taxes, and cuts in regulation, especially costly environmental regulations.

Congressional Republicans' strenuous efforts on behalf of their voter and interest group base contrast sharply with the halfhearted efforts and tepid legislation Democrats have offered their base voters. From the mid 1970s on, the Democrats provided weak representation on economic issues to their working-class and middle-class supporters. The Democrats retreated from nearly every major economic proposal that might have been welcomed by their voter base, despite growing cohesion among congressional Democrats. Proposals for universal health insurance all but vanished from mainstream Democratic politics from the very beginning of the Carter presidency until President Clinton's failed effort in 1994. The retreat from New Deal, Fair Deal, Great Society, and other Democratic economic programs in the Carter years sparked Senator Ted Kennedy's challenge to President Carter's renomination in 1980.

The Pluralists' Weak Parties story does not explain the difference between the parties in their propensity to be responsive to their base voters. The Republicans fought fiercely for their base. The Democrats did not. As a result, the Democrats lost control of both houses of Congress in the four elections between 1994 and 2000, a majority of governorships, and half the state legislatures. So, it is difficult to accept the Pluralists' Weak Parties theory, since only one party, the Democrats, exhibited growing weakness. If the cause of growing party weakness was the increase in members' reliance on incumbency advantages and constituency service, the period should have witnessed proportionate increases in the weaknesses of both parties. But that did not happen.

It follows that the weaknesses of the American party system are not inevitable. Neither the Democrats' main weakness nor the Republicans' main weakness result from the pluralistic diversity of the electorate, the inherent advantages of interest groups in the political process, nor the independence of legislators from their party. Rather, Republicans' weakness flows from their opposition to the economic preferences of most Americans.[15] The Democrats' weakness flows from their failure to champion those same popular preferences with any gusto. Witness the Gore-Lieberman proposal in the 2000 campaign to spend a mere $17 billion a year more on education, as cited above. If the Pluralist story is false, and if contributors would be much less influential after campaign reform, then reform might indeed trigger major policy changes through the agency of a strengthened Democratic Party.

A seventh argument provides the strongest reason to *accept* the Pluralist theory that the weaknesses of parties would persist even after passage of campaign reform. This argument focuses on the fact that interest groups do not rely only on campaign contributions to gain influence in Congress. Other sources of influence are also valuable to them, including issue ads, grassroots lobbying, informing legislative committees, and legal effort. But after effective reform, ordinary citizens could use these same tools on a much more equal footing if, and only if, well represented by more independent political parties, as the next chapter shows. Currently, private campaign contributions compound many times over the power of interest groups relative to the power of parties and voters.[16]

Who Needs Parties? Is Divided Government Enough?

Perhaps weak divided parties are not an obstacle to effective government. But perhaps strong parties are not really needed to get things done. Perhaps strong parties per se are not the only remedy for government's failure to meet the challenges that voters would have them meet. Some recent analyses laud the accomplishments of divided governments—governments in which one party controls Congress, and the other controls the White House.[17] Divided governments get a lot done, these studies say.

To judge whether divided or unified governments have been successful, some clear standard of success is required against which to judge their performance. The standard itself should not be an ad hoc standard, but rather must have a fundamental basis.[18] The appropriate standard is whether a government has enacted into law policies that have significantly increased U.S. security, productivity, reduced inequality, increased social cohesion, and, in general, succeeded in promoting collective ends. Against this standard, divided governments have failed by an enormous margin.[19] Evidence of this failure lies in three trends. Three Brookings economists, Baily, Burtless, and Litan, note,

> For nearly two decades the U.S. economy has been plagued by two disturbing trends: anemic productivity growth and growing inequality in the distribution of income [and wealth]. . . . In the next decade and beyond the nation faces no more urgent economic challenge than reversing these two trends.[20]

Arguably, these two trends have now lasted closer to three decades, as chapter seven shows. Third, an equally powerful indication of government failure is found in the many polls asking voters about their trust in government. These polls show that most American voters believe that government has failed, and that belief has grown dramatically over the last several decades.[21]

It is true that bipartisanship buttressed such major governmental initiatives as the Marshall Plan, the containment of communism, and building the national highway system.[22] Yet, many other major governmental initiatives were primarily the work of one party, including Medicare, Medicaid, aid to education, civil rights, and governmental protection of the environment, consumer safety, and worker safety. Overall, it seems clear that the public sector investments and social insurance that most voters prefer deeply divide the parties.

For these reasons, one can only reject the thesis that divided government works.[23] And so it is necessary to consider the claim that only strong parties can govern well. Making that assumption leads one to ask what conditions, if any, would lead to strong party governments in the United States in the twenty-first century. The passage of effective campaign finance reform would strengthen at least one party, the Democratic Party.

Conclusion

In sum, how the political system would react to campaign reform depends on whether the Pluralist view of inherently weak parties is valid. If interest groups are bound to dominate congressional parties, reform or no reform, then it is correct to say campaign reform probably will not have major consequences. For then, even after campaign reform, interest groups and wealthy individuals would continue to capture the resources reformers hope will be used to fund popular programs and national needs. But what if campaign reform allowed at least one political party, the Democratic Party, to be more independent from those interest groups whose influence is derived primarily from their campaign contributions? Then, that party would be able to subordinate many interest group demands to national needs, and provide much more democratic representation of voters' preferences. After reform, popular programs and national needs could be funded with monies recaptured from what interest groups had previously captured using their contributions to members of Congress as the principal lever. If these implications hold true, then campaign reform is likely to have dramatic consequences for the political parties and for public policy.

The Strong Parties Theory

As embodied in classic studies by Key, McConnell, Schattschneider, and others cited in the introduction, the Strong Parties theory puts forward the view that strong parties might effectively represent the main preferences of most Americans, and overwhelm the party-fragmenting forces discussed in this chapter. A contemporary basis for asserting the Strong Parties theory is examined in the next chapter.

Chapter 6

Nine Party-Unifying Forces

There are many reasons for all of this chaos, but chief among this is the compulsion to put a partisan bent on every single issue. . . . There is rarely a consensus even on the most practical and ideologically neutral matters. Why in the name of heaven should tobacco or the environment or education be partisan issues? . . . It's rare for more than two or three senators to cross party lines on a vote. Nothing could more starkly demonstrate the fog of partisanship that has enveloped the Senate.
—Retiring Senator Dale Bumpers (D-Arkansas)[1]

THIS CHAPTER DRAWS ON INTERVIEWS IN 1991 AND 1992 WITH 70 DEMOCRATIC members of the House of Representatives, and with a large number of senior staff. Interviewees were chosen primarily from key committees and the party leadership structure. Interviews were carried out with two of the four top party leaders, members of the leadership staff, leaders of the whip organization, the House Democratic Caucus, the Democratic Study Group, and all 20 members of the Gephardt "Message Board." Over half of the Democratic members of the Ways and Means, Appropriations, Rules, Budget, and Energy and Commerce committees were interviewed. The interviews are not used here as a source of systematic data to test hypotheses; rather they inform this study with insights and understandings that influenced the arguments presented below.[2]

The interviews showed that, excepting unhappy southern Democrats, a number of whom openly disdained their congressional party, Democratic members' partisanship was quite strong. Their partisanship was an indication that their party's potential for pulling together behind a popular program may be stronger than it has appeared. Yet, if partisanship in Congress is strong, why have congressional Democrats failed to propose popular programs such as universal health insurance? Having lost control of Congress and of a majority of governorships continuously from 1994 to 2000, and having failed to reverse the erosion in its voter base, why haven't the Democrats offered more attractive policies with which to rebuild their voter base and recapture control of Congress?

The theory proposed here claims strong partisanship and strong parties would normally occur at both the elite and voter levels because of the nine party-unifying forces described in this chapter. The combination of campaign reform and these nine party-unifying forces would overwhelm the party-fragmenting forces described in the previous chapter. This chapter shows that, freed of the need to raise campaign funds, members would have strong partisan incentives to reallocate resources to serve partisan and national goals.

Nine Party-Unifying Forces

To pass legislation, majority coalitions must be formed somehow, and accommodations must be made to produce those majorities. Notwithstanding the great diversity present in American society, majority coalitions reflect concerns that unify voters and politicians from diverse congressional districts and states. The Social Security issue resonates in Billings, Montana; East Los Angeles; Cherry Hill, New Jersey; and Galveston, Texas. In the same way, many other issues resonate across diverse districts, bringing together voters and parties, when parties provide leadership.

Party goals are championed by legislators who are elected from partisan congressional districts that elect their congresspersons from the same party in election after election. A story emphasizing party-fragmenting forces fails to explain how 68.7 percent of congressional districts returned a representative to Congress from the same party for five consecutive elections through much of the period from 1914 through 1980.[3] Between 1968 and 1994, an average of only 6.8 percent of all seats changed party per election. Even in the dramatic election of 1994, only 14 percent—60 House districts—changed party, which was the most since 1954.[4] These patterns suggest most members come from partisan districts that instill members of Congress with partisan incentives to work together in a party organization seeking power. What follows outlines nine party-unifying forces.

The First Unifying Force: The Party Vote

Members of Congress win elections by drawing support from both their personal vote and their party vote. Again, the personal vote is derived from members' endless efforts at constituency and district service, self-advertisement, and fund-raising. The party vote, on the other hand, consists of the votes of party identifiers who regularly vote for the party's candidates across elections and across offices.[5] Democratic party identification has diminished sharply over the last several decades.[6] But party voting still matters. The percent of party-line voters, defined as party identifiers who vote and vote for the candidate of their party, has averaged 75 percent, 74.9 percent, and 75.3 percent in elections for president, senators, and representatives respectively from 1956 through 1996. In the 1990s, the figures were, respectively, 74 percent, 75.3 percent, and 74 percent.[7] The presence of party voters gives congresspersons a powerful incentive to support party policies that would meet the concerns of party voters.

During the redistricting process members' behavior reveals their desire to maximize the size of the party vote in their districts to ensure their reelection:

> Congressional lawmakers play a key role in redistricting, not least because their political survival could be at stake. Redistricting is a rare instance in which members must curry favor with lesser-known state legislators. Among other things members are expected to contribute to state campaigns. "You'll see congressional delegations aggressively raising money and doing things for state legislative candidates they normally don't [care] about," said Cole, who was an Oklahoma state senator in the last redistricting round.[8]

Thus, members of Congress do all they can to influence the drawing of their own district's lines, so as to maximize the number of their party's voters included in their district. From a member's perspective, the more party voters, the safer their seat.

At times over the years, some Democratic politicians, especially conservative southern Democrats, have disassociated themselves from their party's president, their party's national image, and some of their party's more visible national interest groups. Yet, no one has made the claim that these politicians have run away from their party's more loyal base voters. Nor would anyone claim these same politicians have run away from the main economic policies long identified with the core of Democratic politics. It is more than a little puzzling, therefore, why anyone would downplay members' concern for the party vote relative to the personal vote. They are both important. But the importance of party voters to the individual member predisposes members to support party goals and party leaders. Whatever the differences among Democratic members' districts, issues of common concern to party voters in different districts and states, especially economic issues, shape party cohesion in Congress.

A Second Unifying Force: The Need for a Party Message

Members' need for a party message is a second source of a members' support for party goals and party leaders. Members of Congress want a party message to mobilize party voters. The party message enables a member to present herself and her party as responsive to party voters' concerns. Interviews for this study in 1991 and 1992 with all of the members of then-Majority Leader Dick Gephardt's 20-member "Message Board" revealed sizable, intense, and persistent efforts being devoted to message formulation and projection by some of the most influential and energetic members of the House Democratic Party. These interviews made it plain that efforts to link legislating to message formulation and projection was accorded the highest priority by the party's leaders. Observers tend to underestimate this activity because many of the messages are not funneled primarily through the main national media channels. Rather, they show up in local news programs, press interviews, members' speeches, town meetings, one-minute speeches at the beginning of each legislative day, and party leaders' press conferences and speeches. These messages are both internal and external signals. They are coordinated to affect the climate of opinion near the time of legislating bills and electing members. Party messages enable members to sing from the same hymn book. Party activity is impossible to understand without taking account of party message activity.

According to one view, some national congressional elections have little to do with party messages. Such elections, especially midterm elections, are taken to be a sum of local races that fail to engage national party issues. Some analysts have argued that persistent 90 percent incumbency return rates allow most members to sidestep national tides that hurt the party in their bids for reelection. They argue what accounts for members' high return rates is their ability to run primarily on local issues. A better explanation is that, in districts dominated by partisan voters, which are most districts, members can withstand national tides because of strong partisan support for them in their districts.

Unlike the past, members often court the party vote without ever mentioning their own party affiliation. Members' ads no longer say, "Vote for Candidate X, a Democrat." Perhaps, then, party messages matter little, and most members easily deviate from party positions when it suits them. But this view ignores members' need to mobilize party voters. Party messages are more prevalent than they seem. Instead of using old-fashioned party labels, party messages now use indirect party cues that emphasize "social security" and "patient rights" rather than "Democrat," or "choice" and "prayer" rather than "Republican." They qualify as party cues because they are primarily associated with one party or the other. They are honed to appeal simultaneously to party voters, potential defectors from the other party, and independents. When one party tries to preempt the rhetoric of the other party, it is constrained by its commitments to its base voters and contributors. It can't promise anything. And it is incumbent on the party whose rhetoric is stolen to demonstrate the difference between the parties on the preempted issue, something some analysts say Al Gore did poorly in the 2000 election.

The importance of party messages is underscored by the intense involvement of congressional leaders and high-priced consultants in the formulation and projection of party messages.[9] The need for a credible party message is also manifest in the extensive efforts congressional parties make to fit legislative accomplishments to the party's message. Only partisan legislators would endow their party leaders with the support necessary to make extensive efforts to produce a party message.

Presidential messages are often party messages. Any president will go to great lengths to find a message his congressional party can support, since he will seem weak if his congressional party fails to support his message with legislative authorizations and appropriations. A president's top aides and his congressional party's leaders meet continuously to forge legislation that supports the party's message. Such party messages function as party-unifying mechanisms, and as rally points.

The importance members attach to their party's message is reflected in the tendency for congressional leaders to be selected because of their ability to shape and deliver party messages. At least since the 1980s, this ability has been crucial in leadership selection. Senator George Mitchell (D-Maine) became Majority Leader of the Senate in part because other senators of his party thought him unusually effective in message formulation and projection. He gained this recognition in part from his replies for the Democrats on national television to several State of the Union addresses by President Reagan. Similarly Congressman Dick Gephardt (D-Missouri) was widely seen as unusually effective in constructing and delivering the party's message, and was elevated to the leadership in part because of it. The *National Journal* put a picture of then-Democratic Majority Leader Gephardt on its cover with the caption: "Delivering The Democrats' Message."[10] The same can be said of the current Senate Minority Leader Senator Tom Daschle (D-South Dakota).

The importance of party messages to legislators was revealed in a failed revolt against Speaker Thomas Foley in 1991. Many Democratic members were frustrated over the failure of the House Democratic leadership to legislate bills that would support a party message in 1992. That frustration led to a revolt against Speaker Foley in the Democratic Caucus that summer, which had some chance of ousting him from the speakership, and sent him scurrying. The intensity of the frustration with Speaker Foley was evident in interviews for this study with Democratic members. Speaker Foley, on the other hand, blamed lack of cohesion within the party for the failure to produce a program and a message, as the speaker's press secretary, Jeffrey Biggs, made clear in several long interviews for this study. Others saw Foley, a moderate conservative from a conservative district east of the mountains in Washington state, as ideologically out of tune with the progressive majority in his own party. Whatever the truth of this matter, there is no way to appreciate these events without acknowledging the intensity of members' demand for an effective party message.

A number of members interviewed for this study expressed concern that the chairpersons of some control committees regularly blocked legislation that would have supported a party message. In 1992, a revolt against the power of the committee chairs took the form of a report from the Democratic Study Group of the House, headed then by Congressman, now Governor, Bob Wise (D-West Virginia), and a milder report from the House Democratic Caucus Committee on Organization, Study, and Review (OSR), chaired then by Congresswoman Louise Slaughter (D-New York). They proposed "radical rules changes" shifting power from the committee chairmen to the Caucus. The DSG proposals concentrated on two goals:

> (1) to strengthen the ability of the party and its leadership to develop an effective policy agenda [read party message]; and (2) to enhance the accountability of those who serve in positions of authority as agents of the Caucus [read committee chairs who block legislation that would support a party message].

One key provision was to allow any 50 Democratic members in the Caucus to move a vote of no confidence in a committee chairman. The committee chairmen felt threatened by these moves, and they reacted forcefully in concert with the help of Speaker Foley.[11] The insurgents clearly seemed to place a higher value on legislation supporting a party message than did the chairmen and the speaker. Reformers seeking to strengthen the party at the national level have long hoped to weaken committees in relation to the Caucus and the party leadership so as to produce a partisan program and message.

In recent years, power has been centralized in the Republican-controlled House. Committees were subordinated under Speaker Newt Gingrich, and a six-year term limit was imposed on committee chairs, leading to the departure of a number of chairpersons at the beginning of the 107th Congress in January 2001. The departure of Gingrich was accompanied by some shift in power from the speaker back to the committee chairs. But a relatively small group of Republican party leaders and committee chairs continues to dominate the coordination of policy and politics in the House.[12] Under Speaker Dennis Hastert, the subcommittees are subordinate to the speaker and key committee leaders. These events indicate a conviction that centralization increases party power, especially the power to formulate and project a national party message.

The House Democrats have also centralized power since 1995. They have created a Policy Committee for agenda setting, framing policy proposals, and communications strategy. This new effort reflects the same concerns that drove the 1992 DSG and OSR reports cited above. At one time, such efforts would have threatened the control over information and policymaking jealously guarded by the committee chairs. The Democrats have also eliminated subcommittee leaders' right to appoint staff, which right has been transferred to full committee ranking members, subject to the approval of a committee's Democrats.[13] These various changes indicate somewhat greater leadership control over Democrats on committees and subcommittees. Majority Leader Gephardt's Chief-of-Staff Lawrence O'Donnell stated in 1995, "we're a lot more centralized than before."[14] Even on the more decentralized Senate side, Senate Democrats have continued the trend toward greater use of task forces. This trend indicates a willingness to reduce the information advantages and autonomy of committees somewhat.[15]

Overall, these events indicate members value a more centralized party as a tool for legislating programs that support a party message. Legislators want a party message to unify the party's leaders and voters, activate the party's base voters, attract swing voters, energize activists, convince interest groups, stimulate candidate recruitment, and attract contributors. However, a top Democratic National Committee official, later a top White House official, emphasized in a 1991 interview for this study that, although there was no problem in getting a party message out to where it would do the most good, formulating the message was another matter, and this went to the deeper problems of the party. He recalled how, in the search for an effective party message, the DNC had brought together all the best Democratic consultants and asked them what to do about the party message. The result, he said, was "a cacophony" he contrasted with the harmony among Republican consultants, and added, "But they are all on retainer."

A Third Unifying Force: Party Services to Candidates

According to a study by the Annenburg Public Policy Center of Advertising, over half of the issue ads broadcast in the last two months before the 1998 election were attack ads. According to this study, the political parties paid for 70 percent of such ads airing after September 1, 1998.[16] Thus, parties have become important in providing campaign services. In addition to paying for election advertising, other party services include candidate training, opposition and issue research, campaign management, media services, and polling.[17] Moreover, some vital party services are unrecorded, as when potential contributors are directed by party officials to send their contributions to key races in appropriate ways at appropriate times (especially early money and money to counter end-of-election media attacks). The influence of parties with their candidates has grown accordingly, and may continue to grow.

A Fourth Unifying Force: Party Leaders

A fourth source of partisan behavior in Congress is the increasing influence of party leaders. Roger H. Davidson notes by the time Tip O'Neill became speaker in 1977, "he commanded far more extensive formal powers than did Rayburn, his illustrious predecessor."[18] Increased party cohesion creates greater opportunities for party leaders, and cohesion among the congressional Democrats has increased in recent decades, due to the following events.[19]

First, the Voting Rights Act of 1965 led many southern conservatives to leave the Democratic Party, as African Americans began voting in large numbers. As a result, many congressional seats previously held by southern Democrats came under Republican control. The proportion of conservatives in the Democratic congressional delegation fell accordingly,[20] the remaining Democrats became more cohesive, and party unity scores rose in the late 1970s.[21] Race is as important as ever in southern politics,[22] but the Democrats in Congress have become cohesive on racial issues, since many white southern Democrats now depend on African-American votes to beat Republicans. Then, in the late 1980s and early 1990s, an alliance between some African-American groups and the Bush Justice Department was successful in obtaining judicial support for increasing the number of so-called majority/minority congressional districts following the 1990 Census. African-American voters were taken out of districts where they made the difference in keeping white conservative Democrats in office, and were put into new majority/minority districts. The number of African-American representatives increased substantially. The Democratic Party in Congress was affected in two ways: (1) the increase in majority/minority seats increased the number of Republican-controlled seats in the South, which helped the Republicans become the majority in the House after the 1994 election; (2) the Democratic delegation became even more cohesive, which might have helped their party leaders to develop a more popular party program if they had not lacked the money to fund such a program.

Second, the congressional reforms of the 1970s, which liberal Democrats constructed to reduce the power of the southern conservative Democrats, succeeded in shifting power to the more moderate and liberal factions in the party. These reforms took a good deal of power away from the few committee chairmen and gave it to the many subcommittees. The reforms also created significant new powers for majority party leaders, who gained influence using committee assignments, multiple bill referral to and time limits imposed on committees, control of the Rules Committee, enhanced scheduling power, and an elaborated party whip system. After these reforms, each speaker made more use of the new processes than had his predecessor, with the possible exception of Speaker Foley.[23] The powers of the party leaders were also enhanced by a more active Caucus, a new Steering and Policy Committee, and an active campaign committee. Leaders expanded their assistance to members in raising funds, getting media exposure, and promoting their careers, all of which increased the leaders' ability to call on those members for support.

In the Senate, when Senator Robert Byrd (D-West Virginia) became Majority Leader in 1978, he concentrated power in his own hands. He chaired the Democratic Steering Committee that controlled committee assignments, dominated scheduling of legislation as chairman of the Senate Democratic Policy Committee, and presided over the Senate Democratic Caucus. His successor George Mitchell (D-Maine) used many of the same instruments to exert leadership, as has his successor Senator Tom Daschle (D-South Dakota) using the more restricted powers of the Minority Leader.[24] Senate majority leaders also gained leverage from constructing unanimous consent agreements. Since 1997, the increased number of hard-line conservatives within the Senate Republican delegation has endowed their leaders, Senator Trent Lott (R-Mississippi) and Senator Jim Nichols (R-Oklahoma), with increased opportunities for more unified Republican strategies. In general, both Senate and House Democratic and Republican party leaders are now better positioned to assert party interests over narrower interests than in the past.

Third, the economic environment of slower growth and big budget deficits in the 1980s and 1990s altered internal power relations inside Congress to the advantage of party leaders. Writing in 1987, Davidson described "a new centralization" of power in Congress that made the parties "more cohesive and hierarchical than portrayed in scholarly and journalistic accounts." He noted increased leadership influence over budgeting, following a shift in power from authorizing committees to Budget and Appropriations committees under pressure from the large Reagan deficits; increased leadership influence through negotiating budget deals with the White House; and increased leadership influence through constructing large Budget Reconciliation bills that packaged together many policy decisions.[25]

Party leaders also exert influence over committees through post-committee changes in legislation, and by bypassing committees through various devices.[26] Committee leaders lack the means on their own to build chamberwide coalitions. Constructing inter-committee logrolls require the active efforts of the majority leadership.[27] The more important an issue is to non-committee members and their constituents, the less committees enjoy independence from party leaders.[28] Party and chamber use a number of devices to control committees that overrepresent the interests of committee members and committee constituencies. These include making committee assignments that keep committees representative of the party's ideological center of gravity, especially on control committees; making committee assignments that reflect party concerns and that reward party loyalty;[29] and, on rare occasions, restricting the seniority rights of a member to become or remain a committee chairperson.[30] Majority party leaders use scheduling as a bargaining chip to gain changes in the content of committee bills, especially at the end of a congressional session when many bills compete for scarce time. All of these mechanisms enhance the influence of party leaders relative to committee leaders.

Party leaders also gain influence from packaging legislation. Narrow provisions are linked together in a single larger bill. Party leaders do the packaging, and these leaders are mindful of longer-term coalition needs of the party. Omnibus bills, hundreds and even thousands of pages long, routinely provide support for political interests that could never succeed alone. As Davidson and Walter Oleszek point out,

> Party leaders command the resources and authority to exercise coordinative and substantive influence over the packaging process. As a result, rank-and-file members look to Party Leaders for assistance in formulating a package acceptable to at least a majority of members. House and Senate Leaders often appoint ad hoc party task forces to mobilize support behind these priority matters.[31]

Omnibus bills usually involve policies with the greatest impact on the nation.

The question is often raised whether party leaders can coerce ordinary members of their party. Members are independent because they can get themselves reelected and so can refuse the demands of party leaders if they need to so as to satisfy constituent pressures. But members win because they are responsive to constituents' demands for a legislative product.[32] They need the support of their party leaders to pass the legislation their constituents demand. Hence, leaders have crucial leverage over things crucially important to members. The apparent independence of members is qualified by what they need from their leaders. Thus, party leaders and followers in Congress have great incentives to cooperate, which tends to unify and strengthen the parties.

A Fifth Unifying Force: Partisan Interest Groups

The view of congressional committees as independent of parties but dependent on interest groups "permeates congressional scholarship more than any other model."[33] This literature assumes parties are weak because interest groups and their committee allies pull members away from party agendas. Jack L. Walker argued a contrary view, *denying* most interest groups are competitors with or antagonists of the parties. Walker stated,

> As the circle of participants in the dialogue over public policy grows and the political system becomes increasingly polarized along ideological lines, each individual interest group will be under pressure to encourage the fortunes of the political party that affords it the best access to government. Pressures will increase for all interest groups of liberal persuasion to form loose alliances during elections to work for the political party that best represents their views. For most citizens there will be no other path to influence. Groups that have developed close cooperative relationships within subgovernments increasingly will be pressed to take sides in the partisan struggle.[34]

Robert H. Salisbury also finds interest groups traditionally have aligned themselves with parties, and are not independent of them. He notes,

> [A] substantial majority of interest group lobbyists active in Washington are rather strong partisans. In our study of lobbyists in four policy domains, my colleagues and I found that . . . many of them have been involved in partisan campaigns, they often have held political or partisan office themselves, and they have contributed money to campaigns and raised it for others. If their political background and present commitment is Republican, they tend quite strongly to be conservatives on economic questions. Interest group representatives who are or have been active Democrats are generally quite strongly liberal. Moreover, liberal Democrats tend to know and work with other liberal Democrats, and the opposite is true of conservative Republicans. Working colleagues tend to share the same partisan and ideological perspective, and their network connections with notable lobbyists follow similar paths.[35]

If Walker and Salisbury are correct, many and perhaps most interest groups, especially the more influential ones, have mutually supportive relations with one party or the other but not both.

These ideologically compatible and durable alliances between parties and certain interest groups are a major party-unifying force. But, again it is essential to recognize that many other interests that make campaign contributions are allied unnaturally to parties, since their alliance is based only on their campaign contributions, the related quid pro quo, and frantic need of political candidates to raise campaign funds.

A Sixth Unifying Force: The Role of Ideology

One major source of doubt about the potential strength of parties comes from an enduring dispute among scholars about the nature of congressional coalitions.[36] Perhaps party leaders' capacity to lead is undercut by coalitions in Congress that are ever-shifting or multidimensional. Faced with ever-shifting coalitions, parties would have weak cohesion and therefore weak influence on its members. According to the Pluralists' ever-shifting view, congresspersons who vote on the conservative side on one issue will vote on the liberal side of the next issue. Supporting an ever-shifting coalition model is the image of lawmakers as individual entrepreneurs, operating in a vast short-term political auction market, who ignore the transaction costs of long-run coalition formation.[37] In this world, politicians exhibit little loyalty to their party, and all bargaining over legislation starts from scratch.[38]

Abundant anecdotal evidence, however, suggests politicians place a high value on political loyalty. Confirmation of the importance of loyalty to politicians is found in the work of scholars who claim congressional behavior better fits models with partisan/ideological coalitions. Some studies show ideological coalitions operating across issues, in a large number of consecutive Congresses across long periods of time.[39] Ideological conflicts are shown to reflect partisan and regional divisions, and operate on most issues.[40] Other studies show the important role of U.S. senators' ideologies as a determinant of their voting patterns in the Senate, and one finds "ideology is the primary determinant."[41] Moreover, a recent study shows the role of ideology among voters is expanding. Using National Election Study data, it shows that over the last 20 years, ideology has played an increasing role in shaping voters' partisanship, and ideology cuts across traditional New Deal social group cleavages.[42] Moreover, ideology has become more important among the parties' more intense partisans.[43]

The ideological model of congressional politics has the unique virtue of being able to explain shifts in the balance between liberal and conservative clusters of members within each party as well as within Congress as a whole. Such a shift occurred in the ideological balance in the Senate as a result of the 1996 elections. A significant shift to the right occurred among Senate Republicans. A number of Republican moderates, notably Alan K. Simpson, Mark Hatfield, William S. Cohen, Nancy Kassenbaum, and Robert Dole, left the Senate prior to 1997, while a number of new Republican senators were quite conservative, notably Sam Brownback, Pat Roberts, Wayne Allard, Jeff Sessions, and Chuck Hagel.[44] This shift to the right permitted Majority Leader Trent Lott to challenge the Democrats more directly. If such shifts are real,[45] it would make little sense to also claim each senator is now a liberal on one issue, now a conservative on another, as the Pluralist, multidimensional model claims. So the ideological model fits the facts better than the multidimensional model.

What makes ideology so powerful as a party-unifying force is that broad ideological principles saturate many specific issues. Durable alliances result among advocates for different issues, cemented by ideological linkages, based on overarching principles such as the desirability of smaller government or greater equality. The seemingly narrow issue of educational vouchers, for example, became an icon for conservatives because the voucher issue is saturated by such themes as the desirability of smaller government, government (school) incompetence, the ineffectiveness of government regulation, and resistance to higher taxes.

Such an ideological saturation of narrower issues by broader issues occurs when an objective basis is found for linking issues together and accordingly linking groups together in a coalition. As a coordinating mechanism for drawing interests together for long-run mutual support, ideology has cash value. Because ideologies are rally points, they reduce the transaction costs of searching for and winning compliance from coalition partners. Ideologies enable politicians and parties to build and maintain bonds with other politicians and groups, thereby increasing their power. Ideologies, therefore, can help unify parties.[46]

A Seventh Unifying Force: The Need to Reduce the Transaction Costs of Coalition Formation

Putting together a winning legislative coalition requires time, effort, money, and information, i.e., transaction costs.[47] To pass legislation, party leaders depend on the support of the party's loyal legislators, those who do not have to be courted on every vote. The complex process of learning party members' real preferences, and combining these preferences into support for legislation, is greatly simplified by members' partisanship. Their partisanship reduces the time, effort, money, and information costs their party leaders must expend to create a coalition behind a piece of legislation.

By way of contrast, any system in which every legislator's vote is up for grabs on every vote and must be won over with bargaining and logrolling on every bill to re-form every coalition would collapse under the weight of excessive transaction costs. Durable party coalitions greatly reduce the quantity of bargaining necessary with uncommitted members to pass legislation.[48] Members need to participate in party coalitions embodying low transaction costs, so that political markets clear and deals get done that satisfy constituents' demands for legislation. This need helps overcome the abovementioned forces that fragment parties. Cox and McCubbins note,

> If creating a winning coalition is costly, then already formed coalitions will be stabilized because potential defectors must pay a cost to assemble a new winning coalition—so the policy benefits gained by defection must exceed the coalition formation costs in order to be worth the effort . . . We already know from the work of Sloss (1973) that adding transaction costs to the basic spatial model can in principle produce structurally stable cores . . . We think in fact the game is . . . more reliant on transaction costs to induce stability.[49]

The great stability of party coalitions is reflected in the historical evolution of Federalists and Anti-Federalists into Whigs and Democrats and then into Republicans and Democrats, based on the continuous support of roughly the same economic groups across centuries of American history, especially labor and business.

It is useful to draw on economic theory to explain why parties and party loyalties are normally stable. How are party coalitions in legislatures that depend on loyal partisans different from ever-shifting coalitions? They differ in the same fundamental way that distinguishes customer markets with implicit contracts from auction markets.[50] A buyer or a seller in an auction market only seeks information about the terms of the immediate transaction. A buyer or a seller in a customer market seeks much more information. In customer markets, customers develop good long-term relationships with suppliers. These customers pay premiums for information about such things as (1) future product reliability or (2) future delivery time reliability. A buyer in a customer relationship with a seller can expect to be relatively high on the list of those who will receive goods when those goods are in short supply. Similarly, a seller can expect a "good customer" will stick with the supplier at least long enough to ride out short-term fluctuations in prices, even if competitors lower prices. Customer market relations are distinguished by implicit contracts that allow someone to avoid the high costs of spelling out and negotiating explicit contracts concerning unspecified future contingencies.

The relationship between a congressperson and her party is a customer market relationship. A legislator supports her party leaders today in return for an implicit contract promising that if she is loyal, the party will support her bills and advance her career more than a disloyal member could expect. The contract is incomplete regarding various contingencies,[51] which interferes with easy measurement of incentives for partisanship. That is why, perhaps, the payoffs of partisanship have received less attention than they deserve.

Abundant evidence, including the interviews done for this study, confirms that partisanship in Congress is strong, if underestimated in the past. *The Strong Party theory argues that strong party coalitions, strong party loyalties, and strong party leaders are best understood in relation to the economic theory of transaction costs, customer markets, and implicit contracts. On the basis of this foundation, it is clear that partisanship is the normal mode, and deviations from partisanship are unstable in the long run.*[52]

An Eighth Unifying Force: The Relation between Income and Party

Over the last 30 years, the correlation between the income level of a congressional district's voters and which political party wins in that district has increased. At the same time, the correlation between a district's ethnic composition and its party choice has decreased. In other words, the relationship between party and income, like the relationship between ideology and party, is becoming closer as time goes on.[53] Schlozman and Verba concluded the party system is "divided more or less on economic lines."[54] Miller and Shanks showed lower-income individuals regularly vote for Democrats, while higher-income individuals regularly vote for Republicans.[55] Stonecash and Lindstrom have summarized this literature, and they too show a strong and growing relationship between voters' income and their party choice.

The broad implication is that the common needs of constituents in the same income range tends to draw legislators of the same party together, and thus provide a basis for party unity.

A Ninth Unifying Force: Collective Interests

A political system is only successful when its collective interests overwhelm less productive narrow interests. Collective interests include the national defense, democracy itself, increased productivity growth, reduced inequality, the full utilization of labor and capital, the reduction of conflict, social justice, social cohesion, the rule of law, and the reduction of environmental dangers.[56] Yet, some theorists seem to believe the triumph of particular interests over the general interest is all but inevitable most of the time. Particular interests are highly mobilized and have a clear understanding of what they want and how to get it.[57] Voters, presumably, lack information about their collective interests, which suggests collective interests are apt to be shortchanged. This story ignores different elites' and voters' awarenesses of the value of collective goods.

Congress has often changed the political process itself to make collective interests more attainable. Sometimes a change in the legislative process is necessary before collective goals can compete successfully with narrower interests. Base closings, trade legislation, Omnibus Reconciliation bills, and financing of the Federal Reserve all required a new extraordinary legislative process, specifically the Base Closing Commission, Fast Track legislation, Omnibus Reconciliation rules, and the funding mechanism for the Federal Reserve. In the last case, for example, the independence of the Federal Reserve Board's control over monetary policy was protected when Congress voted to allow the Fed to finance its operations from fees on its transactions. Ordinarily the Fed would have been required to request annual appropriations from Congress like other agencies of government. In superseding the normal appropriations process, lawmakers made monetary policy decisions immune to influences by members of Congress who might hold monetary policy hostage to narrower interests. The dominance of the collective interest over particular interests was institutionalized and could not be readily undermined.

Collective goals are sometimes so important they bring people together in a national movement. Other times collective goals bring people together behind one political party, as with the environmental movement. Therefore collective goals often act as unifying forces within parties when they fail to unite the nation.

Conservative Democrats and Party Unity

The nine party-unifying forces discussed above prevent fragmentation from being the central problem of political parties. The weaknesses of parties do not result from being fragmented by interest groups' dissention in the ranks, a diverse voter population, or the independence of members of Congress from their party's leaders. The parties are weak for other reasons. The Republicans' overriding weakness is they are attached to an economic agenda that is popular with Republican stalwarts but unpopular with average voters. They oppose appropriations for public goods that voters want. The Democrats' main weakness is that, symbolic reassurances and token programs to the contrary notwithstanding, they lack the money with which to supply the public investments and social insurance voters want and the economy needs. This weakness is reflected in the dramatic decline in Democratic voters' partisanship, and the dramatic decline in congressional seats controlled by the Democrats.

But there is a second reason why the Democratic Party has been weak. The congressional Democrats' conservative wing continually undercuts the party. This wing of the party consists mostly of some southern, mountain, and western conservatives who are close to business interests. Conservative Democrats, though reduced in numbers, still play an obstructionist role within the congressional party. In the House in 2000, 29 members belonged to the Blue Dog Democrats, the organization of conservative Democrats.[58] Though not a cohesive group on every issue, they are strongly committed to one brand of fiscal conservativism: achieving balanced budgets by cutting programs, including public investments, rather than by raising taxes or cutting contributor waste. There is no comparable group organized in the Senate. The Blue Dogs have had a major impact. Because the party seat balance in the House has been close in recent congresses, the Blue Dogs' votes have provided the margin of victory on many important votes.[59]

It is important to emphasize that the Blue Dogs are not the only conservative Democrats in Congress. Depending on what legislative votes or issues one chooses as a gauge, more Democrats than just the 29 Blue Dogs could be identified as conservatives.

Although the differences within the party on civil rights has all but disappeared, the conservative southerners are still a distinct deviant faction in the House Democratic Party.[60] When asked on which issues they disagreed with their party most, southern Democrats replied the most important were economic issues, including capital gains taxes, child care, family leave, and generally issues affecting small business and labor unions. Similarly, on many social and foreign policy issues, conservative southern Democrats have been notably more conservative than other Democrats.[61]

These differences between Democratic factions are obscured by party unity scores measuring unity on bills put to a vote. But these votes occur after progressive Democrats have already made concessions to the conservative Democrats. When Democratic leaders accommodate their conservative wing, that forced collaboration obscures the real preferences of the party's base voters and many Democratic lawmakers. The impact of the conservative Democrats is therefore greater than indicated by standard measures of party cohesiveness. Cohesion on a shrunken agenda hides the majority's capitulations.

The strength and policy positions of this conservative Democratic faction has often been viewed as inelastic. According to the conventional wisdom, nothing will change the strength of this faction enough that it would take on the more progressive views of their northern colleagues. And so the national Democratic Party is seen as likely to remain proportionately incohesive and weak. At the root of this argument is the widely held view that members reflect their districts, and conservative members reflect their conservative districts. This static reasoning is open to serious question. It assumes that progressive Democrats cannot be elected to the southern seats now held by conservative Democrats. Yet, like most of the country's voters, roughly 75 percent of whom lack a college degree, most southern voters share economic interests with people of similar income levels in northern districts. Ballot access aside, it remains a mystery why, after campaign reform, a progressive Democratic candidate for Congress who embraced his national party's progressive economic agenda would be less viable in a southern congressional district or state than in a northern one. The current absence of an appealing Democratic Party economic program reduces the salience of economic issues, while raising the salience of conservative social, especially racial, issues that play especially well in the South.[62] But Bill Clinton successfully changed the relative salience of different issues,[63] proposing moderately progressive economic positions offensively while taking moderately conservative social issue positions (for example, the death penalty) defensively.[64] Progressive Democrats may yet prevail in southern congressional races using progressive economic proposals to change relative issue saliencies. Then the gap between many southern Democrats and mainstream progressive Democrats in the Democratic delegation to Congress would be narrowed. Greater party unity within the congressional Democratic Party would emerge accordingly, provided the Democrats took enough money from federal waste to fund what they proposed.

Conclusion: Two Theories of Congressional Party Weakness

Pluralist theory sees parties as endemically weak, because interest groups are strong, because legislators are individual entrepreneurs who only join together in ever-shifting coalitions, and because American society is a patchwork quilt of social and economic differences. If congressional parties are perpetually weak for these reasons, then passing even a best possible campaign finance reform into law will have little effect. After enacting reforms, weak parties would continue to be dominated by strong interest groups, and would continue to misallocate resources to those groups.

This view of parties is contradicted by a second view, which sees both parties as undermined by campaign contributions, the Democrats more than the Republicans, and also sees the Democrats as weakened by their conservative faction. But, because of the nine party-unifying forces described in this chapter, enacting effective campaign reform would strengthen political parties in Congress, making them more responsive to voters and to the needs of the commonweal. Operating under campaign finance reform, the Democrats would be willing and able to recapture from campaign contributors what they need most: a great deal of money to apply to public investment and social insurance. So with campaign reform accomplished, the nine party-unifying forces would incentivize a resurgent Democratic Party.

The power of party-unifying forces relative to the power of party-fragmenting forces has never been systematically measured, statically or dynamically. Yet, the discussion above suggests party-unifying forces are underestimated. *A transaction costs / customer markets / implicit contracts theory suggests strong parties in Congress are likely most of the time.* Passing legislation to satisfy constituents requires legislative majorities, building majorities requires allies, and long-term allies reduce transaction costs much more than short-term allies. If so, a congressional party in partnership with its president should normally provide greater leadership to the nation than the Pluralist paradigm allows. But even a strong party can be deflected from its path by contributors that coopt its legislators. So effective campaign reform is a precondition of a strong Democratic Party. If that precondition is fulfilled, then the nine party-unifying forces discussed above should produce strong parties capable of effective national leadership.

Chapter 7

Are the Democrats Big Spenders or Big Investors? Inequality and Productivity

CHAPTER FOUR SHOWED THAT CONGRESS WASTES AT LEAST $1 TRILLION A YEAR in a $10 trillion plus economy. Recapturing that money, and adding funds borrowed from a voluntary national saving program, would finance a large increase in new public and private investments. Effective campaign finance reform would give Democrats in Congress the opportunity to reallocate wasted funds over to new public investments. They would be eager to reverse the decline in their voter base and reestablish effective control over governmental institutions by legislating popular programs.

Republicans often charge Democrats with being big spenders who would waste the taxpayers' hard-earned money on unnecessary and corrupt projects. Yet, publicly financed congressional campaigns would remove legislators' incentive to trade wasteful spending for campaign contributions. Nonetheless, many observers are skeptical about public investment. They argue that now wasted funds should be returned to the citizenry in the form of tax cuts instead of spending that money on public investments. But tax cuts would mostly support increased personal consumption by better-off consumers who would get the lion's share, whereas efficient public investments would have large payoffs for the nation. But, if funds that are now wasted are to be reallocated to new public investments, widespread skepticism must be overcome. *A fundamental rationale is needed to support increased public investment.*

It is especially difficult to understand why an expansion of government investment is desirable when the economy has seemed better than at any time in decades. Unemployment and inflation rates are exceptionally low, technological advances are remarkable, and, productivity growth has, arguably, been both better and good since 1995. Stock market portfolios have been swollen with profits, and welfare rates are historically low. In the context of an apparently strong economy, how much would new public investments improve the economy?

The key benefit to the nation that would flow from new public investments is they would enable most individuals to become more productive. By making individuals more productive, the whole economy would become more productive. Efficient public investments, especially human capital investments, ordinarily lead to an increase in productivity.[1] A more productive economy would make the United States both more prosperous and more powerful. Public investments are needed to spur the economy because public investments *complement* private investments. Public highways *complement* private automobiles. Publicly educated workers *complement* the privately owned equipment they run.

The best way to determine the value of new government investments is to identify the largest economic problems new investments would remedy, which is the task of this chapter. Many economists believe the U.S. economy has two major economic problems that may damage the future of the American nation: growing inequality and sluggish productivity growth. In the words of three Brookings economists:

> In the next decade and beyond, the nation faces no more urgent economic challenge than reversing these two trends.[2]

They note employing better education and job training policies would increase equality and raise productivity at the same time.[3] Many economists argue that a wide range of public sector investments in human capital, knowledge capital, and physical capital would raise productivity. What progress is achieved in reducing inequality and increasing productivity growth will benchmark the political parties. Solving these two problems would give campaign reform a fundamental justification, second only to fixing democracy itself.

These two problems are best understood in a historical perspective. Driven by productivity growth, a remarkable increase in U.S. living standards occurred in the decades following World War II.[4] Per capita income more than doubled between 1947 and 1974, a mere 27 years.[5] In the nearly three decades since 1973, however, productivity growth rates have been quite low. Some analysts believe the period 1995 through 2000 saw an uptick in the rate of growth in productivity, reflecting the impact of new technologies. Other analysts argue the evidence does not yet support the view that productivity has accelerated. This dispute is reviewed below.

Whatever the truth about the productivity growth rate since 1995, an optimal public policy would so allocate resources between consumption and investment as to maximize productivity growth. Maximizing productivity growth should be the goal of government policy no matter how high the level of productivity already is. Economists estimate that if a 2 percent rate of growth in productivity could be sustained, a rate lower than obtained in the 1950s and 1960s, the median U.S. family income, which was $35,353 in 1990, would rise to $52,533 in 2010, more than a

48.4 percent increase in only 20 years. But if incomes only rose 0.5 percent a year, the median income would only be $39,061 by 2010, a mere 10.5 percent increase in the same amount of time. This median income is roughly 37 percent lower than the median income at the higher 2 percent rate of growth in productivity, and is $13,472 lower in real terms.[6] Hence, a prudent nation will do all it can to increase productivity.

While U.S. productivity suffered low growth rates in recent decades, inequality increased sharply in those same decades. Inequality is now at quite high levels relative to the past and relative to levels in other advanced nations. Most male workers have only a high school education or a little more, and they have experienced sharply declining wages over several decades. The wages of female high school graduates were steadier, but at a lower level. The decline in wages is likely to continue, reflecting technological innovation and globalization. Poorly educated and poorly trained workers now have little chance of getting ahead, and in fact are losing ground.[7] The growth in inequality can at some point threaten a nation's political stability and its tranquility.[8]

What follows considers in greater detail the problems of growing inequality and low rates of growth in productivity. Solving these two problems would require a large reallocation of wasted resources over to public and private investment. No such reallocation will occur without effective campaign finance reform.

Growing Inequality

According to one leading study, income inequality has grown "enormously" in the United States over the last several decades.[9] The largest increase occurred in the gap between the earnings of men who did not go beyond high school and men with a college education.[10] This growing gap reflected falling demand for unskilled workers, which resulted from technological change and globalization. In 1996, the average high school educated man between the ages of 45 and 54 earned approximately $30,963, down from $36,217 in 1986.[11] Median male hourly wages fell 14.7 percent between 1979 and 1993, and wages fell 19.9 percent for low-wage men. Men in the 60th income percentile and below suffered wage deterioration between 15 percent and 20 percent between 1979 and 1993. James Heckman notes, "Standard measures of earnings inequality understate the severity of the problem because they exclude non-earners. Among the least skilled, nonemployment and lack of earnings has substantially increased."[12] So the real growth in inequality is even greater than these numbers show.

Frank Levy highlights the growth in inequality by comparing income growth in two generations:

In 1949, the average thirty-year old man . . . had an income of about $16,800 [in 1997 dollars] . . . a little more than the poverty standard for a family of four. Twenty years later, however, this average man, now fifty, was making almost $40,000. His income had more than doubled in twenty years. . . .

Jump ahead to 1976. . . . Among thirty-year-old male high school graduates, . . . average wage and salary income rose modestly and then fell, ultimately moving from *$27,600 at age thirty to $28,400 at age fifty.* [italics added][13]

Women's wages show a different pattern. Female high school graduates' wages fell slightly, and hours worked increased. Female wages as a percent of male wages rose from 65 percent in 1973 to 78 percent in 1993. However, more than 70 percent of the narrowing was due to declines in male wages and less than 30 percent to female wage growth. Higher wage women alone had significant wage increases between 1979 and 1989.[14] Most important, percentage gains in the earnings of women in the highest group were three times as large as those of women in the bottom group.[15] All of this contributed to growing inequality.

In recent decades, falling wages were offset by increases in the number of hours worked, by marrying later, by having fewer children, and by saving less.[16] Most of all, falling wages were offset by the addition of married women to the work force in higher percentages than had been common earlier. But families have run out of additional earners who can join the labor force, are carrying all the debt they can service, and are working all the additional hours they can reasonably be expected to work. Thus, most American families have used up what assets they could use to offset a future decline in wages. So further wage declines will be more painful than past wage cuts, especially to the less affluent in the Democrats' voter base.

Declining wages and growing inequality reflect falling demand for unskilled labor, and rising demand for skilled labor. Technological innovation substitutes equipment and skilled labor for unskilled labor, causing much of the increase in income inequality.[17] But conventional differences in education and experience account for less of the growth in inequality than differences in skills within narrowly defined education and labor market experience groups, which makes optimal policies harder to ascertain.[18]

After skill-based technical change, the other principal causes of growing inequality in the United States have been globalization (foreign trade), immigration of low-skilled workers, shifts from manufacturing to service industries, declining union membership, subcontracting, a lower real minimum wage,[19] and the declining bargaining power of labor.[20] Paul Krugman argues the impact of globalization on inequality has been minor so far, since exports and imports together are only roughly 12 percent of the U.S. economy. Moreover, the United States trades mostly with advanced countries where wage rates approximate U.S. wages, and so cheap labor abroad has not put downward pressure on U.S. wages.[21] However, some economists fear inequality may increase in the future, if capital and technology flow out of the United States to low-wage countries at an increasing rate. Domestic wages would then be bid down, reflecting "factor price equalization,"[22] U.S. wage rates would fall, and inequality would increase.

The causes of growing family income inequality are somewhat different than among individuals. The income of the bottom 80 percent of families declined 7 percent between 1977 and 1995, while the income of the top 20 percent of families grew 26.4 percent.[23] This increased inequality among families resulted in part from (1) the increase in families with two high income earners, and (2) the increase in lower-income one-parent families, mostly female headed. But changes in these two groups only explain about one-fifth of the increase in family income inequality from 1973 through 1993.[24] Among families with a spouse between 18 and 64 years-old, the increase in earnings inequality among working males caused about one-third of the increase in family income inequality after 1969.[25] From 1973 to 1993, inequality among families was increased by the growth in the number of women getting college degrees, combined with a sharply increased tendency for college-educated higher-income men to marry college-educated women who earn more. One-third of the growth in income inequality among families is explained by growth in earnings from a female earner.[26] Overall growth in income was concentrated among high-income families, many of them well educated.[27]

Inequality among individuals and among families continues to grow in the United States, especially between better-educated workers and unskilled workers lacking a two-year or four-year college degree. The best remedy for boosting the earnings of lower paid workers is to increase investments in their education and training, mostly in the public sector. But such investments would require massive new funding.

Wealth Inequality

In the United States, some human capital investments are funded from personal financial assets, some are financed with personal debt serviced with current or future income, and some are financed by government. Personal financial assets enable some families to ease the transition from lost jobs to new ones, cope with uninsured health crises, and prepare for retirement and elderly care. Most Americans, however, have little wealth with which to meet these crises or to invest in the educational development of their children or themselves. In 1983, the last year of available data, 54 percent of families had zero or negative net financial assets.[28] Thus over half of families in the United States were living paycheck to paycheck. They had little or no economic security other than their jobs and illiquid equity in their houses.

The low level of most Americans' wealth accumulation is accompanied by very large inequality in the distribution of wealth. Edward N. Wolff, the editor of the journal *Review of Income and Wealth*, shows in the 1989 distribution of financial wealth[29] the top 20 percent held 94 percent of the wealth, or the bottom 80 percent of the population only held 6 percent of all U.S. financial wealth, not counting owner-occupied housing, autos, and other consumer durables. The top 1 percent held 48 percent of all the U.S. financial wealth in 1989.[30] More than 66 percent of the gains in financial wealth between 1983 and 1989 went to the top 1 percent.

Wolff finds the distribution of wealth in the United States is considerably more unequal than in other advanced nations. The significance of this greater wealth inequality is compounded by another factor. Wolff notes that in Europe, many of the things one would spend one's personal wealth on—education, training and retraining, health insurance, and pensions—are provided by the state, reducing the need for personal wealth. Most Americans not only lack personal wealth, they also lack the benefits that governments in Europe provide. Wolff points out that earlier in this century, the U.S. wealth distribution was much more egalitarian than in European nations. Today the United States has a much higher concentration of wealth, and it is Europe that is relatively egalitarian.[31]

The degree of wealth inequality found in the United States ensures most Americans will not be able on their own to find the funds to pay for human capital investments to increase their ability to function and contribute more productively to the U.S. economy.

Cross-National Comparisons of Income Inequality

Differences in inequality between the United States and Western Europe are instructive. According to Richard B. Freeman and Lawrence F. Katz:

> Only in the United States was the rise in inequality associated with quite large declines in real wages for low-wage workers (even those in year-round, full-time employment). The huge decline in the real earnings of low-paid workers in the United States has been associated with sharp increases in family income inequality and growing rates of poverty among working families.[32]

Why was did the United States alone experience large declines in the wages of lower paid workers in recent decades? According to Freeman and Katz, the biggest difference between the United States and other advanced countries is the United States invests much less in the education and training of its non-college educated workers than do Germany, Japan, and some other advanced countries. Moreover, the United States has lower minimum wages and less union wage setting, which in other countries raise the living standards of less skilled workers.

The big difference in income inequality between the United States and other advanced countries is in the growth in inequality between the 90th percentile of male workers and the 10th percentile. The 90/10 income ratio is very large in the United States compared with the same ratio in other OECD countries. The 90/50 ratio in the United States appears to be only slightly larger than in other advanced countries.[33] However, when inequality is measured by consumption, which fluctuates less because of transient events, the 90/50 ratio grew as much as the 90/10 ratio.[34]

In addition, the distance between the rich in the United States and the rich abroad has been growing dramatically. Timothy Smeeding finds high income Americans had real living standards far above those of the same percentile—the ninetieth and ninety-fifth—in other rich nations. Smeeding concludes the rich in the United States "are far better off than the rich in other nations, and its poor are not as well off as the poor in other nations."[35] If the rich in the United States enjoy a larger proportion of their nation's income than in previous decades, and a larger proportion than the rich of other nations, is there less investment in public goods in the United States than in Europe in part because the wealthy and the well-off in the United States consume so much larger a proportion of national income? In this context, it is vital to note most income is consumed, and only a small proportion is saved and invested, even by the wealthy.

However dramatic the growth in inequality may be, its implications are not obvious. We turn now to the effects of inequality on individuals and on the national economy.

The Significance of Inequality: (1) Harm to Individuals

Looking beyond the deprivations visited on the poorest decile of the income distribution, where the harm is fairly clear, it might be argued inequality matters less now than it used to. Most Americans are at least modestly prosperous, and quite prosperous when compared with Americans 50 years ago, or compared with living conditions in most other nations. Gains in longevity indicate the enormous gains most Americans have derived from the growth in prosperity. Perhaps inequality in the United States today has few consequences, even if the well-off have an increased share of national income.[36] Does it matter if some people live in smaller houses, have smaller cars, and take cheaper vacations than other people? Or is there more to it than that? A number of recent studies show inequality has consequences that go far beyond smaller houses and smaller cars.

A study by Bruce P. Kennedy and others[37] shows that differences in income inequality among the 50 states of the United States are associated with increased mortality. Such states as Texas, Louisiana, Mississippi, Alabama, and New York show both high mortality and high inequality, while states like Utah, Hawaii, Minnesota, and Wisconsin are lower on both scales. The larger the distance within a state between the incomes of the wealthy and the poor, the higher the mortality rate. The differences among the states in these distances are correlated with differences in mortality rates. One measure of inequality, the Robin Hood Index, was positively correlated ($r=0.54$; $P<0.05$) with total mortality adjusted for age, and with infant mortality, coronary heart disease, malignant neoplasms, homicide, and causes of death amenable to medical intervention, including infectious diseases, hypertensive disease, tuberculosis, pneumonia, and bronchitis. The relationships were "just as strong for white people as for black people." The authors conclude a redistribution of incomes that reduced inequality 5 percent would be associated with about a 25 percent reduction in mortality from coronary heart disease, and a total reduction in mortality of about 7 percent.[38] Increased mortality is only the most extreme effect of greater inequality. Those who have less education, less training, and poorer health care also experience greater vulnerability to job loss, have inadequate family resources to meet family needs, and suffer more assaults on their dignity even if they do not die from these problems. Their anxiety and stress levels are accordingly higher, which affects their health. Clearly, then, inequality matters.

What is of central relevance here is that the authors of these studies conclude differences in income distribution may be a proxy for differences in access to human capital investments. They suggest communities that tolerate greater inequality may also underinvest in education, health care, and other public goods. R. G. Wilkinson argues that in developed countries, the absolute standard of living is less important than relative differences in living standards within a country. That is because these differences coincide with higher rates of depression, isolation, insecurity, and anxiety, as well as more disability, more violence, less health insurance, less education, less literacy, and in general more difficult lives.[39] A study by George A. Kaplan and others[40] confirms these findings. They conclude,

> Variations between states in the inequality of the distribution of income are significantly associated with variations between states in a large number of health outcomes and social indicators and with mortality trends. *These differences parallel relative investments in human and social capital.* Economic policies that influence income and wealth inequality may have an important impact on the health of countries. [italics added]

Researchers have found similar relationships for other countries.[41]

Human capital investments could remedy the deprivations and insecurities that are the byproduct of highly unequal societies. Who doubts a better educated and healthier person is more likely to find a better job? The more practical issue is whether the money can be found to pay for such investments. Without campaign finance reform, and the reallocation of resources that reform would trigger, such investments are unlikely to be made.

The Significance of Inequality: (2) Harm to the Economy

Efficient public investments in education, job training, health care, child care, and other public goods would reduce the harm to individuals flowing from inequality. It is much less obvious, if Congress fails to make such public investments to reduce inequality, that substantial harm to the economy would also occur. Some degree of inequality is, after all, economically desirable to create incentives to work, save, and invest. What is at issue is how much inequality is good for the economy, and how much inequality is bad for the economy.

Perhaps, whatever the value of public investments, they are less valuable than private investment. Not a few politicians, interest groups, and economists strongly prefer tax cuts to human capital investments. It is often claimed that putting government revenues into tax cuts rather than into public investments would aid capital formation and hence would grow the economy. But as the Nobel Laureate Robert M. Solow notes,

> [T]ax reduction—especially income tax reduction—fattens the disposable income of households. *Most of it flows into consumption*; only a small fraction is saved. The choice between [federal] debt reduction and tax reduction as ways of disposing of a budget surplus is mainly a choice between adding to investment and adding to consumption, between provision for the future and enjoyment for today. [italics added][42]

Nor are the increases in consumption from a tax cut enjoyed equally by all. Rather the quantity of increased consumption is greater the greater the income tax forgiven. Even at a flat income tax rate, higher-income people get a larger dollar amount from a tax cut than lower-income people, and hence the increase in their consumption from such a tax cut is proportionately greater. It follows tax revenues spent on efficient public investments would dollar for dollar increase capital formation far more than income tax cuts would, since the latter tend to increase consumption most of all. Solow also notes, "Spending on public investment—like transportation and communication infrastructure, schools, urban amenities—are a direct way of adding to the nation's stock of real capital."[43]

It follows that the failure to make such public investments, including investments that would reduce inequality, harms the economy over the long run. Capital of any kind produces a flow of services over time. The failure to accumulate public capital causes the loss of such services to the economy.

The magnitude of the benefits that flow from increases in at least some public investments are far larger than generally understood. Let one indicator suffice here to make the point. John Bishop calculates that increasing the time spent in school from 6.25 hours per day to 7 hours, and from 180 days a year to 200, has the following effects:

> [I]ncreasing time in school by 275 hours per year is estimated to eventually raise the productivity of adults by $3,276 per year (15.6 percent of mean compensation). Because a one year cohort contains 3.5 million people, the benefit is about 11.5 billion dollars a year [for just one cohort of the 13 cohorts in school]. *The real rate of return on the taxpayer contribution to the additional learning investment is 33 percent per year . . . Only investments in R&D have social rates of return this high.* [italics added][44]

Other nations have school years lasting as much as 240 school days. A school year that lasted 240 days would raise these productivity gains even more. So, the magnitude of the payoff from such an additional investment in education is extraordinary. The failure of the U.S. Congress to fund a longer school day and year has the effect of passing up an investment having a net return of 33 percent per year. Only Congress as it is presently constituted would turn down a net return on an investment of 33 percent a year. Wall Street never would, assuming reasonable risk.

So, failing to make those public investments that would reduce inequality can only harm the U.S. economy over the long run. By failing to make such public investments, the nation foregoes the income that would have flowed from such investments. Giving up that income implies that the nation will also give up some portion of its national economic capacity to solve its problems and achieve its dreams.

II. Productivity Growth

The level and rate of growth in productivity are the best indicators of the strength of a nation's economy. Over the long run, a higher rate of growth in productivity transforms a nation by raising its living standards and by increasing the capacity of its economy to afford public goods like defense, medical research, environmental safety, and a better-educated and trained workforce.

Productivity growth boosts living standards in several ways: (1) If a product is produced more efficiently, its price goes down, allowing consumers to buy it more cheaply. The consumer then has money left over to buy other things not previously affordable. (2) If a product like a car or washing machine is produced with qualitative improvements, it may break down less, need servicing less, or allow safer use. Such improvements free up time and money that can be devoted to other productive activities. (3) New technologies generate activities that previously could not be done at all, creating new sources of valuable income and new satisfactions. Examples include air conditioning, which helped revive the economy of the southern states; public sanitation, which increased health; refrigeration, which reduced food spoilage and increased health; and of course electricity, autos, chemicals, and the telephone. (4) Greater national productivity increases tax revenue derived from growing profits and growing wages, which expands government's capacity to provide public goods. (5) As growing efficiency increases the value of a business's products, the value added by an employee also goes up, making the employee more valuable to the firm, which can boost her wages. In firms that fail to increase their productivity, wages are more likely to stagnate or decline.

The benefits of productivity growth are distributed unequally. The rich get more of the increase in output than other income groups. Yet, everyone benefits enormously from increases in productivity over the long run. From 1000 A.D. to 1700 A.D. real per capita income increased at a rate of 0.016 per year, and living standards scarcely changed over this period. The technologies of ancient times were essentially unchanged in 1700, with such notable exceptions as the musket, printed books, and clocks. From 1700 to 1750, productivity rose to 0.4 percent.[45] Then from 1750 through 1900, productivity accelerated to a rate of between 1.2 and 1.4 percent a year. By the late nineteenth century, productivity growth rates were unprecedented. From 1870 to 1979, the average annual rate of growth in productivity in the leading industrial countries was more than 2 percent, which doubled per capita living standards in a few decades.[46] The best indication of the power of productivity growth to benefit everyone is that average longevity has reached 75.8 years of age in the United States.[47] By comparison, a female born in 1855 could expect to live an average of less than 41 years, and a male 39 years.[48] These gains in life expectancy would not have been possible without the added income from productivity growth becoming available to fund new health-enhancing activities, private and public.

The desirable consequences of productivity gains are captured in the following calculations. Baily, Burtless, and Litan note,

> If productivity growth can be increased, the simple arithmetic of compound interest ensures a powerful and fairly quick effect on future living standards. When the annual growth in output per hour is 0.5 percent a year, twenty years' productivity gains are needed to increase output per hour by 10 percent. If produc-

tivity growth rises to 1 percent a year, twenty years of productivity improvement will boost hourly output by 22 percent. With a 2 percent rate of productivity increase—a rate still lower than the one achieved in the 1950s and 1960s—the increase in hourly output is nearly 50 percent.[49]

Many now unaffordable private and public goods will become affordable when a higher rate of growth in productivity leads to a higher national income. *So a nation ought to do everything possible to maximize its rate of growth in productivity.*

Another major reason to value a higher rate of growth in productivity is that a country stands to lose a great deal when its productivity growth rate is lower than the rate of productivity growth in other countries. A nation's standard of living can both rise in absolute terms and fall in relative terms. A nation with a productivity growth rate lower than other nations over long periods of time can still have low unemployment, and still be able to sell what it makes abroad. Yet, to the extent its productivity is inferior, it will be forced to sell its goods abroad for less than it would have had if its technologies and its workers had been as productive as those of its competitors. At the same time it will have to spend a larger percent of its income to buy goods from countries whose production is more efficient. Hence, a nation with a relatively lower rate of growth in productivity will become a supplier of relatively cheap labor, following a decline in that nation's currency on world markets.[50] A past president of the American Economic Association, William Baumol and his colleagues conclude,

> [A] 1 percentage point lag in productivity growth for one century was sufficient to transform the United Kingdom from the world's undisputed industrial leader into the third-rate economy that it is today. It was also sufficient to cut real wages in the United Kingdom from about *1½ times that in other leading European economies to about two-thirds of the real wages in those countries today.* All this shows that now is the time to worry about America's standing in productivity growth and that, in particular, it is time to worry about that standing half a century hence. *Fifty years from now the deed may have been done. It may then be too late to do much about it.* [italics added][51]

This history of the United Kingdom embodies what is often referred to as the British Disease, a decline in the rate of growth in productivity relative to the same rate in other advanced nations.[52] The danger of such a relative decline in productivity creates a large incentive for a nation to do all it can to raise its rate of growth in productivity. Being third rate in productivity growth, American influence abroad would be eroded in many ways—political, military, and economic. Informed Americans worry about America's unilateral educational disarmament, which may guarantee that America's productivity rate in the future is low relative to other countries' rates. A nation acting in its own interest will do all that is possible to avoid the British Disease.

A poor productivity growth rate is disadvantageous in another way. It is no mystery that a growing pie allows some of the needs and demands of everyone to be satisfied somewhat. A static pie, on the other hand, requires that one group's gain must come at the expense of another's. So productivity growth is important for conflict reduction.

In sum, a low rate of productivity growth weakens prosperity, opportunity, social harmony, and a nation's influence abroad. Consequently, it would be wise to do all that is possible to boost productivity.

The Slowdown in Productivity Growth

It may be desirable to avoid the British Disease by boosting productivity growth. But what if the rate of productivity growth is already good. Perhaps then there is little policy can do to increase that rate. Economists are engaged in a debate about whether the rate of growth in the productivity of the U.S. economy has slowed down after 1973, and whether it has increased speed since 1995. We will quickly review this debate for one purpose. If the rate is below its long-term trend, then there is a greater reason to use saving and investment policies to increase it, if it can be increased through policy. Similarly, if the productivity growth rate has increased since 1995, then perhaps there is less of a need to use policy to increase the rate. Since the major economic rationale for campaign finance reform is to reallocate wasted funds over to investment, public and private, one might conclude, falsely we will argue, that if the rate of productivity is good, then more investment is that much less desirable, and so campaign finance reform is that much less desirable. Instead, however, we will argue that it is desirable to increase investment, public and private, even if the rate of growth in productivity is high compared with some historical benchmark.

Some economists claim that in recent decades the United States failed to invest enough. This Crisis School believes that the United States has been in a productivity growth crisis, or, a large and prolonged slowdown in the rate of growth in productivity. The Crisis view has been stated as follows:

> [A] study of the long-term data has revealed that productivity in the U.S. economy and in virtually all industrialized countries has been growing very slowly in recent years, even in comparison with growth rates that prevailed before World War II. Standard measures show that U.S. productivity growth has been especially slow since 1973.[53]

The Crisis School argues that even if the baseline is the long-term trend in productivity growth going back to the beginning of the century or even earlier, in the period 1973 through the present, the United States has had a productivity growth rate that is lower than the trend rate. Angus Maddison argues U.S. labor productivity

> has not been a simple reversion to historical norms. In Europe and Japan, productivity since 1973 has grown much faster than in the eight decades from 1870 to 1950. By contrast, U.S. productivity growth has fallen well below what was a much more stable long-term norm.[54]

The usual list of factors alleged to have contributed to the slowdown include government regulation, oil and other natural resource prices, sectoral shifts (to services), and a slowdown in investment.

On the other hand, a No Crisis School of economists believes additional investment may be desirable, but not to end a major slowdown in the rate of productivity growth. More investment may be desirable, but it is not urgent. The No Crisis School claims the increase in Gross Domestic Product (GDP) per hour of work in the period from 1940 through 1960 about equally balances the decrease from 1960 through 1979. The higher productivity rates of the 1940 to 1960 period followed decades of depression and war, when savings built up but investment was repressed, and useful technologies sat on the shelf waiting for the economy to pick up. After the war, these accumulated savings and unutilized technologies drove a productivity growth spurt that could not last. Smoothing the long-term trend over these two periods produces a trend rate that was fairly steady until the back-to-back policy-induced recessions of 1979 to 1982, the worst downturn since the 1930s. Baumol concludes, "Thus, the Maddison data themselves . . . display no sign of any long-term decline."[55] The No Crisis story focuses on what it takes to be a relatively constant trend rate of growth in productivity over the last century, after smoothing fluctuations. Most important, if the trend rate is constant, it is more difficult to suppose that government policy can substantially increase that rate over a long period of time. That says nothing, however, about increasing the level of productivity, a different issue discussed below.

A recent version of the No Crisis view focuses on a familiar group of measurement problems. Robert J. Gordon notes measuring inflation has been error prone, making productivity measurements equally error prone, since productivity gains have to subtract inflation to capture real productivity changes. Inflation is difficult to measure because of the difficulties in measuring quality changes in products, pricing of new products, and sectors in which output is harder to measure. Therefore, he notes, the true rate of productivity is understated, not just in one period, but in all. Gordon claims fully correcting for measurement errors could easily double the recorded rate of productivity growth in the non-manufacturing non-farm economy where the productivity problems are concentrated.[56]

Yet still unexplained is why the rate of productivity should appear to be so much worse in the United States since 1973 than before, or why the rate went down across the industrialized world at about the same time. Measurement problems didn't change between the pre- and post-1973 periods. Therefore, despite his analysis, Gordon still concludes there was a slowdown, though from what level and to what level is more mysterious. Gordon asserts the official accounts understate productivity gains prior to 1987 and overstate it after 1987.[57] Gordon and others claim the higher productivity growth rates found in some other advanced countries are merely the convergence of other nations catching up by copying technological advances already achieved in the United States. These foreign rates therefore make U.S. rates appear to be worse than they are. In that case, perhaps government policies aimed at accelerating productivity growth are needed less.

A New Economy

Perhaps government policies aimed at accelerating productivity growth are needed less for another reason. The recent explosion of new technologies—satellites, the Internet, computers, biotechnology, robots, microelectronics, new materials, and others—have led some analysts to hope a new higher rate of growth in productivity has taken hold since 1995, or soon will take hold. No doubt information technologies (IT) are transforming the way many businesses operate, and have the potential to increase their efficiency. Whether these changes will lead to a higher rate of growth in productivity in the future remains to be seen. Perhaps a shift to a faster rate of growth in productivity is already taking place. For thousands of years, the lack of increases in productivity kept all nations mired in poverty. Then the modern era brought rapidly rising productivity and much higher living standards. So a shift occurred between all of recorded history prior to 1700 and the period from 1700 to the present, a shift from negligible rates of growth in productivity to relatively fast rates. Since a shift in the long-term rate has occurred in the past, another such shift may be happening again. New technologies may raise the productivity growth rate above the normal trend rate of the past hundred years to a new and higher normal rate. The issue is whether there is good evidence that such a shift is actually happening.

Some analyses suggest the new economy has in fact arrived. They point to record low inflation combined with very low unemployment, and what appears to be a step-level increase in the rate of productivity growth, from approximately the 1 percent level to a 2.2 percent level since 1996.[58] However, productivity increased in other periods and then fell back in 1975 to 1978 and 1983 to 1986. The increase since 1996 needs to extend over more years before it is possible to call it a new trend. Moreover, low inflation and low unemployment can be explained by other factors beside higher productivity: cheap commodities, downward pressures on labor costs, a strong dollar, increased spending from increases in stock valuations.

Third, and most important of all, a study by Gordon shows virtually all of the improvement in productivity occurred in computer manufacturing. Productivity in this sector was 42 percent a year from the end of 1995 through the beginning of 1999. Manufacturing productivity, which traditionally has provided most productivity gains, grew more slowly—the opposite of what one might expect if a shift to a higher rate of productivity has occurred. Overall, except for computer manufacturing, productivity has been poor in manufacturing and poor overall, according to Gordon, and these trends do not fit with a new economy view. Gordon sees a half point increase in the underlying rate of growth in GDP.[59] But it is not clear whether this increase will last. The rate of productivity gains in computer manufacturing is taken to be unsustainable. Most important, if one takes out computer manufacturing, the rest of the economy shows a continuation of the poor productivity growth rates that have been the object of so much concern since 1973. Gordon also shows the impact on productivity of the technologies that are so promising today pale by comparison with the impact of technologies that accelerated productivity in the early twentieth century, especially innovations in electricity, the internal combustion engine, petrochemicals, plastics, pharmaceuticals, and communications.[60] All this leads to one conclusion: the slowdown may be continuing, and if it is, then increasing government investment becomes more desirable.

Further undercutting claims that productivity growth has accelerated are recent findings that unrecorded overtime hours worked are increasing. As many as 16 percent of workers' hours are now unreported, according to the Bureau of Labor Statistics.[61] The failure to capture overtime inflates estimates of output per hours worked, making productivity look better than it actually is.

Low productivity estimates suggest it would be beneficial to expand public investment to stimulate greater productivity.

Rates versus Levels of Productivity

Care should be taken not to create false expectations about how much public policy can drive up productivity. Economists tend to agree government policy cannot boost the long-term rate of productivity. But economists also tend to agree that additional investments, including public investments, can raise the level of productivity growth and with it the total value of all goods and services produced. What if policy aimed at raising the level of productivity by increasing the same kinds of investments that drove the U.S. rate of growth in productivity so high for the two decades after World War II, namely increases in saving, technological innovation, and human capital (the G.I. Bill)? Then the rate of productivity would increase for a decade or two, leveling off in permanently higher levels of productivity and living standards. But if the level of productivity, unlike its long-term rate, can be raised substantially through policy changes, how much would "merely" boosting the level matter?

Boosting the level of productivity would produce very large payoffs, as the analysis below demonstrates. In what follows, it is assumed that campaign finance reform shifts spending from consumption to investment, raises public and private investment, and so boosts productivity. Again, the rate of growth would "only" go up during a transition period to a higher level of productivity. The length of time of this transition is one technical issue, and the magnitude of the increase in output during this transition is another.[62]

Just how much of a gain can be expected from an increase in the level of productivity as a function of changes in government policy? A recent reckoning by President Clinton's Council of Economic Advisors (CEA) provides a crucial sense of proportion about the effects of an increase in the level of productivity. The CEA invokes standard models in their analysis, as follows:

> To illustrate the difficulty of improving the trend in the growth of the Nation's productive capacity, consider the following example. Suppose that a particular set of policies were to result in an immediate and permanent increase in the investment rate of 1 percentage point of GDP. Given that investment now constitutes about 14 percent of GDP, this would be an impressive accomplishment indeed. Under plausible assumptions, a standard approach to modeling the long-term growth of the economy suggests that such an increase in investment would boost the average annual *rate of growth* of potential GDP only by about 0.2 percentage point per year for the first 10 years. Thereafter the growth effects would diminish, fading eventually to nothing—but leaving the *level* of potential GDP an estimated 3½ percent higher than it would have been without the investment push.
>
> . . . If policies to boost the annual growth of productive capacity by 0.2 percent had been implemented a decade ago, the American economy would now have the capacity to generate an additional $150 billion in goods and services every year. Fortunately, it is not too late to lay the foundations for comparable gains in productivity and incomes 10 years hence. The disappointing growth record of the last 20 years, and the anxieties that so many Americans have about their own and their children's economic prospects, demand that every effort be made today to expand the economy's capacity in the future. [63]

But even more is possible. Consider how politics matters. Note the figure of 1 percent in the above quote: "Suppose a particular set of policies resulted in an immediate and permanent increase in the investment rate of 1 percentage point of GDP." Where does that 1 percent come from? How is it derived? It isn't derived from anything. It is plucked from the political sky. It is derived from what is deemed to be politically realistic. In other words, if political conditions changed, the 1 percent could become 5 percent. If a political upheaval of very large proportions obtained, it might even be 10 percent. Bear in mind the large reallocation of resources by Congress in 1965 and 1966 and again in 1981 and 1982.

After a major political change, say the enactment of public financing of campaigns, it might be possible over 10 to 20 years to dramatically raise the economy's capacity to produce and raise incomes. Instead of the CEA's assumption of a 1 percent increase in the investment rate, assume instead that campaign finance reform allowed a 5 percent increase in the investment rate over the same 10-year period. Then multiply the 3½ percent increase in the GDP achieved in the above CEA calculation by a five times larger increase in the investment rate. The result after 10 years is a 17.5 percent increase in GDP each year and every year forever. Policy-induced increases in productivity growth would then add roughly $1.658 trillion a year, every year, on top of an initial base of a $9.477 trillion GDP.[64] In other words, policy change could increase the productive capacity of the economy by nearly 20 percent a year after a decade.[65] If, instead, the investment rate increased to ten percent after a large political change, the output could increase $3.32 trillion dollars a year, or a 34 percent more productive economy a year every year thereafter in a decade.

These calculations assume linear relationships between increases in the investment rate and the growth of output. If nonlinear, then the amount of growth in GDP for a given increase in the investment rate may be overstated or understated. Either way, the gains in productivity and living standards that would follow from an increase in investment would still be vitally important for the economy. But the above calculations may understate the potential gains from increased investment. New Growth Theory, a prominent economic theory, anticipates higher returns from additional investments than standard models allow.[66] If New Growth Theory is valid, then standard models underestimate the returns to policies that increase investment. One account describes this theory as follows:

> In recent years several variants of a "new growth theory" have proposed that an increase in investment brings with it various productivity-enhancing benefits that are not captured in the return to capital. The new theory hypothesizes that investments by individual firms indirectly provide increased knowledge and other spillover benefits to the economy at large that are not reflected in the

return earned by the investing firm. An increase in investment will consequently speed up productivity and economic growth by more than would be predicted from the standard growth models. . . . The validity of the new theories is still in dispute. . . . [67]

Assuming New Growth Theory, returns to additional domestic business investment might double returns expected under standard models.[68] It was estimated above that a 5 percent increase in the investment rate would increase GDP, currently more than $9 trillion, by $1.658 trillion a year after 10 years, and a ten percent increase in the investment rate might produce a GDP roughly $3.2 trillion a year larger after 10 years. But if new growth models are used, these estimates might double. So, the potential payoffs from additional investments are huge, whether standard models or new growth models are used. The additional income gained from large increases in investment could be devoted to national problems and aspirations.

Should Government Increase Public Investment to Boost Productivity?

In general, new efficient investments, public and private, would raise national productivity, and drive up living standards and national income. Yet, if there is not a productivity crisis, perhaps there is no good reason to promote productivity. Similarly, if new technologies are about to bring about a new higher rate of growth in productivity without accelerating government investment, then again, one might mistakenly conclude there is no compelling reason to increase public investment to promote productivity. In both situations, if there isn't a problem, why do anything?

One reason is that a more productive economy is always more desirable, because it raises living standards and produces more revenue to devote to national priorities. More productivity is always highly desirable, no matter from what level of productivity one starts.

A second reason to support new government policies to spur productivity comes from acknowledging ignorance. There is little confidence among economists concerning estimates of future productivity growth rates. Small mistakes in projecting future rates compound over decades into sizable forecasting errors. The range of estimates about how much inflation distorts the measurement of the growth rate is, by itself, very large. Estimates range from 0.02 to 2 percent a year.[69] Just as extracting an accurate growth rate from inflation data is subject to large errors, so is measuring productivity changes in different industries and sectors. In the face of so much uncertainty, why do anything?

But this argument cuts two ways. The slowdown in productivity growth may be continuing, as Gordon suggests. Perhaps bottlenecks in education, training, and other public capital, after an era of cutting back on government investment, will crimp future growth. Just because the future is uncertain the nation should maximize efficient investment, public and private, to avoid inferior rates of growth in productivity in the future. The nation should make sure that national resources are not inadequate for national goals. Failing to achieve greater productivity and catching the British Disease could inflict serious harm on the United States in the emerging global order. So, if new policies can be funded in relatively painless ways—from waste reduction and higher voluntary saving—there is every reason to do all that can be done.

Conclusion

This chapter has reviewed the evidence that growing inequality and sluggish productivity growth are major problems facing the nation. Inequality in the United States has increased dramatically over the last several decades. In 1996, the average high school educated man between the ages of 45 and 54 earned approximately $30,963, down from $36,217 in 1986. Men in the 60th income percentile and below suffered wage deterioration between 15 percent and 20 percent between 1979 and 1993. Women's wages remained at a lower level than men's wages. Most American families have used up what assets they had with which to offset declining wages, especially a second family member entering the labor force. Hence, future declines in real wages will not be offset by anything that helped up until now, and growing inequality will therefore be more painful in the future, and more politicized. But technological change, globalization, and other factors virtually guarantee that inequality will continue to worsen. The increase in inequality reflects most of all the falling wages of unskilled workers in the context of increasing demands for skills generated by technological innovation. Reskilling would require large human capital investments by government, funding for which is now seen as politically unfeasible.

The harm to individuals from inequality shows up in higher mortality rates and many forms of severe ill health that do not immediately result in death. These health effects are a proxy for the failure of U.S. governments to make human capital investments other governments routinely supply. The harm to the nation from greater inequality, from failing to make enough human capital investments, shows up in lost national productivity and lost national income.

Increases in productivity provide the new income that allows a nation to increase its consumption and its investments that raise future consumption. Over the long run, a higher rate of growth in productivity transforms a nation by raising its living standards. The best indication of the power of productivity growth to benefit everyone is that average longevity has reached 75.8 years of age in the United States, from about 40 years of age in 1855. A nation ought to do everything possible to maximize its rate of growth in productivity. The gains from a faster rate or a higher level of productivity are so large that the nation would be imprudent if it failed to do everything it could to accelerate the growth in productivity.

The potential productivity payoffs from a large increase in efficient public investment are poorly understood. Hence, the gains from reallocating wasted funds over to public investments are also poorly understood. As a result, the economic gains that would result from enacting effective campaign reform are also poorly understood.

At present many analysts believe new public investments, howsoever desirable, are not politically feasible because they would be so costly. But if effective campaign finance reform became law, enough money would become available to support new investment policies. The next chapter briefly surveys some leading public investment options for utilizing these funds to increase productivity and reduce inequality.

Chapter 8

Public Sector Investment

Previous analysis implied that social democratic economic policy in the golden age consisted primarily of demand-side stimulation. Our work has shown that it was, instead, primarily supply side [investments], including public investment directly in human and physical capital and facilitating private investment in physical capital through low interest rates and subsidized interest rates. . . . [1]

THE PREVIOUS CHAPTER DEMONSTRATED THE NATION WOULD GAIN ENORmously from improving productivity and reducing inequality. This chapter describes specific public investments that would achieve those goals.[2] Economists agree that policies that increase saving will drive up productivity, as will policies that promote education, job training, technology, and infrastructure. Howsoever expensive these policies may be, they are less expensive than surrendering the gains in national living standards that greater productivity would provide. No effort is made here to quantify how much each policy would cost. But by the end of this chapter it should be evident these policies would cost many hundreds of billions of dollars a year. So nothing short of effective campaign finance reform would shift enough money from waste to investment to fund these public goods at optimal levels.

The United States underinvests in public goods when government fails to offset market failure. Market failure occurs when markets fail to invest in public goods like education from which business, workers, and the nation would benefit. Market failure is exemplified by worker training that might profit a company, but nonetheless does not take place because the worker might go to another firm. Then the firm cannot appropriate, or recoup the costs of making such an investment. Edwin Mansfield has estimated the social return is more than 50 percent greater than the private return on some investments.[3] The existence of this "appropriability problem" implies that only government has the incentive to make many productive investments, such as those discussed below. Only government can compensate for market failure.

Education

Education and training policies offer the greatest promise for reducing inequality and boosting productivity at the same time:

> The best long-run remedy for the widening earnings inequality in the United States is to improve the skills of workers now stuck at the bottom of the wage distribution. We recommend a fundamental reorientation of the current system for providing non-college-educated workers with improved general occupational skills.[4]

By most accounts the American education system is failing to supply the educated workers the economy requires. Rather than work through all of the statistics that indicate the dimensions of America's education policy problem, it seems more useful to summarize the main findings of some prominent analyses.

The MIT Commission on Industrial Productivity produced an unusually high-powered study of the United States' strengths and weaknesses for increasing the productivity of the nation. On the subject of education they noted,

> We have concluded that without major changes in the way schools and firms train workers over the course of a lifetime, no amount of macroeconomic fine-tuning or technological innovation will be able to produce significantly improved economic performance and a rising standard of living.[5]

Recent trends show the United States has fallen behind other advanced countries in the education of its labor force. According to the 1996 Economic Report of the President,

> Although average scores have been rising in mathematics and science, much of the gain has occurred in lower level computational skills rather than in higher level problem solving. Reading and writing test scores declined slightly for the weakest students during the 1980s. *Perhaps most disturbing, students in the United States continue to lag behind their counterparts in many Asian and European countries in math and science* . . . [italics added][6]

Brookings economist Gary Burtless concludes,

> Since publication of a *Nation at Risk* in 1983, Americans have become increasingly concerned about the quality of their schools . . . Most observers now agree that American schools are in trouble. U.S. high school and junior high school

students stand near the back of their class in international rankings of student knowledge and achievement. The mediocre quality of American education is apparent in a wide variety of measures of student performance. None of these measures is perfect, but many of them point in a similar direction. *Americans leave school knowing far less than typical secondary school graduates in other industrialized nations.* [italics added][7]

Productivity experts Richard R. Nelson and Gavin Wright show investment in education has become even more important for productivity growth than in the past. They note,

> [A] well-educated labor force with a strong cadre of university trained engineers and scientists at the top, is now a requirement. . . . It is not an accident that countries like Korea and Taiwan, which have been gaining so rapidly on the world leaders, now have populations where secondary education is close to universal for new entrants to the work force, and where significant fractions of the secondary school graduates go on to university training . . . *we do not dismiss the possibility that the United States may be in the process of slipping into second, third, or fifth rank in productivity and per capita incomes, and in terms of mastering the application of several important technologies . . . it is entirely possible that a once-dominant nation may slip into social paralysis and decline.* [italics added][8]

Robert Eisner, past president of the American Economic Association, notes,

> [O]*ur largest gains in productivity seem likely to come from investment in human capital, in education and training, and in research.* Free trade does not mean leaving our population ill-equipped for competition with those industries and activities on the leading edge of modern technology. If we do so [i.e., leave our population ill equipped], we will still find it advantageous and profitable to trade. But we will then find our comparative advantage in industries where we are less productive, not more productive than the rest of the world . . . *It would be that failure to invest in ourselves, and not free trade, that would threaten us eventually with second-class economic status in the world.* [italics added][9]

Does Money Matter?

Education may matter, but it does not follow that spending more money on education would improve it. Some experts claim fixing American education would entail major new funding commitments. Some researchers find spending more money increases workers' earnings per year spent in school. But other analysts disagree on whether spending more money raises test scores significantly.[10]

At first glance, the superior educational achievements of other countries do not appear to flow from spending more money than the United States now spends. Some OECD data seem to support the money-does-not-matter viewpoint. OECD data on primary and secondary education show the United States spends as much or more than other advanced countries as a percent of GDP. The United States spends 4.5 percent, Japan 3.2 percent, Germany 3.9 percent, and Sweden 4.7 percent.[11] Eric Hanushek notes,

> [A]ny evidence of effective resource usage is balanced by evidence of other, naturally occurring, situations in which resources are squandered. Moreover, nobody has produced a guide to situations that yield effective as opposed to ineffective resource usage . . . Today, the existing knowledge base does not ensure that any added funds will, on average, be spent wisely. That is true even if some schools may spend their funds wisely.[12]

This money-does-not-matter view is countered by several arguments. First, a better measure for comparing educational spending in different countries is the ratio of expenditures on secondary education per student to GDP per capita and to GDP per worker. On these measures, the United States ranks roughly in the middle of the OECD group of advanced nations. But after taking account of cross-national differences in such education budget items as sports, transportation, and so on, it is estimated the United States would fall even further down in the ranking.[13]

Critics opposed to spending more on education often allude to the doubling of U.S. primary and secondary school spending over the past two and a half decades, accompanied by a negligible increase in test scores. How, they ask, can so much additional money have been spent with so few payoffs? Various studies offer two answers. One study shows that much of the increase in the costs of education over recent decades was driven by increased expenditures for new school missions, including training of the disabled, increasing student health and nutrition, vocational education, and assimilation of non-English speaking students, among others.[14] Moreover, as teachers became older, they were more likely to get master's degrees, which raised their salaries, though gains in competence from master's degrees did not improve performance as much as salaries.[15] So, even though educational spending increased while educational performance did not, the possibility remains that other new spending would raise educational outputs.

Evaluations of the payoffs from past education spending need to take account of the effects of two new burdens on the schools. First, a society with growing social pathologies, family breakup, and diminished authority of institutions generally is bound to send students to school who are more difficult and more expensive to teach. Other advanced social democracies spend a much larger proportion of national income on public investments and social insurance, and, not surprisingly, they put fewer problems on the doorsteps of their schools than does the United States. Second, demands are escalating for higher levels of competence in math, science, computer skills, and other skills that enable workers to deal with an exploding knowledge base and an increasingly interdependent global economy. In such a context, expenditures need to be larger.[16]

The following policies are leading candidates for fixing the ailing U.S. education system, and they are all very expensive.

(1) REDUCE TEACHER-PUPIL RATIOS. "Of all the relations studied in the literature, the link between the teacher-pupil ratio in the classroom and educational attainment is strongest. . . . "[17] Moreover, the increased output flowing from a better teacher-pupil ratio can be leveraged by other complementary inputs, such as teacher quality and parental involvement.

(2) CREATE A LONGER SCHOOL DAY AND A LONGER SCHOOL YEAR. An additional year in school pays off. A longer school day and a longer school year ought to pay off also. A review of the literature shows even disadvantaged students benefit significantly from additional schooling in the summer.[18] These summer students forgot less over the summer, needed to review less afterward, and moved to new work sooner. Reproducing these effects year after year would add up to a significantly better national educational performance. John H. Bishop notes, "The most significant barrier to this reform is cost."

It is worth repeating that increasing the time spent in school from 6.25 hours per day to 7 hours, and from 180 days a year to 200, has the following effects. Bishop shows that

> increasing time in school by 275 hours per year is estimated to eventually raise the productivity of adults by $3,276 per year (15.6 percent of mean compensation). Because a one year cohort contains 3.5 million people, the benefit is about 11.5 billion dollars a year [for just one cohort of the 13 cohorts in school]. *The real rate of return on the taxpayer contribution to the additional learning investment is 33 percent per year . . . Only investments in R&D have social rates of return this high.* [italics added]

With the 240 day school year found abroad, the productivity gains would be even larger. The increased cost nationally at 200 days would be $34.4 billion for primary and secondary public schools, roughly three-fifths of the increase in spending that occurred between 1986 and 1991. An offset would come from reduced child care costs of working mothers, estimated at $8.45 billion.

(3) HIGHER TEACHER SALARIES AND BETTER TEACHER TRAINING WOULD PROVIDE BETTER TEACHERS. U.S. teachers' educational attainments are (1) inadequate relative to other U.S. college graduates; (2) inadequate relative to teachers in other nations; and (3) inadequate relative to standards of acceptable training in their specialties, especially math, sciences, and computer technologies.[19]

American teachers compare poorly to other U.S. college graduates. U.S. teachers come from the bottom of the barrel on test scores and other academic indicators, and their weaknesses are reflected in their pay rates. Compared to other U.S. college graduates, teachers' pay is at the bottom of the scale. Salaries for business, economics, and engineering graduates are double teachers' salaries. Graduates with math and science bachelor degrees earn 77 percent more than teaching graduates. U.S. secondary school teachers earn only 33 percent more than the average worker, whereas most advanced nations pay their teachers 60 to 70 percent more than the average worker. Low salaries in the United States make it difficult to recruit potentially strong teachers trained in math, science, and computer education among other subjects. Whereas American schools seldom recruit the most able college graduates, in Europe and Japan, there is strenuous competition for teaching jobs, and those who win them are highly competitive in the market.[20]

Poor student performance in math and science in the United States reflects poor teaching of these subjects by poorly prepared and less-skilled teachers:

> The quality of people recruited into teaching is very important. The teacher characteristic that most consistently predicts student learning are tests assessing the teacher's general academic ability and subject knowledge (Hanushek, 1971; Strauss and Sawyer, 1986; Ferguson, 1990; Ehrenberg and Brewer, 1993; Monk 1992). Ferguson, for example, found that holding community characteristics, class size, teacher experience and the proportion of the teaching staff with a master's degree constant, that a one standard deviation increase in the TECAT test scores of a school district's teachers increased the reading exam scores of students in third and higher grades by about .20 to .25 of a standard deviation (about one grade level equivalent for senior high students).[21]

That the United States alone among advanced nations underinvests in teacher quality suggests the gap between American workers' productivity and the productivity of workers in other advanced countries will continue to grow. But attracting high-quality teachers nationwide with higher salaries would be very costly, as would be training them properly.

(4) INCREASING STUDENT MOTIVATION BY MEANS OF STUDENT ACHIEVEMENT TESTING WOULD TRANSFORM THE SCHOOL ENVIRONMENT. Most students who

work hard are not rewarded for it in the marketplace or in academic placements. The best indication of student motivation is time spent on homework. In a 1991 survey, only 29 percent of 13-year-old Americans reported doing two or more hours of homework per day, while for most other countries the percent was higher: 79 percent for Italy, 63 percent for Ireland and Spain, more than 50 percent for France, Hungary, Israel, Jordan, and the former Soviet Union.[22] In addition, American students end up with far fewer hard academic courses on their transcripts. American students spend significantly less time in school. American students do not prepare for any particular employment, training, or learning path, and thus have no reason to believe what they learn can help them after they leave school. Lacking any objective benchmark tied to future employment or advanced education, such as achievement tests, parents attach a low priority to achievement in school.

Except for the few students applying to highly selective colleges, high school academic achievements do not affect college admissions or opportunities for better jobs. The opposite is true in other advanced nations. In America, college admission is based on aptitude tests, not achievement tests as in other countries, and on class grades compared with the grades of other students not held to any high standard. Since neither the non-college bound nor most of the college bound experience any linkage between what they study in school and employment, most lack effective incentives to learn.

The usual prescription for all these incentive problems is to test all students' achievements according to some set of standards, rather than test ability. The United States alone does not use achievement tests to raise the incentives of all involved—students, parents, teachers, administrators, school boards, and employers. The tests need to be constructed so learning to pass a test is also valuable educationally. Then employers would have an incentive to hire graduates on the basis of their achievements in school. Achievement test results and grades would be disseminated to employers who would use them to sort labor quality. Parents and students would anticipate employers' reactions. Getting the tests constructed and disseminated would not be expensive. What would be expensive would be getting 15,000 school districts to accept national testing, which would require federal incentive grants large enough to encourage their participation.

(5) SIX OTHER EXPENSIVE EDUCATIONAL IMPROVEMENTS ARE FREQUENTLY RECOMMENDED. First, fund special education classes for those students with disciplinary and other problems. Second, fund more teacher aides, who would improve the efficiency of teachers. Third, increase the participation of all students in athletic programs, which would energize students. Fourth, provide additional funding to help teachers to get parents involved in schools and in furthering their children's progress. Fifth, expand the Head Start Program, which increases its participants'

educational progress dramatically, and/or provide high-quality preschool education for all three- to five-year-olds, which would vastly increase educational achievement in subsequent years. Sixth, make major curriculum changes to equip all high school graduates with basic skills.[23] These improvements are primarily blocked by the lack of money.

States, localities, and businesses lack the incentives to make the needed educational investments. They have consistently failed to make the human capital investments other nations have made routinely. Moreover, putting achievement testing in place would not by itself cause states to raise enough money to buy all the other factors that have to complement testing if testing is to be effective. So, only the federal government is at all likely to fund the educational investments needed for national goals, and then only if campaign reform becomes law.

Job Training

More than ever before, workforce training is central to increasing U.S. productivity growth and to raising living standards. The MIT Commission made plain that the Japanese, German, and many other economies have provided much better national worker training systems than are available in the United States.[24] The United States is only investing one-half of the percent of payroll its main competitors are investing in on-the-job training.[25] In addition, what U.S. companies spend on training is skewed toward the more educated portion of their workforce.[26] The European and Japanese training system, on the other hand, train all strata of workers.[27] More training would increase productivity, increase profits, increase the ability of firms to compete abroad, raise American living standards, reduce inequality, and strengthen social cohesion. Thus the magnitude of benefits foregone from too little training in the United States is simply huge.

However, economists view better education as a prerequisite for better training. According to Baily et al., "The educational preparation of non-college-bound Americans is inadequate to the demands of the modern workplace. And training in the workplace *does not offset* their educational disadvantages" [italics added].[28] In the same vein, James Hechman concludes, "In the long run, significant improvements in the skill levels of Americans, especially workers not attending college, are unlikely without substantial change and improvement in primary and secondary education."[29]

If adequately subsidized by government, employers would train workers much more extensively than they do now. They would make up for education shortfalls by supervising educational catchup in community colleges and other education programs given outside their companies. If companies supervised the choice of courses and programs, it would ensure that only useful learning tied to employers' needs would be chosen. Business training subsidies could be coupled to guidance provided from commissions representing government, business, and labor, similar to the advice the Agricultural Extension Service has provided farmers since the late nineteenth century, with spectacular results.

General skill training teaches those basic skills associated with a good secondary school education—math, sciences, writing, reading, computing, and so on. Employers have a greater incentive to train employees in company-specific skills than in general skills, which they leave to the individual worker, schools, and government. That is because they would lose their investment in general skills training if a worker left for another company.[20] Training carried out outside the company, especially at community colleges, normally provides general skills training, and makes employees receiving that training more attractive to other companies. Training carried on inside the company tends to be firm-specific training. An effective government training subsidy would compensate employers for training their workers in both firm-specific and general skills and hope they would be combined.

Researchers have emphasized four training routes for improving the quality of the workforce through improved training: (1) apprenticeship programs; (2) school-based training; (3) on-the-job training; and (4) an institutionalized student credentials system for use by employers. Expanding these kinds of job training programs would increase U.S. productivity. They too would be very expensive.

The first route for increased training is through apprenticeship programs. These programs increase the motivation to learn in school, and link what is learned in school to the jobs that follow. Apprenticeship programs, of which Germany's is taken to be exemplary, actively integrate general skills training in school with company-specific skills training taught in that company.

Good apprenticeship programs are built on strong education systems. Grades on tests tied to school curricula largely determine who is awarded an apprenticeship in Germany. In the United States, a mere two percent of high school graduates are trained in apprenticeship programs, mostly in construction trades.[31] The United States is alone among advanced nations in not rewarding educational achievement with job placements based on those achievements.[32] Without achievement testing, widespread utilization of apprenticeship programs is unlikely. Without achievement test scores to use as a yardstick for measuring labor quality, an employer does not know whether taking on any particular individual as an apprentice is a good investment.

A second route to increased training is school-based training, primarily community college-based training. Schooling, school-based training, and employer training are complements, not substitutes. Those with stronger educational backgrounds get jobs that offer more employer-provided training, and are better paid.[33] There is always a danger that skills learned in a school will not be used on the next job. Therefore, schooling and school-based training need to be integrated with the actual training needs of companies. Community college or school programs attract trainees when they demonstrate the program offers employment gains after training. An occupation-specific education received in a high school or community college leads to further on-the-job training and increased wages and productivity. This finding is especially applicable to youth and adults changing occupations, and it suggests that devoting more resources to school-based training and training provided by community colleges would be well spent.[34]

Direct subsidies to students, however, do not increasing training effectively. Subsidies offered directly to students are often not utilized by potential recipients. Community colleges enjoy subsidized tuition, but do not attract all the students they might. Of the 5.3 million community college students enrolled in 1991, 42 percent dropped out. A RAND study showed community college dropouts gain few benefits.[35] Nor is it clear students can efficiently choose useful training from the training options offered in the marketplace. So direct government subsidies to schools and employers are likely to be more efficient than subsidies to students.

A third route to increased training is a program of government subsidies to employers to increase on-the-job training. A major objective of any policy involving subsidies to employers is to find technical means of measuring what training employers would supply anyway without the subsidy. Otherwise, the subsidy will be inefficient. A corollary is that any successful training program should deemphasize training of the better educated, better skilled, and more mobile employees, and should target the less skilled who are less apt to be trained without the subsidy. The returns to on-the-job training are very high for those workers who receive such training, even without government subsidies:

> Incumbent worker training that is provided by employers raises worker productivity and wages. Formal and informal training appear to have roughly equal effects on productivity. Probably because it is better signaled, formal training has significantly larger impacts on wages than informal training. *Rates of return (both private and social) are very high* and substantially higher than for regular schooling and non-degree credit school-based training. [italics added][36]

More government subsidized training would close the gap between the inadequate worker training levels found in the United States and the much higher ones found abroad. Given the very high returns to training that now obtain, subsidized training is a major remedy for the growth in inequality and for suboptimal productivity growth in the United States.

Early in 1993, the first Clinton Administration asked Congress for $140 billion in new investment spending, including money for training funds. The proposal was blocked by the Democratic Congress, which was more concerned with cutting deficits. In the end, the administration accepted the claim that "the money just wasn't there."[37]

A fourth route to increased training is an institutionalized student credentials system for use by employers. Such a system would utilize student scores on achievement testing of general skills training and of occupation-specific training. For occupation- or skill-specific credentialing, Germany has set up training curricula in roughly 400 occupational categories, representing 20,000 occupations. Tests for each of the 400 categories are negotiated by officials from government, employers' associations, and unions. The tests are regularly updated. At the end of a training period, the trainee takes a national examination in one of those 400 occupational categories.[38] Passing the exam results in the issuance of a certificate, which provides a prospective employer with a great deal of information about the student or trainee at a low cost. Establishing a credentials system across a wide range of occupations and skills will not occur without government providing a great deal of money to create and continually update standards and tests to reflect new technological innovations. A national training policy would require "a major public and private effort to define and certify necessary occupational skills. . . ."[39]

An employer would be more willing to train a certified worker, because the certificates would help her gauge what she would get for her investment in an individual worker's training. Government subsidies would be less likely to be spent inefficiently if pegged to specific achievement tests and scores. Students would know what they must accomplish to become employed, and what to accomplish to become employed better, thereby increasing the incentives even for lower-quality labor.

Today, high school graduates and dropouts can no longer get well-paying jobs, as they could until the 1970s. In 1993, the median income of 30-year-old male high school graduates was only $20,000 a year—a wage insufficient to support a family. That is down from $27,700 in 1979.[40] The United States has not adapted to this change.[41] To enable graduates to earn higher incomes, they must be better trained. But better training will be very expensive. So, again, the issue of where to find the money is paramount.

Technology Policy

Increases in productivity depend most of all on technological innovations.[42] But many technological innovations, not least the Internet, computers, communications satellites, new materials, and biotechnology were developed through government-sponsored R&D. The role of government in maximizing technological innovation grows out of the large difference between the private return and the social return on technology investments mentioned earlier. Again, Edwin Mansfield found the social return was 50-plus percent greater than the private return on a number of investments. Widely cited, this finding gives a green light to a major government role in technological innovation.[43] Companies will not invest in many potentially productive technologies because often they cannot appropriate or capture enough of the returns to make a profit. Therefore only government is likely to explore and sponsor many new and promising technologies.

Businesses often cannot appropriate enough of the returns to innovation for a number of reasons. First, other businesses may copy inventions, capturing the benefits of invention without having paid its costs. Second, risks of failure are often high, and thus inhibit investment. Third, long-time horizons before an investment pays off increase risks proportionately. Fourth, uncertainty about whether research will lead to commercializable new products deters investment. Investment in basic research, whose time horizons are especially uncertain, is unprofitable for all but a few companies. Hence government bears the brunt of carrying out basic research, often through contracts with universities and national laboratories. Such risks are more easily taken by government because it can spread the risks over all taxpayers.

The desirability of an expanded government role in technology is revealed in a recent study commissioned by the National Science Foundation. It found 73 percent of the papers cited by U.S. industry patents were authored at publicly funded institutions—academic and governmental. Only 27 percent were authored by industrial scientists.[44] That the U.S. Government could effectively spend more on technology is indicated by the many worthwhile research projects identified by panels of scientists and business leaders that remain unfunded or underfunded. Three lists of promising targets are prominent: the Report of the National Critical Technologies Panel, The Department of Commerce List of Emerging Technologies, and the Department of Defense List of Critical Technologies.[45]

The six main categories of federal technology policy are (1) supporting basic research; (2) supporting precompetitive or generic technology development; (3) giving tax credits for commercial R&D; (4) encouraging corporations to increase their time horizons; (5) reforming liability laws; and (6) encouraging joint ventures in R&D.[46]

Some economists have shown the government's use of tax incentives is particularly effective in encouraging private sector R&D. Martin Neil Baily and Robert Lawrence show the Investment Tax Credit boosted corporate R&D spending by eight to ten percent for every ten percent reduction of the cost of R&D due to the credit.[47] They recommend expanded use of tax credits for R&D.

Some critics have argued that very often direct federal spending on R&D is not spent well. Linda R. Cohen and Roger G. Noll have detailed waste in the area of those federal projects aimed at developing new commercial technology for the private sector.[48] They did not explore basic research done at federal labs and universities using government funds. Nor did they examine defense R&D or commercial R&D influenced by tax subsidies. Restricting themselves solely to direct federal subsidies, they found Congress reacted inappropriately to problems, timetables, funding levels, project definitions, changing circumstances, and pilot demonstrations. The resulting projects should have been defined better, scrapped from the outset, or scrapped later, and many projects were underfunded or overfunded. Moreover, big science projects, like the superconducting super collider, because their large facilities and large staffs were important in their communities, were often funded over small science ones even when smaller projects held greater promise. Congresspersons can more easily claim credit for politically visible big science projects. In addition, they found that Congress made bad choices between fundamental and applied research, among technologies, and among institutions and regions.

Other economists, however, describe Cohen and Noll as unduly pessimistic. They acknowledge government R&D is often wasteful, but suggest the following ways to make federal R&D spending more efficient and effective:

> First, project ideas should come from the private sector, mainly corporations and small businesses, but also universities and other nonprofit institutions with strong technological capabilities. This would ensure that the projects are not dreamed up by federal agencies or politicians without any clear sense of their ultimate commercial usefulness. Participating private companies should be required to provide part of a project's funding.... Second, the basic support strategy should include a wide variety of projects directed toward the same general goal, each one of which receives modest funding. This strategy serves a dual purpose. It allows the exploration of many options, rather than encouraging early commitment to a particular technology strategy.... And it reduces the dangers of pork barrel funding because no single project generates enough jobs to be a focus of massive lobbying efforts. Third, congressional oversight should not lead to congressional meddling into exactly which projects are funded and how the research ought to proceed. Congress should determine the rules of the game; it should not call the plays....[49]

The broad implication of all of the above is that much more money could be well spent on federal R&D, and spending it well would lead to large payoffs for national productivity and living standards.

The problems of wasteful government R&D subsidies could be reduced even further if effective campaign reform freed congresspersons from the need to use their committee assignments to harvest campaign money. After campaign reform, it is possible that the selection of government R&D projects would shift toward heavier reliance on expert assessments of the efficiency and effectiveness of different projects.

Infrastructure

Some analyses show some infrastructure spending raises productivity significantly. Other studies claim reducing infrastructure investment may not have lowered productivity growth.[50] It is not clear from the literature whether significantly more spending on infrastructure projects would increase productivity if those projects were chosen more carefully.[51]

What is meant by "infrastructure" includes schools, hospitals, water and sewer lines, bridges, tunnels, roads, highways, railroads, harbors, dams, inland waterways, airports, telephone systems, and cable systems. Some infrastructure is private, but most is (1) publicly owned; (2) involves large capital intensive outlays; and (3) is a natural monopoly. Roughly 75 percent of the stock of narrowly defined nonmilitary infrastructure is owned by state and local governments. Of that, 53 percent goes for schools, streets, and highways. Edward M. Gramlich explains infrastructure input costs are hard to measure because they are not bought in a market. Outputs are also hard to measure. A better road increases security, time savings, and environmental safety, but the value of these benefits is difficult to measure.[52] State and local infrastructure spending grew steadily until the early 1970s, and leveled off since then, in part because the national highway system was mostly completed.[53] But many of the nations' schools are in advanced disrepair, and other infrastructure needs are apparent in different places. The popularity of infrastructure expenditures on Capitol Hill suggests it is frequently used to pass out pork.

There is one large reason why a post-reform Congress might be more willing to create a new process using experts to distinguish productive infrastructure investments from wasteful ones, and appropriate funds to projects ranked by utility. Campaign reform would reduce or eliminate the influences of campaign contributors/contractors and their suppliers on project selection.

Health Insurance

Withholding health insurance from children will affect their future productivity.[54] Yet approximately five million poor children who are eligible for health insurance under Medicaid are uncovered. Another 1.3 million less-than-poor children are not enrolled by the CHIP program that started in 1998, largely due to costs.

Approximately 44 million people, or roughly 17 to 18 percent of the non-elderly population, are uninsured, and this group is increasing at the rate of approximately one million Americans a year. Future policy changes and market-driven changes are expected to add to these numbers. In addition, the extent of underinsurance, people who have coverage for some illness but not others, seems to elude reliable estimates, but one study finds 30 million more Americans who are seriously underinsured, in addition to the 44 million uninsured.[55] "On average an uninsured, low income American now receives only about 50 to 70 percent of the health care that an identical insured American receives."[56] Though not all the uninsured are sick, those who are untreated are less likely to work, and are less likely to be efficient employees if they do work.

The median length of a spell of being uninsured is only about seven months. Nineteen percent of the uninsured do without insurance for two years or more. The uninsured receive about two-thirds of the use of physician services received by the insured, and benefit from 31 to 81 percent of inpatient hospital use of the insured. Young adults are most likely to be uninsured, but they are healthier and lose less time at work from illness. Twenty-two percent of 18 to 34-year-olds are uninsured, compared with approximately 13 percent of those 35 to 64. Fifty-seven percent of the uninsured are full-time workers. The uninsured are also concentrated among less productive workers, as measured by compensation levels. These and other facts do not provide a basis for determining how much U.S. productivity would benefit from supplying health care to underserved subpopulations. Though it would be a positive number, relative to costs, the gains are unclear. If so, then moral reasons may prove to be the primary reasons for extending health insurance to the adult uninsured.

But there is a larger productivity issue in the health care area. Cutting waste in the health system is a major opportunity. Comparisons of the United States with other OECD systems suggest considerable waste in the U.S. health system. The United States spent 14.2 percent of GDP on health care in 1996, but failed to insure more than 44 million of its people.[57] The other OECD countries deliver good health care to all of their citizens, but all spend less than ten percent of their GDP.[58] Defenders of the present system say the additional four percent of GDP the United States pays for such advanced procedures as open heart surgery, cardiac catheterization, and organ transplants that other nations do not ordinarily supply.[59] But with a less wasteful system, the United States could continue to provide these advanced medical procedures, could retain the high pay for researchers and other incentives that drive its more technologically advanced system, but could also provide health insurance to the 74 million uninsured and seriously underinsured Americans.

In the opinion of some analysts, a single-payer government insurance plan would avoid the massive waste generated under the present system—the seemingly endless phone calls, faxes, letters, and forms necessary to get multiple approvals of procedures, negotiate and contest non-approvals, and provide payments for all or part of those procedures through fund transfers among insurance companies, health providers, patients, and government. Moreover, preventive health care is dramatically underfunded in the U.S. system. Prevention would reduce expensive procedures that become necessary because of prior neglect. Additional waste reductions could be achieved by eliminating overutilization of some procedures and tests, excessive drug company profits, excessive medical specialization, and excessive insurance company bureaucracy.

Another major source of health system waste is the excessive spending on treating patients in the last six months of their lives, without regard to how long they can survive treatment, and too often without regard to the level of functioning to which a patient would be restored after treatment. Treatment practices frequently impose both large costs on the system and much unnecessary pain on patients by prolonging life even though there is no reasonable hope of being restored to any acceptable state. Many people in this situation would prefer to have their pain treated and nothing else, but too often such preferences are not honored. The costs of this practice to the system are huge.

These various areas of wasteful health spending point to opportunities to make both the health system and the economy more productive.

Policies to Reduce Inequality Directly

Inequality will continue to increase if a large part of the labor force remains undereducated and undertrained. Increases in productivity may continue to provide little benefit to the bottom eight deciles in the income distribution.[60] Education and training policies, on the other hand, would reduce inequality directly, while racheting up productivity at the same time.

Four other policies would also reduce inequality directly. First, the government might provide jobs to some low-skilled workers. But some economists question how productively government programs can employ low-skill workers, and whether their government job experience would increase their employability in the private sector. These issues are controversial.

Second, Robert M. Solow and others[61] suggest transferring the costs of "social charges" on wages—health care costs, social security contributions, and so on—from employers and employees to the federal government. Doing so would make hiring of less-skilled workers less expensive, and so more hiring would occur. Solow points out most economists believe these social charges fall on the worker anyway, no matter who makes the payment. But the ability of an employer to shift those costs onto workers breaks down with low-skilled workers, due to legal constraints like minimum wage laws. So, low-skilled workers are hired less than they would be if social charges were shifted to the taxpayer.

A third way of reducing inequality is to target the working poor and near-poor with expanded redistributive policies. These policies include a more generous Earned Income Tax Credit (EITC), a higher minimum wage, and universal health insurance. Under the EITC, work is rewarded with a reduced tax on wages. Both conservatives and progressives support EITC,[62] while disagreeing about how generous the EITC should be. Edmund S. Phelps prefers instead a low-wage employment subsidy,[63] as do Robert H. Haveman and others.[64] It appears to encourage employers to hire lower-skilled workers.

Proposals to increase the minimum wage are highly controversial. The politically important small business community of 12 million owners tends to oppose increases. Many economists see a higher minimum wage as likely to reduce jobs by reducing the money available to an employer to hire more workers, thereby pricing some workers out of the market. Other economists do not.[65] Most members of Congress favor modest increases in the minimum wage because of widespread public support for increases. A large increase would significantly reduce the worst effects of inequality on the poorest workers. But how many low-wage workers would lose jobs as a consequence is unclear.

Fourth, unionization would reduce inequality. Unions have become much weaker than they used to be.[66] Union membership in the private sector is down to about ten percent of non-managerial workers. Union members receive higher compensation than comparable workers who are not unionized. But even non-union workers benefit from union activity. In the past, when unions were stronger, non-union firms often embraced union level compensation to avoid unionization, making unions a force for reducing inequality in the wider economy.[67] Unions reduce the differences in compensation among unionized workers in firms, and between management and union workers. Unions reduce inequality most of all as the political force behind efforts to get Congress to defend and extend the so-called social wage—health insurance, social security, disability insurance, survivors' insurance, aid to education and training, pension protection, family leave, poverty aid, and workers' rights. Moreover, unions are the mainstay of efforts to prevent the political process from being changed so as to disadvantage the less powerful. It is for these reasons the labor movement claims common ground with the majority of working people and the middle class. Perhaps most striking of all is the finding by Harvard economists Richard B. Freeman and James L. Medoff, who have shown that, overall, higher union wages and benefits do not come at the cost of decreased economic efficiency, but have actually increased economic efficiency.[68]

A Summary of Productivity Remedies

In addition to policies that increase saving, described in chapter four, the following policies were described in this chapter as likely to increase productivity and reduce inequality.[69] Putting them all together roughly indicates the amount of money that is needed to enable the United States to increase productivity and living standards in the national interest. The money needed will not be available unless and until effective campaign finance reform is enacted into law.

Education Policies

The most promising policies would include (1) national standards tied to achievement testing, linked to federal incentive grants to persuade school districts to adopt such testing; (2) higher teacher salaries to recruit high-performing teachers; (3) more and better teacher training; (4) lower teacher-student ratios in classrooms; (5) a longer school day; (6) a longer school year; (7) high-quality special education classes for students with disciplinary and other problems; (8) expanding the Head Start Program, and/or (9) high-quality universal preschool education; (10) increased quality participation of all students in athletic programs; (11) programs to get parents involved in schools and in their children's progress; (12) major curriculum changes to equip all high school graduates with basic skills; and (13) high-quality low-cost paid child care available to all working parents.

Job Training Polices

The principal public investments needed include (1) apprenticeship programs; (2) school-based training, primarily community college–based training; (3) subsidies to employers for employer-run training programs; and (4) an institutionalized student credentials system made available to all employers.

Technology Policies

The most promising public investments include (1) support for basic research; (2) support for precompetitive or generic technology development; (3) increases in tax credits for commercial R&D; (4) incentive grants to corporations to increase their time horizons; (5) some reform of liability laws; and (6) support for R&D joint ventures among companies and with the federal government.[70]

Infrastructure Policies

Possible public investments include repairs to and upgrading of old facilities as well as new facilities in the following areas: schools, hospitals, water and sewer lines, bridges, tunnels, roads, highways, railroads, harbors, dams, inland waterways, airports, telephone systems, cable systems, school and government Internet connections, and other public facilities where market incentives are insufficient to supply what is needed.

Health Insurance

At least from a moral point of view, if not from a concern with productivity, the most promising public investment is universal health insurance covering the uninsured and the underinsured. Universal insurance would assure every American they no longer need to fear that losing their job will entail that they or their children do without medical treatment. Eliminating the massive waste in the health system could provide much of the resources needed for a more equitable system. Health programs should be considered within the format of alternative rationing schemes. According to many experts, the efficiency of the health system would increase if it were more equitable and less wasteful than it is now with rationing by price, that is, with allocating care according to how much a patient can afford to pay.[71]

Policies to Directly Reduce Inequality

In addition to education, training, and health insurance, several other policies would reduce inequality. These include transferring "social wages" from employers to the federal government, a more generous Earned Income Tax Credit, a higher minimum wage, wage subsidies, and increased unionization.

Conclusion

It is in America's national interest to pursue the productivity-enhancing and inequality-reducing investments described above. The failure to make certain investments in the public sector will reduce the efficiency of investments in the private sector, and weaken the American economy over the long run. America's leaders can choose to fully fund the public investments presented in the previous section, or they can choose to fund public investments at the Spartan levels presented in the Gore-Lieberman 2000 election proposals, including a mere $17 billion a year *total* for all new education spending.[72] Or it can choose to actually reduce public investments by cutting taxes. Whether or not the decline of the Democrats continues will depend on this choice.

The public sector investments listed above would cost many hundreds of billions of dollars. The money needed can only be found in federal waste, increased voluntary saving, and perhaps modest increases in efficient progressive taxes, sketched in chapter four. Unfortunately the national dialogue has assumed it is inevitable the nation will allow campaign contributors to siphon off more than $1 trillion a year in a $10 trillion plus economy, while the national interest is weakened accordingly. That assumption virtually guarantees that the policies outlined in this chapter will be inadequately funded.

Chapter 9

Conclusions

ENACTING EFFECTIVE CAMPAIGN FINANCE REFORM INTO LAW WOULD CAUSE two major changes: First, the Democratic Party would become much stronger, following a decades-long decline in its voter base. Second, the economy of the United States would become much stronger. An effective campaign reform bill can be constructed along the lines outlined in chapter two. Getting an effective bill through Congress is politically feasible if the argument presented in the Epilogue is valid. So the theory presented here offers a new interpretation of the dynamics of the American political system.

What accounts for the decades-long decline of the Democrats outlined in chapter three? Why did the Democrats allow their voter base to decline dramatically when they might have prevented it by offering popular programs like universal health insurance, the way Republicans proposed huge tax cuts for their base? Why have Democratic politicians failed to recover in the 1996, 1998, and 2000 elections the 63 congressional seats lost in the 1992 and 1994 elections? Given the unpopularity of the Republican economic agenda, how else did the Republicans achieve control of the White House, the Senate, the House, and a majority of governorships in the 2000 election except by exploiting the weaknesses of the Democrats?

The decline of the Democrats since 1968 coincides with the arrival of television, after which politicians needed to raise much more money to buy TV advertising time. Then Democratic politicians had no choice but to surrender to the demands of campaign contributors. The Democrats' decline resulted from their use of public monies to pay off their debts to contributors. These public monies might have paid for public investments voters wanted and the economy needed. But Democratic legislators had no other choice if they were to raise the campaign funds needed to compete successfully with the Republicans.

Currently, contributors trade contributions to legislators for quids pro quo, which, when added up, cumulatively waste national resources on a grand scale. Chapter four shows $1 trillion a year in government waste, on budget and off, in five categories: tax expenditures, business subsidies, uncollected revenue from legal activities, rent-seeking, and government program waste. This misallocation of resources has denied the Democratic Party the money it needs to fund the popular programs demanded by its voter base. Public sector investments that would have increased productivity growth and reduced inequality were never made, and will not be made in the future absent campaign reform. This misallocation of resources has weakened the economy in the past, and will weaken it even more over the long run.

Effective campaign finance reform would put an end to this misallocation of national resources. Enacting an effective campaign reform bill into law would change the incentives of members of Congress, thereby enabling them to reallocate federal waste over to national priorities, while refloating the Democratic Party in the process if the recaptured funds went into public investments rather than tax cuts.

But some analysts doubt enacting campaign reform into law would reduce waste. They believe that powerful interest groups would continue to exert influence in Congress even after enacting reform. They note these interest groups have more information than most voters, and can mobilize their members to pressure Congress. Moreover, campaign contributions are not the only tool interest groups use to influence Congress. Other tools include grassroots lobbying, issue advertising, lobbying legislative committees and executive agencies, and legal action. So some analysts believe even a best-possible reform law would fail to prevent interest groups from continuing to dominate the allocation of national resources. And so, from this viewpoint, reform would not work.

The ability of interest groups to undercut effective reform can be counteracted in three ways. First, by providing voluntary full public financing for all election campaigns for federal office, reform would greatly reduce legislators' incentive to be responsive to those demands of interest groups that run counter to the needs of voters. They would no longer incur political debts to contributors. Second, effective reform would reduce inequalities in candidates' opportunities to communicate political information. True reform would reduce the "shouting down" effect embodied in the dominance of those who can afford political advertising over those who cannot. Effective reform would give candidates public funds to match private funding of attack ads, including issue advertising that "directly affects an election." This matching approach has no First Amendment problems, unlike the expenditure limits approach that has bogged down the campaign reform movement. Matching does not require reversing *Buckley v. Valeo*. Chapter two outlines other specific provisions of effective reform, notably low and widely applied contribution limits. Large increases in funding for public broadcasting would also promote democratic debate. These measures would go a long way to free members of Congress to become more responsive to a more informed electorate of ordinary voters.

Full public financing of campaigns would increase the power of parties and voters relative to the power of interest groups. After reform, elected representatives would work together through their party to provide voters with better leadership, especially better information, and then voters would be more mobilized than they are now.[1] Currently, campaign contributions muzzle candidates on the stump. After campaign reform, interest groups would, and should, represent the more intense preferences of organized groups of voters, but would no longer be allowed to use contributions to purchase the legislative parties and weaken them as instruments of representation. An uncoopted political party would be better able to resist interest group demands and better able to represent ordinary voters.

Campaign Reform in the Context of Strong Parties

Whether campaign reform would lead to major policy changes is subject to one additional doubt. Suppose parties were fragmented by the independence of congresspersons from their party and its leaders. Suppose these legislators remained under the influence of many local interest groups, irrespective of most voters' needs. Then the misallocation of national resources after reform may resemble the current misallocation of resources. Then, even after reform, political parties would remain so fragmented as to be unable to put together a coalition strong enough to support party priorities. Interest group dominance would continue.

However, after reform, such fragmentation would be overcome by the nine party-unifying forces described in chapter six, the core of the Strong Parties theory presented here. These party-unifying forces pull congresspersons together in support of their party. Congresspersons need the support of voters who are loyal to their party. So they build party messages to mobilize party voters, while relying on party leaders to pull the party together behind legislation supporting the party message. Passing legislation requires minimizing the transaction costs—the costs in legislators' time, effort, money, and information—of forming legislative coalitions. Party unity behind party leaders is the key mechanism for lowering transaction costs enough to forge coalitions able to win legislative votes. The need to reduce the transaction costs of coalition formation makes political parties a necessity. In addition, each party rallies around policies good for those voters whose economic needs tie them to their party. These nine party-unifying forces normally overwhelm party-fragmenting forces, including the independence of members of Congress from their party leaders.

It is politicians' need for party unity and party effectiveness that makes it likely that campaign reform would achieve its intended effects. Once freed from constraints imposed by campaign contributors, Democratic legislators united by these nine party-unifying forces would have strong partisan incentives to recapture from contributor-driven waste the funds needed to legislate popular programs. That is the core of the Strong Party theory.[2]

The Potential Gains from Reallocating Resources

A large reallocation of wasted federal resources would support a variety of public investments that would increase productivity. The Nobel Laureate Robert M. Solow said recently, "Spending on public investment—like transportation and communication infrastructure, schools, urban amenities—are a direct way of adding to the nation's stock of real capital."[3] Chapter eight suggests what is needed to increase U.S. productivity would easily require many hundreds of billions of dollars every year in new public investments. Only if campaign reform were enacted would such spending be politically feasible. It is possible to increase private investment and public investment at the same time, by cutting waste, running a tight fiscal policy at full employment, and increasing voluntary saving so as to cut consumption, especially the consumption of the well-off.

If new public investments fueled faster growth in U.S. productivity, the incomes of most Americans would increase dramatically over a relatively short period of time. Only by focusing on these income gains is it possible to understand what is at stake economically in whether or not effective campaign reform becomes law. To appreciate the magnitude of the gains from additional investment, consider the following numbers derived from standard models, and summarized from above. Suppose enacting campaign reform into law allowed a 5 percent increase in the national investment rate. Under standard models, GDP would increase by 17.5 percent after 10 years. That increase would add roughly $1.658 trillion a year in additional output to a $9.477 trillion economy (GDP). If the increase in the investment rate were ten percent instead of 5 percent, as could occur after a large political shift, the increase in output would double to $3.2 trillion a year—an economy roughly 34 percent more productive after 10 years. New growth models suggest even larger numbers than standard models. So most Americans have a great deal to gain from enactment of effective campaign finance reform, assuming campaign reform triggers the reallocation of funds from waste to investments that increase productivity. The added income would allow the nation to solve many more of its problems, while achieving many more of its dreams.

Added income from higher productivity would solve another major problem as well. The rapid aging of the population is a major problem looming over the United States. To support a larger proportion of retirees in the population without cutting benefits or raising taxes, only one other option is available. The nation can increase saving and investment to raise productivity, so as to provide more national income to pay for the support of more elderly people. In the context of a rapidly aging population, raising productivity as much as possible becomes a necessity.[4]

Hence a prudent nation will do all it can to increase productivity. It will do so no matter from what productivity rate it starts. Even if productivity is already growing at a good rate, the gains from doing even better would be so great that it would be grossly disadvantageous to fail to enact policies that would help productivity reach a still higher level. So even if a higher rate of growth in productivity has materialized, the United States would still benefit from increases in investments, public and private.

Now campaign reform can be seen in a new light. The main economic effect of campaign reform would be to trigger a reallocation of resources that would increase productivity and reduce inequality, and thus transform the American economy while helping it avoid the British Disease.

The Democrats in the Context of Growing Inequality

If efforts to achieve campaign reform fail, if public investment continues to be Spartan, if productivity growth is suboptimal, and if inequality continues to grow, the Democratic Party could suffer future losses from a source that Democratic strategists seem to ignore. Over the last several decades, real wages have been declining for most American workers. This decline in real wages most affected those workers who only have a high school degree or a little more. These less-educated and less-trained workers in the past mostly voted Democratic. Such workers are most workers in the U.S. economy. In the future, technological innovation and globalization will cause additional shrinkage in the demand for unskilled workers, and so their wages and benefits are bound to fall even further. Thus inequality will probably continue to grow, voter disaffection will also grow, and the Democrats' voter base will decline even more.

In recent decades, one great offset protected the Democrats' base voters from the effects of the decline in real wages. The wages of their families' second earners, mostly wives who entered the workforce more than in the past, offset cuts in the wages of male high school graduates. However, having already budgeted the income earned by a second earner to make up for past wage cuts, there is no third family earner available to provide new income to offset future wage and benefit cuts. Nor will anything else be offsetting. So those who will suffer the effects of declining wages in the future will suffer greater hardships than were suffered from wage declines in the past. These workers may therefore become even less loyal to the Democrats than they have been. Yet the Democrats are not proposing anything like the needed education, job training subsidies, child care, health insurance, and other programs needed to equip high school educated workers to work more productively. So long as the Democratic Party in Congress cannot find the money with which to pay for programs their base voters want, whether those wants are manifest or latent, the Democratic voter base is bound to shrink even further.

At the same time, with inequality growing, the political system may lose some of its democratic legitimacy. Citizens may lose faith in the fairness of the system, and political parties may be perceived as unresponsive. The characteristics of such a weakening democracy are familiar: growing class conflict, growing disrespect for law and order, decay of institutions that depend on common values, proliferation of pathological political movements, and dangerous changes in the political process. The latter include term limits, manipulated ballot initiatives, increased corruption, bitterly contested election outcomes, and ever more clever marketing of personable candidates of questionable ability.

Two Interpretations of Democratic Party Cohesion

Against the backdrop of the decades-long decline of the Democratic Party outlined in chapter three, the strategic situation of the Democratic Party can be interpreted in two quite different ways. First, in the standard interpretation, the erosion of the Democrats' voter base resulted from the realignment of white southerners into the Republican Party, and from the lack of cohesion among the remaining Democratic factions—union members, environmentalists, minorities, women's groups, college educated liberals, and, most of all, non-union white working-class men. Surely, it is said, there is little possibility that these different groups can be cobbled together into an ideologically cohesive force even under the best of conditions, social distances being so great. On the other hand, most Republicans are much more united by an anti-government ideology and shared social class and business affinities. So the already weak cohesion of the Democrats is subject to further fragmentation, and, in this interpretation, greater party strength and unity is unlikely under most conditions.

A second interpretation of the Democrats' decline and lack of cohesion follows from the Strong Parties theory outlined in this study, and focuses on money. There are common goals that under some conditions would draw diverse groups of Democrats together into a potent electoral force. The Democratic Party would come together if the Democrats found a way to finance popular programs of public investment and social insurance. A Democratic Party that delivered universal health insurance, high-quality low-cost child care, universal preschool education, a much more effective national education system, job training subsidies, elderly care, and environmental safety would be very popular with most Americans, as shown by Greenberg's polls among others. Such programs would *override* those differences that now divide voters within the Democratic Party's natural base, and the nine party-unifying forces would provide the structural support for a strong party. Campaign finance reform would trigger the reallocation of the funds now wasted over to needed programs. This theory explains how effective campaign reform would return the Democratic Party to its Jeffersonian-Jacksonian roots and its natural voter base, and at the same time bring about a stronger U.S. economy.

The Future: The Campaign Finance Reform Movement

Because the congressional Democrats' hands are now tied by the need to raise enough money to compete with the Republicans, what happens next depends on *what happens within the campaign finance reform movement.* Only if the campaign reform movement is successful in mobilizing voters behind a truly effective bill will Congress be forced to enact that bill into law. After enactment of reform into law, the Democrats in Congress would have abundant partisan incentives to maintain a campaign reform regime because of the nine party-unifying forces outlined above.

In the end, there are only two models of effective campaign reform. The first counsels that we be "realistic" and do the "doable." Work within existing political constraints, this model recommends. The result of this approach is the six failed campaign finance laws enacted since 1946.

The second model starts with the assumption that only by finding a way to get around existing political constraints can effective reform be enacted into law. To change these constraints, it is necessary to work back from a clearly specified model of effective reform that cannot be loopholed, and from there derive the operational means necessary and sufficient to mobilize enough pressure on Congress to pass an effective bill. Reformers in the end must choose between these two models. The seven steps strategy suggested in the Epilogue that follows presents a rough draft of the second approach.

Epilogue

Is Campaign Reform Politically Feasible?

THE ENTIRE ARGUMENT OF THIS STUDY DEPENDS ON A SINGLE ASSUMPTION, which is open to considerable doubt. This study assumes effective campaign finance reform *can* be forced through the U.S. Congress.[1] Powerful arguments contradict this assumption. If this assumption is indeed false, if true reform is not politically feasible, then it will not matter in the end what efforts reformers make, nor will pro-reform sentiments in the country shape events. However, this Epilogue argues that the campaign finance reform movement could force Congress to enact effective campaign finance reform under certain specific conditions.

A Note on Reform in the States

Twenty-four states have passed full or partial public financing schemes into law. The evidence of so many voters in the states actively supporting reform indicates that support for reform in the country is very large, which suggests reform is politically feasible.[2] Victories in these states have led reformers to target other states that might establish public financing of campaigns. As more states adopt public financing laws, the momentum and enthusiasm behind reform continue to grow, fed by national news reports of elected officials' conflicts of interest and perpetual fund-raising.

However, additional successes in the states might not increase the pressure on Congress to enact effective reform. State victories may be a poor indicator of prospects at the federal level, because many state reforms were passed through referenda, which allowed citizens to bypass elected officials who otherwise would have blocked reform. There is no federal law that allows citizen action to trigger a national referendum. Moreover, the successes achieved so far in some states may not be a good indicator of prospects in large states like California and New York, or in states with different political cultures.

However, achieving reform in more states may increase the salience of the reform issue, encourage reform forces, and extend reform organizations. Moreover, the limited resources now available to reformers can be stretched farther in a few state campaigns than they could in a national campaign to pressure Congress. So a states' strategy used as one component of a longer-term national strategy has much to commend it.[3]

The Feasibility of Forcing Reform through Congress

There is considerable doubt in well-informed circles about the chances of enacting effective campaign finance reform at the federal level. Such doubts are well founded. Many observers believe Congress will never allow effective reform to become law for three reasons. First, any reform law that used public funds to pay for campaigns would be compelled to fund incumbents and challengers alike. By voting for reform, congressional incumbents would fund their own challengers' campaigns, which are now usually underfunded. Thus by voting for reform, incumbent members of Congress would put their careers in jeopardy. So they are likely to vote against reform, unless overwhelming pressure can be put on them. Second, Republicans oppose reform because they are reluctant to give up their advantage over Democrats in attracting contributions from wealthy individuals and businesses. Third, a congressperson's opposition to reform could be motivated by idealism, if she believed the policy differences separating the two parties mattered. She might believe she had a moral obligation to her supporters to prevent the other party from capturing her seat. If she publicly supported reform, she might antagonize contributors who might withhold their contributions and destroy her ability to retain her seat for her party. Until effective reform becomes law, most members must depend on private contributions to survive politically, and so will be unable to openly support effective reform legislation. For all three reasons, any truly effective campaign finance reform is bound to be persistently opposed by a majority of sitting members of Congress of both parties.

Therefore, success in accomplishing effective reform is more likely to result from the efforts of voters and reformers operating outside the two major parties. Only reformers working outside the parties are likely to mobilize public opinion in such a way as to put enough intense and focused pressure on the individual members of Congress that they vote for truly effective reform of the campaign laws.

The main criterion of political feasibility is ordinarily taken to be the likelihood legislation will be passed by Congress, signed into law by a president, faithfully administered by the bureaucracy, and upheld by the courts. Feasibility is usually established by talking to people on Capitol Hill, and by gauging the strength of congressional coalitions supporting and opposing a given piece of legislation. But these methods, though useful for most purposes, are of limited usefulness in judging the feasibility of an effective reform law.

In this instance, a better way to gauge the feasibility of campaign reform is in relation to the fundamental disequilibrium that exists between, on the one hand, congressional opposition to effective campaign reform, and, on the other, the public's deep and durable disdain for the role of money in American politics. The public's disdain, seen in many polls and reflected in the public financing passed by

24 states, is built on what voters see as the violation of a fundamental democratic norm—that votes not be purchased, whether the votes of citizens or the votes of legislators.[4] Voters' discontent is reflected in the dramatic decline of trust in government,[5] in the decline of party voting, and in declining voter turnout in elections. The passage of some form of public financing in 24 states suggests there are at least some conditions under which voters would trump politicians and contributors. The disequilibrium between voter resentments and the influence of campaign contributors creates a large opportunity for entrepreneurial reform politicians, if they can figure out how to provide leadership without being compromised by the contributions they themselves need. If uncompromised reformers can provide strategic leadership, and if the public can be mobilized behind an effective reform plan, perhaps Congress can be forced to enact true reform. The possibilities for transforming this disequilibrium into a new equilibrium define the political feasibility of reform.

The political potential of campaign reform can best be gauged by assessing the relative strengths, actual and potential, of reform and anti-reform forces. Congressional resistance to reform is an impregnable fortress, unless and until reformers organize the public to bring overwhelming pressure to bear on Congress. The elasticity of political constraints is best gauged by determining the potential strength of reformers. This potential can be assessed against two tests: (1) whether voters would support the costs of public funding of campaigns; and (2) whether reformers can formulate a strategic plan with a set of specific steps that would have a good chance of actually bringing about reform. These two tests are considered next.

Will Voters Support the Costs of Reform?

One frequently hears the argument that campaign reform is not politically feasible because voters, under some prodding by anti-reform advertisements, are likely to resent having to pay higher taxes to support public financing of campaigns and matching. This problem has both a simple answer and a complicated one.

The simple answer has two parts. First, voters are likely to accept the costs of public financing and matching if they know these costs will be financed by "*takebacks*"—funds captured from wasteful government expenditures—rather than by higher taxes. Second, if reformers succeed in framing the voters' choice as between having a Congress owned by campaign contributors and having a Congress owned by the American people, voters are likely to support reform.[6] Voters are apt to respond to a warning that "he who pays the piper calls the tune." The reform movement depends on voters' sense of the fundamentals of democratic legitimacy. It remains for a reform movement to bring voters' sense of what is legitimate to bear on specific congressional votes on reform measures.

Whether voters would accept the burdens of public financing has a more complicated answer as well. Suppose, after the enactment of reform, an arms race comes about in which private spending on political attack ads escalates sharply, forcing escalating costs onto the system of public matching of these private ads. Perhaps the public would not accept such escalating costs. Media opponents may play up the rising costs of public financing and belittle its benefits. Yet the taxpayers need not feel their burdens were increasing if these costs were financed from an account funded with takebacks from government waste. However, if Congress set up an account to pay for public financing of elections, and they put too little money in it, aggressive private spending on political advertising could overwhelm it and private spending might indeed bury public financed candidates in an advertising blizzard. The Democracy fund would have to spend as much as private donors were spending on elections to effectively support reform, but prior limits would prevent keeping up.

However, the fund need not operate with a preset limit on the amount of money available for matching. Rather, the fund should be run like the Social Security Trust Fund, as an entitlement whose obligations must be honored so as to preserve a democratic political process. Candidates' requests for matching funds could be honored without regard to the level of funds in the Democracy fund. Campaign funding can and should be an entitlement, so long as public opinion tolerates it, since democracy itself is an entitlement—a set of fundamental rights—and public funding of campaigns is essential to democratic elections. So long as the public funding of campaigns is financed with takebacks, voters would be unlikely to see escalating commitments by their Democracy fund as an increased burden on them.

The importance of this argument cannot be overestimated. This arms-race objection has played a key role in some discussions about the feasibility of matching. The argument caused some reformers to embrace expenditure limits instead, as discussed in chapter two, with all their fatal flaws. So if only matching will do, then the arms-race objection could prove to be the worst obstacle to effective campaign reform.

Another criticism of the matching funds approach has been put forward. If flexible financing of matching causes an increase in the volume of political ads, the voters will become even more bored, annoyed, and disgusted by the increase in political advertising than they already are, at which point support for public financing will wither. The answer to this criticism is straightforward. Reform will change the incentives and recruitment patterns of legislators, after which the content of their ads will change dramatically and for the better. After the massive reallocation of national resources that would likely result from reform, ads would have much more interesting material to promote concerning public investments, social insurance, and the nation's prospects.

Seven Steps to Enacting Reform into Law

The second test of the political feasibility of campaign reform is the test of its strategic plan. The seven steps described below together constitute the conditions under which effective campaign finance reform would most likely be passed by Congress. Reform is only as politically feasible as the feasibility of each of the seven steps taken separately. If none of the seven steps are unfeasible, then reform is feasible, if less than certain.

STEP 1. REFORMERS WOULD NEED TO PRODUCE A DECISIVE PLAN SHOWING HOW TO ACHIEVE PASSAGE OF REFORM IN CONGRESS. These seven steps would serve as a rudimentary starting point. (a) The plan must be effective enough to attract large disinterested contributors. (b) A strategy would be developed showing how enough voters would be mobilized to bring overwhelming pressure on most members of Congress, sufficient to pass an effective reform law. (c) The plan would need to show how reform legislation would permanently close all the loopholes through which private money might exert undue influence despite reform. (d) Scenarios or war games would have to be developed anticipating opponents' efforts to frustrate legislative passage and defeat reform in its administrative and legal phases under varying conditions.

STEP 2. REFORMERS WOULD NEED TO RAISE A GREAT DEAL OF MONEY. Experts must determine, based on a decisive plan, how much money is needed for media, grassroots mobilization, organization, and legislative analysis. Once that is determined, large contributors can be encouraged to contribute. Recent philanthropic contributions of enormous size made by billionaires Warren Buffett, Bill Gates, George Soros, and Ted Turner are indicative of what is possible, as are contributions from groups of less wealthy donors who are civic-minded political contributors. Those with fundamental constitutional concerns would also contribute, as would a broad spectrum of concerned groups. An additional pool of donors would become available if efforts were made to link campaign finance reform to other issues like health, education, and the environment, and if outcomes on these issues were shown to depend on campaign reform for success. Small contributions might also be of some help. There is every reason to believe a great deal of money could be raised from these and other sources.

STEP 3. REFORMERS WOULD NEED TO CREATE LINKAGES BETWEEN THE REFORM ISSUE AND OTHER ISSUES OF CONCERN TO VOTERS. Many voters are now unable to see what benefits would flow from campaign reform, and so they remain less supportive than they might be.[7] Advertising could link campaign reform with other hot button issues. Organized efforts at linkage would accelerate coalition building.

STEP 4. REFORMERS WOULD NEED TO STRUCTURE A NATIONAL ADVERTISING CAMPAIGN TO EXPLAIN CAMPAIGN FINANCE REFORM TO THE PUBLIC. Public cynicism about the present campaign finance regime is already great, and the public is already quite responsive to reform messages, as polls by Mellman and others have amply demonstrated.[8] An advertising campaign would aim most of all at getting voters to demand their representatives in Congress switch sides.[9] Such an ad campaign would be very expensive.

STEP 5. REFORMERS WOULD NEED TO CONSTRUCT A GRASSROOTS REFORM ORGANIZATION AT THE LOCAL LEVEL TO BRING POPULAR PRESSURE TO BEAR ON MEMBERS OF CONGRESS TO SUPPORT REFORM. This has been done before. Conservatives have successfully used grassroots organization to demand candidates "Take the Pledge—No New Taxes." Simultaneously, conservatives fielded trained "truth teams" to make their case on local news shows—an air attack coordinated with a ground attack. Recently, unusually effective mobilization of voters by labor and minority groups in the 1998 and 2000 elections also expanded the political community's understanding of what was possible "on the ground."[10] In the past, an environmental group successfully defeated all of the so-called Dirty Dozen congresspersons with the worst environmental voting records in Congress. An even earlier example of success in organizing grassroots pressure on Congress was the passage of the recorded teller vote reform as part of the Legislative Reorganization Act of 1970.[11] Intense congressional opposition to the recorded teller vote reform was overwhelmed by outside forces. The recorded teller vote reform passed and is law today.[12]

A campaign that successfully brings pressure to bear on individual congresspersons is the only way effective campaign finance reform will ever become law. Reformers need to convince legislators that failing to faithfully support a specific reform package would be inconsistent with their reelection and their public dignity. Ads could attack those incumbent representatives who opposed reform as defending government waste and big interests, and robbing voters of the money to pay for needed programs. Such a nationwide grassroots campaign, if it is to be organized professionally, also will not be inexpensive.

STEP 6. REFORMERS WOULD NEED TO IDENTIFY THEIR BILL WITH A FEW HIGHLY VISIBLE POLITICAL LEADERS, SO AS TO GIVE A HUMAN FACE TO THE BILL.[13] If a president of the United States could be persuaded to use his "bully pulpit" to advance effective reform, the difficulties in financing the seven steps and building support for the plan would shrink dramatically. But a president's obligations to his party's congressional candidates and to his own contributors would likely weaken his ability to lead reform efforts, even in a second term. However, other leaders may be found among reform leaders, retired politicians, interest group leaders, and others. The function of leaders is to provide voters with a point of focus, from which information can be acquired, tactical signals can be taken, and encouragement can be spread. Voters connect more with leaders than with abstract ideas, inversely with how much political information they have, and follow developments by listening to leaders characterize those developments. So visible leadership is essential in developing support for reform legislation.

STEP 7. REFORMERS WOULD NEED TO PRODUCE A FULLY SPECIFIED LEGISLATIVE BILL TO RALLY AROUND, TO HOLD UP AS THE STANDARD OF EFFECTIVE REFORM, AND TO JUDGE LEGISLATORS' BEHAVIOR AGAINST. After extensive deliberation in the reform community and discussion by the public, a perfect bill would serve two functions. A perfect bill, perhaps with measures similar to those outlined in chapter two, would be the best possible rallying point of the reform effort. A perfect bill would have the best chance of arriving in Congress with enough momentum to prevent congressional committees from creating loopholes.[14] Speaker Newt Gingrich's successful efforts in bypassing committees are instructive, as are past speakers' use of inter-committee legislative task forces. The Senate floor offers other opportunities to protect a perfect bill, if coordinated with outside pressures.

If implemented, these seven steps could be sufficient to force Congress to enact effective campaign reform. The seven steps would have a reasonable chance of preventing reform from falling victim to the kinds of compromises exhibited in the fatally flawed reform proposals of the past. Available evidence does not support the conclusion that any one of these seven steps could be blocked by existing political forces. There is no evidence supporting a conclusion that the planning could not get done, that enough money could not be raised, that issues could not be linked, that an ad campaign could not be run, that grassroots organization could not be built, that a few reliable and effective leaders could not be found, or that reformers could not produce a specific bill with enough momentum to bypass congressional committees that would gut it.

Conclusion

If the seven steps are followed, enacting campaign finance reform into law *is* politically feasible, even if enactment is less than certain. Because no one can show empirically that any of these seven conditions cannot be accomplished, each of these seven steps taken separately is politically feasible. If so, all seven together are feasible, and therefore effective campaign reform in the United States is politically feasible. So the discouragement and cynicism, for some a convenience, that plague public consideration of campaign finance reform cannot be reconciled with what is known about political change. Skeptics should explain why the campaign finance movement has less of a chance to be successful than the civil rights movement, the women's movement, the environmental movement, or the anti-Vietnam war movement.

Absent a strategic plan something like the seven steps, the most likely outcome is that reform pressures will be deflected by a carefully contrived make-believe reform bill in Congress. Such a make-believe bill will leave ample room for financially powerful interests to continue to exert disproportionate influence on members of Congress. If reformers are to succeed, their first task will be to mobilize opposition to any bill that is less than effective, on the grounds that if it is less than effective then in all likelihood it has been offered to undercut an effective reform bill. A bad bill deflects efforts to achieve a good bill. Any student of the legislative process knows that the opponents of reform are likely to manufacture a bad bill—a bill with loopholes—and call it a good bill or a "realistic" bill. The acid test of whether reform is effective is not how much private money it takes off the table, but how much money it leaves on the table to distort the incentives of members of Congress after reform has been accomplished.

Appendix

Two Prominent Campaign Reform Plans

TWO LEADING REFORM PROPOSALS FAIL BY A WIDE MARGIN TO MEET THE TWO criteria of effective reform stated above: both the McCain-Feingold bill introduced in the Senate and the Brookings-sponsored Ornstein, Mann, Taylor, Malbin, and Corrado proposal would leave in place the money chase. Under both proposals, the elected representatives of the people would continue to raise large contributions from private contributors, many of them corrupting. Moreover, under these two plans, large inequalities would continue as between, on the one hand, candidates and their allies who spend large sums on political ads, and on the other, candidates who cannot attract contributions from wealthy interests to pay for such advertising. Voters are deprived thereby of their right to hear all sides of issues in equal proportions, and deprived as well of representation of their preferences when those preferences are opposed by wealthy interests.

Six campaign finance laws have been enacted by Congress since World War II.[1] In each of these reform laws, whether by design or inadvertence, Congress left open wide channels through which contributors could influence legislators. These past failures signal obstacles that a successful reform must overcome.

The McCain-Feingold bill was introduced in the Senate from 1997 through 2001. Shays-Meehan, a companion bill, was introduced in the House. Their most important virtue is they would ban soft money—unlimited contributions from corporations, unions, and others to national parties. McCain-Feingold would also ban corporations and unions from financing TV or radio ads that referred to clearly identified candidates within 60 days of an election. But these organizations would be allowed to purchase print advertising, direct mail, and telephone and Internet communications, as well as voter guides. Worst of all, they would also be free to purchase unlimited "issue advertising" affecting elections. Nonprofit advocacy groups would be exempt from any limit on broadcast spending, also a significant loophole.[2] The bill would ban PAC contributions of soft money to candidates or parties, including soft money contributions from nonprofits' PACs and leadership PACs. It would "limit" individual contributions to national parties to $20,000 a year. State parties would be prohibited from spending soft money on federal elections. The bill would create voluntary spending caps on candidates' campaigns in return for some free television time and some subsidized mailings to voters. It would require reliance on in-state funding sources. The bill's proponents claim it would likely reduce campaign costs in the Senate by 46 percent.[3]

McCain-Feingold contains a fatal flaw. Even after becoming law, it would perpetuate candidates' need to raise large amounts of money from private contributors so as to be competitive in elections. While the bill eliminates soft money, it leaves intact legislators' dependence on hard money—federally regulated private contributions[4]—as well as on unlimited spending on issue advocacy ads that affect elections. Ellen Miller has calculated that of the $2.4 billion raised in the 1996 presidential campaign, only 11 percent was soft money, and the rest was hard money.[5] Moreover, money now contributed as soft money would probably be redirected into issue advocacy and other channels if McCain-Feingold became law, thereby largely nullifying even the most positive effects of McCain-Feingold. After McCain-Feingold became law, incumbents would continue to raise much more money than challengers, limiting the scope of competition in congressional elections. McCain-Feingold's provision of some free TV time looks like an important step. But to qualify, Senate candidates would first need to raise $1.6 million in private contributions for a primary and general election in the smallest state, and much more in larger states. House candidates would first have to raise $95,000 in private funds,[6] and not all of a candidate's media expenses would be covered. Other flaws of McCain-Feingold are also significant:

> The voluntary spending limits . . . are only slightly lower than the current average [spending based on contributions]. . . . The current problems are not principally the result of PACs or out-of-state contributions. PACs are now responsible for only 25 percent of funding for congressional campaigns . . . a PAC ban might further slant the playing field: it would disarm labor unions and other interest groups that raise their money from a large number of small contributions from their members. Business interests do not now rely on PACs for their political contributions. If PACs were banned tomorrow, business would simply channel all, rather than most, of its money through large individual contributions. . . . Furthermore, the great majority of funds for these races already come from in-state.[7]

The gap between the Brookings-sponsored Ornstein, Mann, Taylor, Malbin, and Corrado proposal and a truly effective reform plan is also quite large.[8] Their plan has three virtues. First, they propose restructuring the FEC along lines similar to proposals in chapter two. Second, they propose a broadcast bank with vouchers given to candidates and parties to purchase media time without charge. These vouchers would be paid for by contributions of time from broadcasters in exchange for government broadcasting licenses now given to broadcasters without charge, despite their large value. Ornstein, Mann, et al. propose that funding for these vouchers should be equal to the value of all political advertising time sold in a recent two-year election cycle. Challengers and incumbents would benefit equally. This is a major proposal. Yet this plan does not specify how candidates would find the funds required to respond to private attack ads when broadcast bank vouchers are exhausted. Nor are independent expenditures and issue advocacy advertising funded by wealthy interests fully balanced in this proposal, as they would be under the public matching funds proposal described in chapter two. Ornstein, Mann, et al. do not finance many other campaign expenses. So candidates would continue to find it necessary to pursue corrupting contributions attached to quids pro quo.

A third valuable feature of this plan would expand the definition of express advocacy, so as to push some expenditures now claimed to be issue advocacy into the category of express advocacy.[9] Expanding the number of contributions in the express advocacy category and reducing what is counted as issue advocacy would reduce the number of large contributions now escaping such express advocacy regulations as contribution limits, disclosure, and the prohibition on direct corporate and labor contributions. Ornstein, Mann, et al. recommend that Congress pass, and the Supreme Court accept, an expanded list of instances that expressly advocate the defeat or election of a candidate, including use of a candidate's photo or name.

A fourth feature would, like McCain-Feingold, abolish soft money, defined as unregulated, undisclosed, and unlimited contributions to political parties. Abolishing soft money ranks high on every reformer's list of targets, and the means to accomplish this are simple and widely agreed upon, as noted above.

However, at the same time, to promote political parties, an important goal, Ornstein, Mann, et al. would increase the limits on individual contributions to parties. They propose a new $25,000 limit on what individuals could give to parties. This amount may be added to the $5,000 individuals are permitted to give to all individual races combined under present law. This adds up to a total individual limit of $30,000 per contributor that could be given to candidates and parties.[10] Even this new limit could be circumvented by those who gave multiple contributions in these amounts in the names of family members, each allowed to give $30,000. Four family members could together give $120,000 per election, election after election. These limits do not restrict unlimited contributions to independent committees to purchase issue advertising that affects an election. This proposal moves far away from the spirit of one person one vote.

The proposal by Ornstein, Mann, et al. to raise the limits on individual contributions to parties assumes money given by parties to their congresspersons does not corrupt them. Their reasons for making this assumption are not stated. But contributions to parties do corrupt members of Congress when parties broker contributions to specific legislators in return for legislative favors to contributors. This proposal also ignores the huge disparities in influence between those who contribute to political parties and most ordinary citizens who do not. This plan should be contrasted with relying instead on direct public financing of parties as sketched in chapter two.

The fifth feature seeks to encourage "small" contributions, so as to offset the sharp increase in the number of large contributions relative to small ones that has occurred in recent years. They propose creating,

> a 100% tax credit for in-state contributions to federal candidates of $100 or less. The credit would apply to the first $100 an individual gave to candidates—in other words, $25 given to each of four candidates would result in a $100 credit. It would not apply to large contributions; it would be phased out if an individual gave more than $200 to the candidate.

They propose paying for the tax credit with a ten percent fee on large contributions, offset by increasing the limit on individual contributions to a single candidate from $1,000 to $2,500 or $3,000, which seems quite large when the limited number of people capable of contributing even $1,000 once, let alone on a regular basis, is taken into account.

The tax credit itself has several problems. Citizens who take advantage of it are likely to be wealthier than those who do not. Many voters who take advantage of the credit will respond to a solicitation from a sophisticated fund-raising firm asking the credit be sent to a candidate. Groups who can afford to hire such firms are apt to be wealthy. Professional fund-raisers will combine contributions benefiting from the Ornstein, Mann, et al. tax incentive with other contributions to max out the impact of a contributor's dollar. These professional fund-raisers will also find it most efficient to approach those most likely to contribute, primarily wealthier individuals already known to the fund-raiser. So wealthier individuals and groups are more likely to take maximum advantage of this tax credit.

The tax credit by itself may not increase the number of contributions of $100 to candidates. It is worth repeating the evidence cited earlier showing it is primarily a very thin affluent layer of the electorate that now makes most contributions, even small ones. In the 1996 election cycle,

> [L]ess than one-fourth of 1 percent of the American people made a campaign contribution of $200 or more to a federal candidate. Only 4 percent made any contribution of any size to any candidate for office—federal, state, or local. On average, only 20 percent of the money came from individuals giving contribu-

tions of less than $200 per candidate. That means that an astonishing 80 percent of political money came from the tiny group of donors who gave $200 or more.[11]

There is nothing now preventing most ordinary Americans from making small contributions, but that does not happen. It is true that under the Ornstein, Mann, et al. tax credit it would be essentially costless for a citizen to assign $100 of his tax liability to support a candidate's campaign. But current levels of political cynicism and disaffection should be taken into account. Again, distrust in the political system in the United States has been growing steadily and dramatically for decades.[12] Moreover, 92 percent of Americans believe special interest contributions buy votes of members of Congress, and 88 percent believe people who make large contributions get special favors from politicians.[13] In this context it is less likely the Ornstein, Mann, et al. tax credit would incentivize a major increase in small contributions from people of modest incomes. These voters are unlikely to believe their contribution would compete successfully for influence with those who make the large contributions this plan feels constrained to tolerate. Moreover, why would someone make a contribution to a candidate or a party if she believed neither was responsive to her real concerns? Not just because there was a tax credit. Declining utilization of the existing tax checkoff for presidential elections also supports the conclusion that the proposed tax credit would be underutilized by people with ordinary incomes.

Taking account of the various channels this proposal leaves open to large contributors, their opportunity to exert disproportionate influence over governmental decisions would remain very great even after the plan's tax credit took effect. People with unequal incomes would continue to contribute unequally, and so wealthy interests would continue to exert disproportionate influence over legislation. That would not be the case with full public financing of campaigns.

Conclusion

Overall, the Ornstein, Mann, et al. proposal suffers from the same liability as the McCain-Feingold proposal. It leaves the money chase largely in place, and so gives grossly unequal representation to financially unequal voters. At best their plan is realistic in the narrow sense of conforming to present political constraints. But the whole point of campaign reform is to change those constraints. Ornstein, Mann, et al. do not examine the elasticities of present political constraints, and so they beg two questions: (1) what remedies, if any, would create fully effective reform, and, (2) under what conditions would attempts to legislate a fully effective campaign reform law be successful? Both of these questions have been examined in this study.

Notes

Chapter 1: Introduction

1. *Business Week*, February 15, 1999, 64.

2. Anthony Corrado, Thomas E. Mann, Daniel R. Ortiz, Trevor Potter, and Frank J. Sorauf (eds.), *Campaign Finance Reform: A Sourcebook* (Washington, DC: Brookings Institution Press, 1997), 31–32. They claim that in the 1956 elections, total campaign spending equaled about $155 million, and $9.8 million was used for TV and radio. Media spending increased almost 600 percent by 1968, and overall spending nearly doubled. Such spending continued to increase in subsequent decades.

3. In the presidential debates of the 2000 election, Governor George W. Bush continually taunted Vice President Al Gore with the accusation that in eight years, the Democrats had not gotten anything done, referencing Medicare and Social Security reform, a patient's bill of rights, education, and middle-class tax cuts. His polling undoubtedly told him his claim was credible. See http://www.debates.org/index.html

4. What the economy "needs" is used here as having empirical content rather than normative content. For example, that too little education is supplied has as a referent changes in the ratio of wages paid educated and trained workers—say computer programmers—relative to the wages for undereducated workers. Measures of the "readiness to learn" of school children, broken down into health, diet, and other measures are correlated with test scores. Similarly, lists of promising basic research and technology projects put together by panels of scientists, bureaucrats, and business representatives contain many items that go unfunded because of budget constraints. The resulting R&D gap is an empirical measure of the R&D shortfall relative to what the economy could utilize. Suboptimal saving rates due to rent seeking by the securities industry are described in chapter four.

5. This decline is outlined in chapter three. Cf. Ruy Teixeira and Joel Rogers, *America's Forgotten Majority: Why the White Working Class Still Matters* (New York: Basic Books/Perseus Books Group, 2000), 15–18, 31–34, 85, 121; John J. Coleman, *Party Decline in America: Policy, Politics, and the Fiscal State* (Princeton: Princeton University Press, 1996); William G. Mayer, *The Divided Democrats: Ideological Unity, Party Reform, and Presidential Elections* (Boulder, CO: Westview Press/HarperCollins, 1996).

6. Susan Rose-Ackerman, *Corruption and Government: Causes, Consequences, and Reform* (Cambridge, UK and New York: Cambridge University Press, 1999). See her discussion of bribery as an allocative tool that causes misallocations of resources large enough to make a country poorer, while delegitimizing government. Most discussions ignore reform's economic consequences, and hence, underestimate the potential demand for reform that might be activated if it were widely perceived that reform would cause wasted funds to be reallocated to new spending on national priorities. Cf. Mancur Olson, *The Rise and Decline of Nations* (New Haven: Yale University Press, 1982).

7. Studying the dynamics of the party system entails examining counterfactuals, if we are to avoid assuming that the future will be just like the past. Cf. Roderick M. Chisholm, "The Contrary-to-Fact Conditional," *Mind*, Vol. 55 (1946): 289–307, reprinted in Herbert Feigl and Wilfred Sellars (eds.), *Readings in Philosophical Analysis* (New York: Appleton-Century Crofts, Inc., 1949), 482–497; Philip E. Tetlock and Aaron Belkin, "Counterfactual Thought Experiments in World Politics: Logical, Methodological, and Psychological Perspectives," *Social Science Research Council Items*, Vol. 50, No. 4, (December 1996); http://www.ssrc.org/decemitems1.htm. These authors note, "We can avoid counterfactuals only if we eschew all causal inference and limit ourselves only to strictly non-causal narrative of what actually happened. . . ." See also James D. Fearon, "Counterfactuals and Hypothesis Testing in Political Science," *World Politics*, Vol. 43, No. 2 (January 1991) 169–195. Economists' dynamic models routinely embody counterfactual claims.

8. Cf. Anthony H. Birch, *Concepts and Theories of Modern Democracy*, 2nd ed. (London and New York: Routledge, 2001); George E. Marcus and Russell L. Hanson (eds.), *Reconsidering the Democratic Public* (University Park, PA: The Pennsylvania State University Press, 1993).

9. Cf. David B. Truman, *The Governmental Process* (New York: A. A. Knopf, 1951); Robert A. Dahl, *Who Governs* (New Haven: Yale University Press, 1961); Robert A. Dahl, *Dilemmas of Pluralist Democracy* (New Haven: Yale University Press, 1982); Aage Clausen, *How Congressmen Decide: A Policy Focus* (New York: St. Martin's Press, 1973); Bradley Smith, "Faulty Assumptions and Undemocratic Consequences of Campaign Finance Reform," in Corrado et al., op. cit., 104–112. See also William E. Connelly (ed.), *The Bias of Pluralism* (New York: Lieber-Atherton, 1973).

10. Max Frankel, "Pay-Pay-Pay-Per-View: TV Transmits Lucrative Political Lies and Invests Nothing in Our Enlightenment," *New York Times Magazine*, November 8th, 1998, 36.

11. Smith, op. cit., 107.

12. Ibid.

13. Alan J. Auerbach and William G. Gale, "How Big Is the Prospective Budget Surplus?" http://www.brookings.edu/comm/PolicyBriefs/Pb064/pb64.htm.

14. Leaders routinely lead at least as much as they follow. Cf. Lawrence R. Jacobs and Robert Y. Shapiro, *Politicians Don't Pander: Political Manipulation and the Loss of Democratic Responsiveness* (Chicago: University of Chicago Press, 2000).

15. Jerrold E. Schneider, *Ideological Coalitions in Congress* (Westport, CT: Greenwood Press, 1979); Keith T. Poole and Howard Rosenthal, *Congress: A Political-Economic History of Roll Call Voting* (New York: Oxford University Press, 1997). For contrary views, see chapter six, "A Sixth Unifying Force: The Role of Ideology." Perhaps the most prominent contrary view comes from the 2000 Nobel Laureate James J. Heckman and coauthor James Snyder in "A Latent Linear Factor Model of Voting," prepared for the Quandtfest, Princeton University, May 17, 1995, 31, 35. See also their "Linear Probability Models of the Demand for Attributes with an Empirical Application to Estimating the Preferences of Legislators," *The RAND Journal of Economics*, Vol. 28, No. 0 (Special Issue '97): S142–S189. However, they note that the ideological model "*has gained wide acceptance among congressional scholars. . . .*" [italics added], Quandtfest paper, 31, 35.

16. The following analyses of public opinion polls anchors the main argument of this study: Stanley B. Greenberg, *Middle-Class Dreams: The Politics and Power of the New American Majority* (New Haven: Yale University Press, 1996); and his "The Popular Mandate of 1996," post-

election national survey for the Campaign for America's Future, Washington, DC: Greenberg Research, November 12, 1996. Greenberg was President Bill Clinton's pollster.

17. See chapters seven and eight. Cf. Robert H. Frank, *Choosing the Right Pond: Human Behavior and the Quest For Status* (New York: Oxford University Press, 1985); and his *Luxury Fever: Why Money Fails to Satisfy in an Era of Excess* (New York: Free Press, 1999); Juliet Schor, *The Overspent American: Upscaling, Downshifting and the New Consumer* (New York: Basic Books, 1998).

18. E. E. Schattschneider, *The Semisovereign People: A Realist's View of Democracy in America*, reissued with an Introduction by David Adamany (Hinsdale, IL: The Dryden Press, 1975).

19. V. O. Key Jr., *Politics, Parties, and Pressure Groups*, 5th ed. (New York: Thomas Y. Crowell, 1964). Cf. Milton C. Cummings Jr. (ed.), *V. O. Key, Jr and the Study of American Politics* (Washington, DC: American Political Science Association Evron M. Kirkpatrick Monograph Series, 1988).

20. Grant McConnell, *Private Power and American Democracy* (New York: Alfred A. Knopf, 1967).

21. Committee on Political Parties, American Political Science Association, 1950. "Toward A More Responsible Two Party System," *American Political Science Review* 44: supplement to the March issue. Cf. Leon D. Epstein, "What Happened to the British Party Model? APSA Presidential Address, 1979," *American Political Science Review*, Vol. 74, No. 1 (March 1980) 9–22; Cf. Evron M. Kirkpatrick, "Toward a More Responsible Two Party System: Political Science, Policy Science, or Pseudo-Science?" *American Political Science Review*, LXV, No. 4 (December 1971): 965–990.

22. Albert Einstein, "Autobiographical Notes," in Paul Arthur Schilpp, *Albert Einstein: Philosopher-Scientist* (New York: Tudor Publishing Company, 1951), 3–95.

23. Thomas E. Patterson, *The American Democracy*, 4th ed. (Boston: McGraw Hill, 1999), 554. Patterson notes with respect to universal health care and other proposals, "All of these proposals have failed to win broad support, mainly because they run counter to Americans' belief in individualism." Brookings economist Gary Burtless shows why, despite Americans' views about personal responsibility and the availability of abundant opportunities to get ahead, Americans would nonetheless favor universal health insurance. First, growing income disparities threaten to undermine political equality and social cohesion. Second, greater inequality contributes to higher mortality rates and poorer health among those who are lower in the income distribution. Third, humanitarian concern for people at the bottom would move one to favor universal health insurance. See Gary Burtless, "Growing American Inequality," in Henry J. Aaron and Robert D. Reischauer (eds.), *Setting National Priorities: The 2000 Election and Beyond* (Washington, DC: The Brookings Institution, 1999), 141–142.

24. The size of the benefits that would accrue from a given increase in the level of productivity is summarized in chapter nine of this study, and is spelled out in greater length in chapter seven.

25. *Prosperity for American Families: The Gore-Lieberman Economic Plan*, Addendum: The Gore-Lieberman Federal Budget and Surplus Plan, Table 3: Investments in Priorities ($Billions), 182. See http://a1604.gakamai.net/7/1604/1614/v 00000001 www.algore.com/pdf/gore-prosperity.pdf. This chart lists $170.2 billion total for "Investing in Education and Learning" over the

ten-year period 2001 to 2010, or roughly $17 billion per year. For school districts in the United States, see U.S. Department of Education, Digest of Education Statistics, 1999, Table 5: Educational Institutions by Level and Control, 14.

26. For the approximately 90,0000 schools in the United States, Gore-Lieberman's $17 billion per year would only fund an additional three teachers per school at $60 thousand a year per teacher, leaving out all the other education budget items they themselves acknowledge are needed, and more besides. Compare the list in chapter eight. The problem did not suddenly appear in 2000. Dionne notes,

> Bill Clinton's 1992 victory and the large vote given to Ross Perot reflected public frustration with the retreat from practical government. Clinton was elected not only in reaction to the failures of George Bush but also because he seemed to promise a plausible approach to the problems that most troubled the country. He pledged to use job training and education to ease the transition of individuals from the old economy to the new, reshape the health care and welfare systems and to reform the political system to reduce the influence of special interests and expand the public's democratic capacities.
>
> But in the two years after the 1992 election the Democrats failed fundamentally. Health care, welfare, and political reform all fell victim to divisions within the party. Budget constraints never allowed the Clinton job-training and education initiatives to get off the ground. . . . To many Americans, the Democrats seemed to have become a dysfunctional party. E. J. Dionne, Jr., *They Only Look Dead: Why Progressives Will Dominate the Next Political Era* (New York: Simon and Schuster, 1996), 13–14.

Similar budget constraints and their elasticity lie at the heart of the analysis of party dynamics presented here.

27. Theodore Marmor and Mark Goldberg, "A Drug Benefit Has Sour Aftertaste," *Wilmington News Journal*, October 22, 2000, G1.

28. Greenberg, op. cit.

Chapter 2: Would Campaign Reform Work?

1. David Donnelly, Janice Fine, and Ellen S. Miller, *Money and Politics: Financing Our Elections Democratically* (Boston: Beacon Press, 1999), 7. Cf. Ellen Miller, remarks at the Brookings Working Group on Campaign Finance Reform, Round 6 of Discussion, Topic: House Republican and House Democratic alternatives to McCain-Feingold, page 5, http://www.brook.edu/ GS/CAMPAIGN/round6.htm. Federal candidates do not have to report contributions of less than $200, and so the incomes of those who contribute less than $200 are not known. But it is a reasonable extrapolation that smaller contributions are also made disproportionately by wealthier people.

2. Edward N. Wolff, *Top Heavy: A Study of the Increasing Inequality of Wealth in America, A Twentieth Century Fund Report* (New York: The Twentieth Century Fund Press, 1995), 59–60.

3. Anthony Corrado, Thomas E. Mann, Daniel R. Ortiz, Trevor Potter, and Frank J. Sorauf (eds.), *Campaign Finance Reform: A Sourcebook*, op. cit.; Thomas Ferguson, *Golden Rule: The In-*

vestment Theory of Party Competition and the Logic of Money-Driven Political Systems (Chicago: University of Chicago Press, 1995); Charles Lewis and the Center for Public Integrity, *The Buying of Congress: How Special Interests Have Stolen Your Right to Life, Liberty, and the Pursuit of Happiness* (New York: Avon Books, 1998); Elizabeth Drew, *The Corruption of American Politics: What Went Wrong and Why* (Woodstock and New York: The Overlook Press, 1999); and her *Politics and Money* (New York: Macmillian, 1983).

4. This argument is made by Thomas E. Mann, "A Plea for Realism," in Donnelly, Fine, and Miller, op.cit. 74–77.

5. *Buckley v. Valeo*, 424 U.S. 1 (1976); *Austin v. Michigan State Chamber of Commerce*, 494 U.S. 652 (1990). In Corrado et al., op. cit., 65, 70, 73–74, 82–86.

6. Frank Sorauf, remarks at the Brookings Working Group on Campaign Finance Reform, Topic: House Republican and House Democratic alternatives to McCain-Feingold, page 10, http://www.brook.edu/GS/CAMPAIGN/round6.htm. These remarks embody the traditional Pluralist view.

7. Senators John Glenn (D-Ohio), John McCain (R-Arizona), Dennis DeConcini (D-Arizona), Donald Reigle (D-Michigan), and Alan Cranston (D-California) took large unregulated contributions from Arizona businessman Charles Keating, the owner of the Lincoln Savings and Loan in California. Later they defended him before Federal regulators when his bank took excessive risks with its depositors' money and imposed losses of $2 billion on them, which the taxpayers made good to the depositors. Only the intervention of these Senators prevented Federal bank examiners from closing Keating's bank down earlier than it was, which would have stemmed the massive losses that occurred subsequent to the Senators' intervention. Keating later went to jail, *and the senators apologized.* Brooks Jackson, *Honest Graft: Big Money and the American Political Process* (Washington, DC: Farragut Publishing Company, 1990), 314–317.

8. Haynes Johnson and David S. Broder, *The System: The American Way of Politics at the Breaking Point* (Boston: Little, Brown and Company, 1996), 194–235.

9. Pippa Norris (ed.), *Critical Citizens: Global Support for Democratic Governance* (New York: Oxford University Press, 1999), 5–6 ff.

10. David B. Magleby and Candice J. Nelson, *The Money Chase: Congressional Campaign Finance Reform* (Washington, DC: The Brookings Institution, 1990).

11. Public Campaign, The Power of Public Opinion, http://www.peoplefirst.org.pubop. html#CRP.

12. Jeffrey H. Birnbaum, *The Money Men: The Real Story of Fund-Raising's Influence on Political Power in America* (New York: Crown/Random House, 2000), 252–253.

13. Quoted in Ellen Miller, remarks at the Brookings Working Group on Campaign Finance Reform, Round 3 of Discussion, Topic: Interested Money, page 9, http://www.brook.edu/GS/CAMPAIGN/round6.htm.

14. Ferguson, op. cit.; Lewis, op. cit.

15. Justice Clarence Thomas, concurring in the judgment and dissenting in part, joined by Chief Justice William Rehnquist and Justice Anthony Scalia, in *Colorado Republican Federal Campaign Committee v. Federal Election Commission*, 116 S. Ct. 2309 (1996), in Corrado, et al., *Campaign Finance Reform: A Sourcebook*, op. cit., 91.

16. Ibid., 339.

17. Ibid., 346.

18. Cf. Linda L. Fowler and Robert D. McClure, *Political Ambition: Who Decides to Run for Congress* (New Haven: Yale University Press, 1989); Burdett Loomis, *The New American Politician: Ambition, Entrepreneurship, and the Changing Face of Political Life* (New York: Basic Books, 1988).

19. *Buckley v. Valeo*, in Corrado et al., op. cit., 73–74.

20. As the term *matching* is used here, it does not refer to seed money, or public grants given as an incentive to an individual candidate or organization to raise private grants on a matching basis, or as start-up money to do the same.

21. Congressman Richard Gephardt, *Parade*, September 21, 1997. Challengers requesting public funds would have to meet the usual standard of either winning a specified number of votes in a previous election, or getting a specified number of signatures on a petition. Contributions that purchased the services of professional firms who solicit petition signatures would also need to be balanced.

22. In the majority's decision in *Buckley v. Valeo*, independent expenditures, that is expenditures on campaigns made independent from any coordination with a candidate or her campaign organization, are declared an improper object for expenditure limitations imposed by statue. This decision states the 1974 Federal Election Campaign Act amendments, which limited to $1,000 a year independent expenditures by individuals and groups in support of a candidate, "precludes most associations from effectively amplifying the voice of their adherents, the original basis for the recognition of First Amendment protection of freedom of association. . . ." Moreover, the Court stated, "Advocacy of the election or defeat of candidates for federal office is no less entitled to protection under the First Amendment than the discussion of political policy generally or advocacy of the passage or defeat of legislation." *Buckley v. Valeo*, in Corrado et al., op. cit., 67, 73, 74.

23. *Buckley v. Valeo*, op. cit.; *Austin v. Michigan State Chamber of Commerce*, 494 U.S. 652 (1990), in Corrado et al., op. cit., 65, 82–86.

24. Cf. Jamin Raskin and John Bonifaz, "Equal Protection and the Wealth Primary," reprinted from *The Yale Law and Policy Review*, Vol. 11, No. 2 (Winter 1993–1994): 273–332. Also at http:// world.std.com/~nvri/BonYale.html, 28–33.

25. *Buckley v. Valeo*, 424 U.S. 1 (1976), and *Regan v. Taxation Without Representation*, 461 U.S. 540 (1983).

26. *Day v. Holahan*, 34 F.3D 1356 (8th Circuit, 1994). See also the Brief by the Minnesota Attorney General Hubert H. Humphrey III et al. What if the Supreme Court reversed itself and found speech promoted by the matching subsidy reduces candidates' speech? If so, it would still have to decide whether matching would reduce speech more or less than candidates' speech is already reduced by the absence of enough funding to advertise their views as much as their opponent does, especially when these candidates refuse potentially corrupting campaign contributions. It is likely the courts do not know how to measure how much speech is chilled or inhibited by matching, versus how much speech is inhibited by the lack of matching. It follows that what is involved is what the Court has called "a political question" that ought to be resolved by a legislature rather than by a court. Moreover, matching is probably content neutral, in which case it engages a

lower level of scrutiny, under which First Amendment protection may be countered by a compelling state interest such as promoting democracy and the right to vote. Cf. Report of the Twentieth Century Fund Working Group on Campaign Finance Litigation, *Buckley Stops Here: Loosening the Judicial Stranglehold on Campaign Finance Reform,* report drafted by E. Joshua Rosencranz of the Brennan Center of New York University School of Law, 1998.

27. Corrado et al., op. cit., 9, 16–17, 227–239. Soft money would be left outside a matching scheme, since most reform proposals would abolish soft money. See the Appendix, "Two Prominent Reform Proposals." Soft money expenditures are unregulated, unlimited contributions, usually quite large and undisclosed in amount or source, that corporations, unions, other organizations, and individuals give to parties, supposedly to carry on party-building activities.

28. I am indebted to Theodore Kleinman, Esq. for his views on these matters.

29. Corrado et al., op. cit., 229.

30. Cf. ibid. 230–236 for a discussion of the 9th Circuit's important *Furgatch* ruling.

31. Ibid., 341. Cf. Michael J. Malbin and Thomas L. Gais, *The Day after Reform: Sobering Campaign Finance Lessons from the American States* (Albany, NY: The Rockefeller Institute Press, distributed by the Brookings Institution, 1998), esp. 60–61. Vermont's law only applies to the elections for Governor. I am indebted to Derek Cressman of U.S. PIRG for explaining what laws apply in these states. See U.S. PIRG, "The State PIRGs' Political Reform Update," February 2000.

I do not attempt here to compare the various states' experiences with campaign reform. The literature is at an early stage of development. Moreover, state reform experiences reflect conditions quite different than the conditions obtaining at the national level, especially using state referenda to enact reform into law, which is not legally possible at the federal level. For one viewpoint, see Malbin and Gais, op. cit.

32. Ellen S. Miller, "Clean Elections, How To," *The American Prospect,* January/February 1997, 56–59. Cf. David Donnelly, Janice Fine, and Ellen S. Miller, "Going Public," *Boston Review,* Vol. 22, No. 2 (April/May 1997): 3–7. Reprinted in Corrado et al., op. cit., 365–370. Matching would require mandatory disclosure of expenditures on election campaigns and advertising so administrators of public matching funds would know what to match and when. However, a matching scheme might be judged legally vulnerable because, in relying on coerced disclosure of campaign expenditures, First Amendment rights might be violated by virtue of a chilling effect on those making the expenditures. The decision in *Shelton v. Tucker* showed the Supreme Court was concerned such an effect might result when coerced revelation of sources of information occurs. *Shelton v. Tucker,* 364 U.S. 479 (1960); *NAACP v. Alabama,* 357 U.S. 449 (1958). Cf. *Talley v. California,* 362 U.S. (1960). The right to anonymous publication is necessary because exposure of the names of printers, writers, and distributors would lessen the circulation of literature critical of the government). Organizations have a right to protect members from disclosures that might lead to retaliation and harassment. *NAACP v. Alabama,* 357 U.S. 449 (1958). However, no First Amendment problem would arise from the public disclosure of actual spending on political communications that affect elections. The spending itself, specifically for attack ads, is public knowledge as soon as advertisements are broadcast or printed. All that would be asked is that those who run the ads (a TV station), who may keep the identity of sponsors a secret, help the government

identify when such communications are purchased and how much they cost, so those who wish to respond can ask for matching funds. Once so informed, administrators of public matching funds can proceed to match privately financed campaign-related communications whose targets lack the funds to reply to their opponents without the provision of matching funds.

33. The McCain-Feingold bill is analyzed in the Appendix to this study.

34. Douglas Phelps, "Setting Limits," in Donnelly, Fine, and Miller, op. cit., 53–55.

35. One calculation has shown $10 per person per year would guarantee funding for all candidates' campaigns—federal, state, and local—an amount low enough that voters would be unlikely to find it unacceptable. See Dan Clawson, Alan Neustadtl, and Mark Weller, *Dollars and Votes: How Business Campaign Contributions Subvert Democracy* (Philadelphia: Temple University Press, 1998), 223. But merely referring to higher taxes might be the kiss of death.

36. Reform opponents might claim funds taken out of waste should be returned to the taxpayers rather than pay for public financing of campaigns with matching. But this would be a false choice. Without publicly financed elections, elected officials will depend on private contributions whose donors will demand and receive payoffs similar to the waste listed in chapter four, after which these funds would not after all be returned to the taxpayers. The only available choice is between continuing such waste and capturing some of it to fund publicly financed campaigns.

37. Report of the Twentieth Century Fund Working Group on Campaign Finance Litigation, *Buckley Stops Here: Loosening the Judicial Stranglehold on Campaign Finance Reform*, report drafted by E. Joshua Rosencranz, the Brennan Center of the New York University School of Law, 1998.

38. Corrado et al., op. cit., 64.

39. Ibid., 65, 82–86.

40. *Buckley Stops Here*, op. cit., *Buckley v. Valeo*, in Corrado et al., op. cit., 73–74.

41. Cf. Theodore L. Glasser (ed.), *The Idea of Public Journalism* (New York: The Guilford Press, 2000). Cf. James Ledbetter, *Made Possible By. . . : The Death of Public Broadcasting in the United States* (New York: Verso Press, 1997).

42. Cf. John Stuart Mill, *On Liberty, and Other Essays,* edited with an introduction by John Gray (New York: Oxford University Press, 1991).

43. Max Frankel, "Pay-Pay-Pay-Per-View: TV Transmits Lucrative Political Lies and Invests Nothing in Our Enlightenment," *New York Times Magazine*, November 8, 1998, 36. Cf. Edwin Baker, *Advertising and a Democratic Press* (Princeton: Princeton University Press, 1994).

44. Cf. Philip E. Converse, "The Nature of Belief Systems in Mass Publics," in David E. Apter, *Ideology and Discontent* (New York: Free Press, 1964).

45. Cf. Norman J. Ornstein, Thomas E. Mann, Paul Taylor, Michael Malbin, and Anthony Corrado, "Reforming Campaign Finance," in Corrado et al., op. cit., 383–384.

46. Cf. *Vannatta v. Keisling*, 899 F. Supp. 488 (D. Ore. 1995), in Corrado et al., op. cit., 363–364.

47. Corrado et al., op. cit., 34, 59.

48. Ibid., 167.

49. Cf. Norman J. Ornstein, Thomas E. Mann, Paul Taylor, Michael Malbin, and Anthony Corrado, "Reforming Campaign Finance," in Corrado et al., op. cit., 10, 379–384. Re: McCain-Feingold, compare page 177.

50. Derek Cressman, Testimony on Campaign Finance before the Senate Rules Committee, representing the U.S. Public Interest Research Group, March 29, 2000.

51. *Nixon v. Shrink Missouri Government PAC (98–963) 161 F.3d 519*, reversed and remanded. Also see http://supct.law.cornell.edu/supct/html/98-963.ZS html.

52. Elizabeth Drew, *The Corruption of American Politics: What Went Wrong and Why* (Woodstock, NY: The Overlook Press, 1999), 276.

53. Ellen Miller, "The Hard Truth about McCain's Soft Money Ban," *The American Prospect* Vol. 11, No. 9 (March 13, 2000): 12.

54. Cf. an exchange among Gary C. Jacobson, Donald Philip Green, and Jonathan S. Krasno, in the *American Journal of Political Science*, Vols. 32 and 34 (1988 and 1990) concerning the effects of money on incumbents' chances.

55. Reform should not seek to eliminate incumbents' advantages over challengers based on past service and experience. Experience should be rewarded, lest the result be an inexperienced legislature prone to legislating unintended consequences, and lest incentives be increased for leaving legislative service.

56. Justice Clarence Thomas, op. cit.

57. Arthur M. Okun, *Equality and Efficiency: The Big Tradeoff* (Washington, DC: The Brookings Institution, 1975), 22–31.

58. Ibid.

59. See the discussion of coalitions in chapter six.

60. Cf. John Stuart Mill, *On Liberty, and Other Essays,* edited with an introduction by John Gray, op.cit.; John Stuart Mill, *Utilitarianism, Liberty, and Representative Government* (New York: E. P. Dutton, 1951); Amy Guttman and Dennis Thompson, *Democracy and Disagreement* (Cambridge, MA: The Belknap Press of Harvard University Press, 1996).

61. Cf. Kalman H. Silvert, *Essays in Understanding Latin America* (Philadelphia: Institute for the Study of Human Issues, 1977), 12.

Chapter 3: The Decline of the Democratic Party

1. In 1996 the Democrats picked up nine seats net in the House and lost 1 seat net in the Senate. In 1998, they gained five seats net in the House and zero seats net in the Senate. Norman J. Ornstein, Thomas E. Mann, and Michael J. Malbin, *Vital Statistics on Congress, 1999–2000* (Washington, DC: A. I. Press, 2000), 55–56.

2. In the 2000 election, the Democrats did gain five seats in the Senate. But the Republicans who lost their Senate seats were "exposed." Four of the five were weak incumbents who rode the tide of the 1994 Republican sweep. Hence their defeat was not a sign of a Democratic resurgence. In 2001, the Republicans control 29 of the governors' mansions. See http://www.nga.org/Governor/elections2000.asp. In 2001, the Democrats and Republicans each control 17 state legislatures, a loss of two for the Democrats, and split control of 15 others.

3. Jacobs and Shapiro, *Politicians Don't Pander: Political Manipulation and the Loss of Democratic Responsiveness,* op. cit., 224. Legislation regarding a patient's Bill Rights and prescription drug benefits are important bills, but do not deal with the problems of the 44 million Americans

with no health insurance, the 30 million more with inadequate coverage, and the one million who are projected to lose coverage every year. Also neglected are other major problems in the health system, including rampant waste, described in chapter eight, and the systemic failure to provide preventive health care.

4. Robin Toner, "Health Impass Souring Voters, New Poll Finds," *New York Times*, September 13, 1994, A1.

5. Cf. John H. Aldrich, *Why Parties? The Origins and Transformation of Party Politics in America* (Chicago: The University of Chicago Press, 1995), 165–178; Charles H. Franklin, Richard Brody, and Paul M. Sniderman, "Special Issue on Party Identification," *Political Behavior*, Vol. 14, No. 3 (1992): 193–360.

6. Bruce Cain, John Ferejohn, and Morris Fiorina, *The Personal Vote: Constituency Service and Electoral Independence* (Cambridge, MA: Harvard University Press, 1987), 9.

7. Racial issues became a major cross-cutting cleavage among Democrats in the 1968 election. Edward G. Carmines and James A. Stimson, *Issue Evolution, Race and the Transformation of American Politics* (Princeton: Princeton University Press, 1989); but see Alan I. Abramowitz, "Issue Evolution Reconsidered: Racial Attitudes and Partisanship in the U.S. Electorate," *American Journal of Political Science*, Vol. 38, No. 1 (February 1994): 1–24.

8. The question used by NES reads as follows: Generally speaking, do you usually think of yourself as a Republican, a Democrat, an Independent, or what? If Republican or Democrat: Would you call yourself a strong . . . or a not very strong . . . ? If Independent: Do you think of yourself as closer to the Republican or Democratic Party? Data are drawn from Miller, Warren, and the National Election Studies. AMERICAN NATIONAL ELECTION STUDIES CUMULATIVE DATA FILE, 1952–1992 [Computer file]. 7th release. Ann Arbor, MI: University of Michigan, Center for Political Studies [producer], 1994. Ann Arbor, MI: Inter-university Consortium for Political and Social Research [distributor], 1994. Table 2.1. Updated through 1998 from "The NES Guide to Public Opinion and Electoral Behavior: Party Identification 7 Point Scale 1952–1998." 12/1/2000. http://www.umich.edu/~nes/nesguide/toptable/tab2a_1.htm. Leaners—those who answer independent but closer to one party or the other—are not included. With leaners excluded, the decline between the two periods equals 8.4 percent. The samples were drawn from the general population, rather than just registered voters or actual voters.

9. Unleaned, among the general population. The question used was: In politics today, do you consider yourself a Republican, a Democrat, or an Independent? Data do not include 1969 through 1971, 1973 through 1974, 1977 through 1998. Ladd notes, "When those independents who say they lean to one party or the other are added into the respective bodies of partisans, the Republicans' relative position almost always is shown improving slightly, in recent polls." Everett Carl Ladd, "Party Identification: The Idea and the Measure," *The Public Perspective*, May/June 1991. The data from The Gallup Organization also do not give continuous cross-time data on leaners.

The literature raises questions about the Gallup question wording, particularly the phrase "as of today," which may make the measure more sensitive to short-term changes in presidential popularity and the health of the economy at the time of the polling. Richard G. Neimi and Herbert F. Weisberg, *Controversies in Voting Behavior*, 3rd ed. (Washington, DC: CQ Press, 1993), 272 ff. But this seems less troubling given the similarity in results arrayed above.

Keith et al. have claimed that if leaners—self-described independents who say they lean to one party or the other—were included with party identifiers, the decline in partisanship would be seen as not having declined as much as some interpretations conclude. But leaners should not be lumped together with partisans. The decline in self-identified partisans without leaners added more validly captures the true trend. The growth in the number of leaners relative to partisan identifiers is indicative of declining commitments to political parties. When a triggering event occurs, leaners more easily desert the party they lean toward than would party identifiers, whether weak or strong. Bruce E. Keith, David B. Maglby, Candice J. Nelson, Elizabeth Orr, Mark Westlye, and Raymond E. Wolfinger, *The Myth of the Independent Voter* (Berkeley: University of California Press, 1992).

10. The similarity between NES and Gallup data is noted in Harold D. Clark and Motoshi Suzuki, "Partisan Dealignment and the Dynamics of Independence in the American Electorate, 1953–88," *British Journal of Political Science*, Vol. 24, Part 1 (January 1994): 76.

11. *The Public Perspective*, May/June 1991, 92.

12. Poll Releases, April 9, 1999, "Independents Rank as Largest U.S. Political Group," The Gallup Poll, http://www.gallup.com/poll/releases/pr990409c.asp. This poll used telephone interviews.

13. Andrew Kohut, "Questioning Party Identification," *The Public Perspective*, September/October 1991, 21–22. Larry Hugick, "Party Identification: The Disparity Between Gallup's In-Person and Telephone Interview Findings," ibid., 23.

14. Niemi and Weisberg, op. cit., 268–281.

15. A ten percent decline in the party's base vote is equal in theory to giving up all of the winning victory margin in every congressional election where a seat was won by 60 percent or less. Roughly one-quarter of House seats and one-half of Senate seats were won by 60 percent of the vote or less between 1974 and 1992. So, if all of the ten percent of Democratic voters who ceased being party identifiers, whether because of generational replacement or other factors, had instead remained loyal and had voted Democratic in 1994, the Republicans would very likely not have taken control of the Congress. Norman J. Ornstein, Thomas E. Mann, and Michael J. Malbin, *Vital Statistics on Congress, 1997–1998* (Washington, DC: American Enterprise Institute, 1998), Tables 2–12, 2–13, 68–69.

However, such arithmetic neglects how such votes would have been distributed across congressional districts and states. So it is not possible here to translate a loss of party identifiers into a loss of congressional seats. However, the decline in Democratic identifiers that occurred between 1982 and 1992 did not show up in the loss of Democratic seats in Congress prior to the 1994 election. Democratic identifiers declined in this period, but Democratic seat totals in Congress did not reflect this decline.

16. Cf., for example, Robin Toner, "The Conventions Are Over. The Party Is Just Starting," *New York Times*, August 20, 2000, 14 WK; Harold W. Stanley, "The Parties, the President, and the 1994 Midterm Elections," in Colin Campbell and Bert A. Rockman (eds.), *The Clinton Presidency: First Appraisals* (New York: Chatham House, 1995), 202; Charles Cook, *The Cook Political Report*, August 20, 1997, 2.

17. Ruy A. Teixeira, *The Disappearing American Voter* (Washington, DC: The Brookings In-

stitution, 1992), 58–105. Cf. Ruy A. Teixeira and Joel Rodgers, *America's Forgotten Majority: Why the White Working Class Still Matters* (New York: Basic Books, 2000).

18. Walter Dean Burnham, "Realignment Lives: The 1994 Earthquake and Its Implications," in Campbell and Rockman, op.cit., 384.

19. *The Public Perspective*, September, October 1993: 13. Cf. Martin P. Wattenberg, *The Decline of American Political Parties, 1952–1992* (Cambridge: Harvard University Press, 1994), 120–124. However, voters under 30 voted for Clinton in 1996 by a margin of 53 to 34, in part because of Bob Dole's age. But it is not clear if this youth vote was a function of transient images of these candidates or of more enduring themes and loyalties.

20. Gary C. Jacobson, *The Electoral Origins of Divided Government: Competition in U.S. House Elections, 1946–1988* (Boulder: Westview Press, 1990).

21. Wattenberg, op. cit.

22. Cf. Ornstein et al., op. cit., Tables 2–15 and 2–16, 70–71.

23. Jacobson, op. cit., Figure 2.6., 12–15.

24. Ibid., 15.

25. Ibid.

26. Ibid., 42.

27. Ibid., 76–77.

28. "Party Registration Report—1994–1998," Republican National Committee, Computer Services Division, Political Analysis Department, Research Division. Democratic registration equaled .417 percent, .427 percent, and .428 percent of the two party vote, and .329 percent, .327 percent, and .321 percent of the two party vote plus "other" in 1994, 1996, and 1998. Thus, the decline in Democratic registrations relative to Republican registrations leveled off in these three election cycles.

29. Rhodes Cook, "GOP Shows Dramatic Growth, Especially in the South," *Congressional Quarterly Weekly Report*, January 13, 1996: 97–100.

30. Http://www.tarrance.com. Battleground Polls 11 and 12, August 23–25, 1998, and July 12, 1999. I am indebted to Todd Vitale of Tarrance Group for discussing these polls.

31. *Battleground '96: Key Points and Charts*, The Tarrance Group/Lake Research, April 1995.

32. Rhodes Cook, "Dixie Voters Look Away: South Shifts to the GOP," op. cit., 3230–3231.

33. Paul Allen Beck, "Party Realignment in America," in Maureen Moakley, *Party Realignment and State Politics* (Columbus: Ohio State University Press, 1992), 259–278.

34. Cook, op. cit.

35. Giroux, *Congressional Quarterly Weekly Report*, op. cit., 347.

36. Michael Barone and Grant Ujifusa, *The Almanac of American Politics: 1998* (Washington, DC: National Journal, 1997), 5–12; http://www.nga.org/Governors/GovMasterList.htm; and above citations.

37. Cook, op. cit.

38. Ibid.

39. Ibid.

40. Ornstein et al., op. cit., 61.

41. The lagged effects of the 1991 to 1992 House Bank Scandal mattered. But that scandal lacked substance. The so-called House Bank scandal concerned some members who had run up huge unpaid balances. But these balances were financed by other members' positive balances, and not at all by taxpayers. The press however largely reported the scandal as if a lot of congresspersons were enjoying interest free loans at the taxpayer's expense.

42. Robin Toner, "Health Impass Souring Voters, New Poll Finds," op. cit.

43. Ornstein et al., op. cit., Table 2–2, 48.

44. Ibid. Table 1–19, 43. After the 1998 election, the new balance in the House was 223 Republicans to 212 Democrats, including one independent, Bernie Sanders (I-Vermont). By 1999, the gap was reduced to six seats. In the Senate after the 1998 election, the new balance was unchanged at 55 Republicans and 45 Democrats. "Post Election Extra: Guide to New Members," *Congressional Quarterly Weekly Report*, Vol. 56, No. 44 (November 7, 1998): 3004, 3010.

45. *Wall Street Journal*, October 16, 1995, A14.

46. See Stephen Ansolabehaare, David Brady, and Morris Fiorina, "The Marginals Never Vanished?" *British Journal of Political Science* (January 1992): 121–138. They note, "But there is no doubt in our minds that the composition of the House of Representatives is less responsive to changes in national sentiments today than a generation ago."

47. *The Popular Mandate of 1996: The Voter's Concerns That Decided the Election and That Will Shape the Future Agenda*, a national post-election survey sponsored by The Campaign for America's Future, conducted by Greenberg Research, November 12, 1996, 3. Stanley B. Greenberg, "Popularizing Progressive Politics," in Stanley B. Greenberg and Theda Skocpol (eds.), *The New Majority: Toward Popular Progressive Politics* (New Haven: Yale University Press, 1997), 286. Greenberg's polling shows the Democrats do best with familiar but expensive economic policies. Fifty-nine percent of voters in 1996 cited Clinton's support for domestic programs—education, Medicare, and the environment—as the prime reason they voted for him. The public is deeply concerned with protecting Medicare and Social Security against major cuts, and is concerned with guaranteeing health insurance to all Americans, according to Greenberg's polls. This data also shows very strong support (65 percent in favor) for massive investment in education paid for by greater taxation of the wealthy and corporations.

48. Ornstein et al., *Vital Statistics on Congress, 1997–1998*, op. cit., Table 2–5, 57.

49. Citizens' main means of influencing members of Congress is by responding through voting and other activities to the opposition's broadcast attacks on incumbents. R. Douglas Arnold, *The Logic of Congressional Action* (New Haven: Yale University Press, 1990), 272.

50. Party unity among all House Democrats went down from the mid-sixties, and rose sharply from 1979 through 1996. Ornstein et al., op.cit, 211–212. The same pattern obtains among Senate Democrats across this period.

51. Ibid., Table 2-19, 74. Gerald Pomper, "The Alleged Decline of American Parties," in John G. Geer (ed.), *Politicians and Party Politics* (Baltimore: Johns Hopkins University Press, 1998), 14–39.

The intense partisanship exhibited in recent years by both parties is not indicative of fragmentation. In the House dining room under the Capitol Dome, Democrats and Republicans very rarely sit together, which does not fit well with a story about fragmented parties. Cf. Dennis W. Johnson, *No Place for Amateurs: How Political Consultants Are Reshaping American Democracy* (New York and London: Routledge, 2001).

52. For a skeptical view of this argument, see Fiorina, *Congress: Keystone of the Washington Establishment*, 2nd ed. (New Haven: Yale University Press, 1989), 124–129.

53. "Senate: The Balance of Power in 2002 and Beyond," *CQ Weekly Report*, Vol. 58, No. 44 (November 11, 2000), 2625.

54. Poll Releases, November 2, 2000: Clinton approval remains high after eight years: Comparable to Eisenhower but higher than Reagan at end of two terms. Gallup News Service, http://www.gallup.com//poll/releases/pr001102.asp.

55. It is less surprising a good economy did not help the Democrats recapture the House or Senate in 1996 or 2000. The effect of the economy on presidential elections normally does not carry over to congressional races, at least absent a recession. Alberto Alesina and Howard Rosenthal, *Partisan Politics, Divided Government, and the Economy* (Cambridge, UK and New York: Cambridge University Press, 1995), 227.

56. Robert Dreyfuss, "Rousing the Democratic Base," *The American Prospect*, Vol. 11, No. 23 (November 6, 2000): 20–23.

57. Daniel M. Shea, "The Passing of Realignment and the Advent of the 'Base-less' Party System," *American Politics Quarterly*, Vol. 27, No. 1 (January 1999): 33–57. According to a recent poll, 75 percent of the public believes the government is pretty much run by a few big interests looking out for themselves, and is not run for the benefit of the people. Steven Kull, *Expecting More Say: The American Public on Its Role in Government Decision Making* (Washington, DC: Center on Policy Attitudes, May 10, 1999), 4. Also cited are other prominent polls that find essentially the same findings.

58. Greenberg, op. cit.

59. Ruy Teixeira, "Gore's Tenuous Bond with Workers," *The American Prospect*, Vol. 11, No. 24 (November 20, 2000): 16.

60. Haynes Johnson and David S. Broder, *The System: The American Way of Politics at the Breaking Point* (Boston: Little Brown and Company, 1996), 11. Cf. Theda Skocpol, *Boomerang: Health Care Reform and the Turn against Government* (New York: W. W. Norton, 1997); Jacob S. Hacker, *The Road to Nowhere: The Genesis of President Clinton's Plan for Health Security* (Princeton: Princeton University Press, 1997), esp. 77–99 and Note 56, 211. James A. Marone and Gary S. Belkin (eds.), *The Politics of Health Care Reform* (Durham: Duke University Press, 1994).

61. Toner, "Health Impass Souring Voters, New Poll Finds," op. cit.

Chapter 4: Would Campaign Reform Yield Enough Money to Refloat the Democrats?

1. Derek Bok, *The State of the Nation: Government and the Quest for a Better Society* (Cambridge, MA: Harvard University Press, 1996), 418.

2. What is most remarkable is that pennies buy treasure chests; contributors' returns on their investments in politicians are huge relative to the size of their contributions. *The Nation* offered

compelling examples. Between 1992 and 1994, AT&T contributed $90,000 to the Democrats, and received $34.2 million from the Commerce Department. Boeing gave $127,000 and received $50.9 million. Other examples are presented in the same vein. See Donnelly, Fine, and Miller, "Going Public," op. cit., 8–9. That the process generates waste is described in Jeffrey Birnbaum, *The Lobbyists: How Business Gets Its Way in Washington* (New York: Crown Publishing Group, 1992). What makes these ratios plausible is that legislators give away other people's money, not their own.

3. Alan J. Auerbach and William G. Gale, "How Big Is the Prospective Budget Surplus?" http://www.brookings.edu/comm/PolicyBriefs/Pb064/pb64.htm; Robert D. Reischauer, "The Dawning of a New Era," in Henry J. Aaron and Robert D. Reischauer (eds.), *Setting National Priorities: The 2000 Election and Beyond* (Washington, DC: The Brookings Institution, 1999), 12–14; U.S. Government, Congressional Budget Office, *The Budget and Economic Outlook*, July 2000, Summary Table 2, xii; U.S. Congress, Congressional Budget Office, *Long-Term Budgetary Pressures and Policy Options* (Washington, DC: U.S. Government Printing Office, 1998), 2–3.

4. Joseph A. Pechman, *Federal Tax Policy*, 5th ed. (Washington, DC: The Brookings Institution, 1987), 355; U.S. Government, *Budget of the United States Government: Fiscal Year 1998: Analytical Perspectives* (Washington, DC: U.S. Government Printing Office, 1997), 71–98. Cf. Stanley S. Surrey and Paul R. McDaniel, *Tax Expenditures* (Cambridge, MA: Harvard University Press, 1985).

5. Pechman, op. cit., 356, 363.

6. U.S. Congress, Congressional Budget Office, *Reducing the Deficit: Spending and Revenue Options*, February 1995, 3. Citizens for Tax Justice arrives at a similar figure for 1996: $454 billion for tax expenditures. See Citizens for Tax Justice, *The Hidden Entitlements: An Overview of Tax Expenditures* (http://www.ctj.org/hid_ent/part-1/part1.htm#foot1), 3.

7. Ibid. Measuring the economic value of tax expenditures is difficult. Most studies lack any numbers totaling their amount. That is because separately eliminating two different tax expenditures might produce a different revenue estimate than the sum of the separate amounts for each item, because of economic interaction effects. Another source of confusion is whether, and to what extent, any given tax expenditure or subsidy increases saving and investment, in the context of a dynamic general equilibrium model. U.S. Congress, House of Representatives, Committee on Ways and Means, *Where Your Money Goes: The 1994–95 Green Book* (Washington: Brassey's, 1994), 676.

8. Jonathan Gruber and James Poterba, "Fundamental Tax Reform and Employer-Provided Health Insurance," in Henry J. Aaron and William G. Gale (eds.), *Economic Effects of Fundamental Tax Reform* (Washington, DC: The Brookings Institution, 1996), 125–170.

9. Joel Slemrod and Jon Bakija, *Taxing Ourselves: A Citizen's Guide to the Great Debate Over Tax Reform* (Cambridge, MA: The MIT Press, 1996), 39.

10. Robert J. Shapiro, *Cut-and-Invest: A Budget Strategy for the New Economy: Progressive Policy Institute Policy Report No. 23.*, 23. Cf. U.S. Government, *Budget of the United States Government: Fiscal Year 1998: Analytical Perspectives* (Washington, DC: U.S. Government Printing Office, 1997), Table 5–1, 74.

11. Pechman, op. cit., 269.

12. Denis Kessler and Andre Masson, "Bequest and Wealth Accumulation: Are Some Pieces of the Puzzle Missing?" *Journal of Economic Perspectives,* Vol. 3, No. 3 (Summer 1989): 141–152.

13. Slemrod and Bakija, op. cit., 190–191.

14. Pechman, op. cit., 123–127, 256–298.

15. Slemrod and Bakija, op. cit.

16. Citizens for Tax Justice, op. cit., part-2/part2-2htm.

17. Jane G. Gravelle, *The Economic Effects of Taxing Capital Income* (Cambridge, MA: The MIT Press, 1994).

18. U.S. Government, *Budget of the United States Government: Fiscal Year 1998: Analytical Perspectives* (Washington, DC: U.S. Government Printing Office, 1997), Table 5–3, 79.

19. See Organization for Economic Co-operation and Development, *Tax Expenditures: Recent Developments* (Paris: OECD, 1996), 7–19, 107–117.

20. Where the amounts are duplicative, they have been removed from the final tally.

21. Shapiro, op. cit.

22. Ibid. Studies cited include Gary C. Hufbauer and Kimberly A. Elliot, *Measuring the Costs of Protection in the United States* (Washington, DC: Institute for International Economics, 1994) and U.S. International Trade Commission, "The Economic Effect of Significant U.S. Import Restraints," November 1993.

23. Citizens for Tax Justice, op. cit., part-2/part2-1.html.

24. Ibid., 2/part2-3.htm.

25. Ibid.

26. Ibid.

27. Joseph E. Stiglitz, *Economics* (New York: W. W. Norton, 1993), 357–358, 403–404, 451–452, 603–604.

28. Edward N. Wolff, *Growth, Accumulation, and Unproductive Activity: An analysis of the Postwar U.S. Economy* (Cambridge: Cambridge University Press, 1987).

29. William J. Baumol, Sue Anne Batey Blackman, and Edward N. Wolff, *Productivity and American Leadership: The Long View* (Cambridge, MA: The MIT Press, 1992), 273–277. Wolff, op. cit.; cf. Mancur Olson, *The Rise and Decline of Nations* (New Haven: Yale University Press, 1982); David C. Colander (ed.), *Neoclassical Political Economy: The Analysis of Rent-Seeking and DUP Activities* (Cambridge: Ballinger, 1984).

30. Slemrod and Bakija, op. cit., 147.

31. Ibid., 152.

32. U.S. General Accounting Office, *GAO Transition Series: Internal Revenue Service, December 1992,* 15–16.

33. Slemrod and Bakija, op. cit., 154.

34. U.S. Congress, Congressional Budget Office, *Reducing the Deficit: Spending and Revenue Options* (Washington, DC: U.S. Government Printing Office, 1997).

35. Ibid., 9–294. Not included in this tally are Social Security, Medicare, or Medicaid administrative cuts, tax increases, and tax expenditure cuts.

36. William D. Nordhaus, "Budget Deficits and National Saving," *Challenge,* March–April 1996: 48. *Washington Post* editor Brian Kelly has assembled a useful set of examples of egregious

waste in his book, *Adventures in Porkland: How Washington Wastes Your Money and Why They Won't Stop* (New York: Villard Books: 1992).

37. U.S. House of Representatives, Democratic Caucus, Task Force on Government Waste, Rep. Byron L. Dorgan, Task Force Chairman, *The Challenge of Sound Management*, June 1992, 1–57.

38. Aaron and Gale, op. cit., 5.

39. Jeffrey H. Birnbaum, *The Lobbyists: How Influence Peddlers Get Their Way in Washington* (New York: Random House Times Books, 1992).

40. Congress of the United States, Congressional Budget Office, *The Economic and Budget Outlook: Fiscal Years 2000–2009* (Washington, DC: U.S. Government Printing Office, January 1999), Table 4–1, 62.

41. Baumol et al., op. cit., 168–176.

42. *Economic Report of the President*, February 1999, Table B32, 364. Cf. 71–73, 125, 167–169, 365. Of great concern to some economists is that the personal saving rate remains low, at 0.2 percent, down from a seven to nine percent level in the 1960s and 1970s. Many countries, notably Japan in past decades, have run bigger government deficits than the worst U.S. deficits without harmful consequences, because their high saving rates created a large enough pool of capital that government borrowing to finance deficits did not crowd out as much private investment as would have been crowded out if the saving rate had been lower.

43. Robert Eisner, "Divergences of Measurement and Theory and Some Implications for Economic Policy," *American Economic Review*, Vol. 79, No. 1 (March 1989): 3–5. Eisner finds mismeasurement of saving in the National Income and Product Accounts (NIPA) hides much income and savings, and concludes the level of saving in the United States is much higher than the NIPA indicate. Mismeasured NIPA items include income from capital invested by government, the effects of inflation and currency changes on foreign assets in the United States and on U.S. assets abroad, income created by unpaid household work, and many employee benefits. He argues if these items were properly measured, the estimate of national saving would be considerably higher. Cf. William D. Nordhaus, "Budget Deficits and National Saving," *Challenge*, March–April 1996, 48.

However Stiglitz argues the amount of U.S. saving may well be overestimated, if the focus is put on productive saving, as it should be. He notes:

> America does not have a problem with the *level* of household savings, but with the form the savings take. Savings are largely in the form of capital gains for housing, which do not allow for a flow of resources into manufacturing production. . . . And it does not resolve the basic problem: how to increase the flow of funds available to be invested in the new machines and new enterprises that would increase the productivity of the economy.

Stiglitz, op. cit., 1007. Cf. J. Bradford DeLong and Lawrence H. Summers, "Equipment Investment and Economic Growth," *Quarterly Journal of Economics*, Vol. CVI, Issue 2 (May 1991): 445–502.

44. The Nobel Laureate James Tobin has emphasized how much lower the American saving

rate has been in recent decades than it has been in other advanced countries, notably Japan, Germany, Italy, and France. Tobin has pointed out it is no accident the productivity growth rate of each of these countries surpassed the U.S. rate. He argues raising the national saving rate is of the utmost importance for increasing productivity and national income. James Tobin, *Full Employment and Growth* (Brookfield: Edward Elgar, 1996), 254–277, esp. 258–265. Many other economists also emphasize the very high correlation among nations' domestic saving rates and their productivity growth rates. Compare Angus Maddison, "Growth and Slowdown in Advanced Capitalist Economies: Techniques of Quantitative Assessment," *Journal of Economic Literature*, Vol. XXV (June 1987): 649–698, 55 and Jeffrey G. Williamson, "Productivity and American Leadership: A Review Article," *Journal of Economic Literature*, Vol. XXIX, No. 1 (March 1991): 51–68. Baumol et al. also show when differences among nations in saving rates persist, the country with the weaker saving rate will over time have a weaker national capacity to produce, lower productivity growth rates, and lower living standards. Studies by Maddison and Lipsey and Kravis also show the accumulation of capital through saving is very highly correlated with productivity growth. They suggest the rapid growth of the Japanese economy in recent decades owed a substantial amount to its uniquely high saving rate, and less to other factors. Baumol et al., op. cit., 163–171, 195–206.

Some observers believe that the real saving rate is higher than official measures, because of large capital gains in stock portfolios in recent years. Yet these gains have reduced the need that owners of equity have to save as much, and that decrease in saving should be subtracted from any gains from portfolio increases. Moreover, a market downturn could wipe out some part of these capital gains, perhaps a large portion of them, which would cut investment. What is most important to note is that increases in the valuation of assets derived from past saving are not new savings. If it is desirable to increase productivity and living standards as much as possible, then the main objective should be to stimulate the rate of new saving as much as possible, and by some accounts that rate is low. Cf. James Schembari, "Midstream: Beyond the Savings Rate," *New York Times*, July 25, 1999; Klaus Friedrich, "The Real American Saving Rate," *New York Times OP-ED*, May 4, 1999; Robert J. Shapiro, "Piggy Banks, Then and Now," *New York Times Op-Ed*, August 19, 1999, A21.

45. James M. Poterba, Steven F. Venti, and David A. Wise, "How Retirement Savings Programs Increase Saving," *Journal of Economic Perspectives*, 10 (Fall 1996), 91–112. See also, James M. Poterba, Steven F. Venti, and David A. Wise, "Targeted Retirement Savings and the Net Worth of Americans," *American Economic Review, 84* (May 1994): 180–85.

46. Cf. Eric M. Engen, William G. Gale, and Ciru E. Uccelo, "The Adequacy of Household Saving," in *Brookings Papers on Economic Activity* 2(1999): 65–166, and especially the comments of other economists on this paper, 166–187.

47. In David L. Laibson, Andrea Repetto, and Jeremy Tobacman, "Self-Control and Saving for Retirement," *Brookings Papers on Economic Activity* 1(1998): 91–172.

48. Martin Browning and AnnaMaria Lusardi, "Household Saving: Micro Theories and Micro Facts," *Journal of Economic Literature*, Vol. XXXIV (December 1996): 1797–1855. The issue of whether an increase in the rate of return on saving would in fact increase saving is contro-

versial and highly technical. See Olivier Jean Blanchard and Stanley Fischer, *Lectures on Macroeconomics* (Cambridge, MA: MIT Press, 1990), 135 ff.

49. B. Douglas Bernheim, "Rethinking Saving Incentives," in Alan J. Auerbach (ed.), *Fiscal Policy: Lessons from Economic Research* (Cambridge, MA: MIT Press, 1997), 260.

50. R. Glenn Hubbard and Jonathan S. Skinner, "Assessing the Effectiveness of Saving Incentives," *Journal of Economic Perspectives*, Vol. 10, No. 4 (Fall 1996): 73–90.

51. Bernheim, op. cit.

52. Ibid. Cf. James M. Poterba, Steven F. Venti, and David A Wise, "How Retirement Saving Programs Increase Saving," in ibid., 91–113. And Eric M. Engen, William G. Gale, and John Karl Scholz, "The Illusory Effects of Saving Incentives on Saving," in ibid., 113–138.

53. John B. Shoven and David A. Wise, "Extending the Consumption-Tax Treatment of Personal Retirement Saving," *American Economic Review, Papers and Proceedings*, Vol. 88, No. 2 (May 1998): 197.

54. James Poterba, Steven F. Venti, and David A. Wise, "401(k) Plans and Future Patterns of Retirement Saving," *American Economic Review, Papers and Proceedings,* Vol. 88, No. 2 (May 1998): 179–184.

55. Steven F. Venti and David A. Wise, "The Cause of Wealth Dispersion at Retirement: Choice or Chance?" *The American Economic Review, Papers and Proceedings*, Vol. 88, No. 2 (May 1998): 191.

56. Sania Siwolop, "When Saving for Retirement Comes with the Job," *New York Times*, May 18, 1997, F4.

57. Cf. Sylvester J. Schieber and John B. Shoven (eds.), *Public Policy Toward Pensions: A Twentieth Century Fund Book* (Cambridge: MIT Press, 1997).

58. Joel Slemrod, "What Do Cross-Country Studies Teach about Government Involvement, Prosperity, and Economic Growth?" *Brookings Papers on Economic Activity* 2(1995): 373–431. He specifies examples of where the existing literature gets entangled in measurement errors, missing variables, and interaction effects, while making dubious causal inferences and being overwhelmed by poor data and conceptual problems.

59. William G. Gale comments on Slemrod in *Brookings Papers on Economic Activity* 2(1995): 416.

60. Steven M. Sheffrin, "Perceptions of Fairness in the Crucible of Tax Policy," in Joel Slemrod (ed.), *Tax Progressivity and Income Inequality* (Cambridge, UK: Cambridge University Press, 1994), 309–334. Joel Slemrod and Jon Bakija, *Taxing Ourselves: A Citizen's Guide to the Great Debate over Tax Reform* (Cambridge, MA: The MIT Press, 1996), 10. Frank Newport and Lydia Saad, "Americans Still Feel They Pay Too Much on April 15th," *The Gallup Poll Monthly* (April) 1993: 18–21.

61. Were taxpayers aware of the extent of the growth in inequality, particularly Wolff's finding that 94 percent of the financial wealth is now held by the top quintile, or, only 6 percent of the wealth is owned by the bottom 80 percent of the wealth distribution, they would be even more determined to deny that the only reasonable policy choice was benefit cuts or tax increases on average voters.

62. Nordhaus, "Budget Deficits and National Saving," op. cit., 45.

63. Ibid., 398. William Easterly and Sergio Rebelo, "Fiscal Policy and Economic Growth: An Empirical Investigation," *Journal of Monetary Economics,* 32(3): 442.

64. David M. Cutler, "Review of John M. Quigley and Eugene Smolensky (eds.), *Modern Public Finance* (Cambridge, MA: Harvard University Press, 1994)," *Journal of Economic Literature,* Vol. XXXIV (June 1996): 778–779. Cf. Peter K.Clark, "Tax Incentives and Equipment Investment," *Brookings Papers on Economic Activity* 1(1993): 317–339. Clark argues tax policy probably does not significantly affect investment. For other views, see Eric Engen and Jonathan Skinner, "Taxation and Economic Growth," in Joel Slemrod (ed.), *Tax Policy in the Real World* (Cambridge, UK and New York: Cambridge University Press, 1999), 305–330; Alan J. Auerbach, "Measuring the Impact of Tax Reform," in Slemrod, op. cit., 285–292; and Kevin A. Hassett and R. Glen Hubbard, "Tax Policy and Investment," in Alan J. Auerbach (ed.), *Fiscal Policy: Lessons from Economic Research* (Cambridge, MA: MIT Press, 1997), 339-375.

Chapter 5: Are Weak Parties Inevitable?

1. Senator Mitch McConnell (R-Kentucky), the chairman of the National Republican Senatorial Committee in the 105th Congress, and the chief foe of campaign reform in the Senate, quoted in "A Choice in the Senate," *Washington Post,* November 29, 1998, C6.

2. Cf. David B. Truman, *The Governmental Process* (New York: A. A. Knopf, 1951) and Robert Dahl, *Dilemmas of Pluralist Democracy* (New Haven: Yale University Press, 1982). See also William E. Connelly (ed.), *The Bias of Pluralism* (New York: Lieber-Atherton, 1973); Theodore J. Lowi, *The End of Liberalism: The Second Republic of the United States,* 2nd ed. (New York: W. W. Norton, 1979); Robert H. Salisbury, "Parties and Pluralism," in Eric M. Uslaner (ed.), *American Political Parties: A Reader* (Itasca, IL: F. E. Peacock Publishers Inc., 1993), 30–54. For a particularly clear summary of the central thesis of the Pluralist paradigm, see Gary W. Cox and Mathew D. McCubbins, *Legislative Leviathan* (Berkeley: University of California Press, 1993), 1–14, regarding how weak parties pay large inefficient transaction costs. Also see Clarence N. Stone, "Group Politics Reexamined: From Pluralism to Political Economy," in Lawrence C. Dodd and Calvin Jillson (eds.), *The Dynamics of American Politics: Approaches and Interpretations* (Boulder: Westview Press, 1994), 277–296.

3. Bruce Cain, John Ferejohn, and Morris Fiorina, *The Personal Vote: Constituency Service and Electoral Independence* (Cambridge: Harvard University Press, 1987).

4. Norman J. Ornstein, Thomas E. Mann, and Michael J. Malbin, *Vital Statistics on Congress, 1997–1998* (Washington, DC: Congressional Quarterly, 1998), 61–62, 72.

5. Morris P. Fiorina, *Congress: Keystone of the Washington Establishment,* 2nd ed. (New Haven: Yale University Press, 1989), 39–47, 85–97.

6. Jackson, *Honest Graft: Big Money and the American Political Process,* op. cit.

7. Dahl, *Dilemmas of Pluralist Democracy,* op. cit.; Cf. Arnold, op. cit., 11, 92–98; Cf. W. John Moore, "Trade Groups' Tirade over New Tax," *National Journal,* February 3, 1999: 418–419.

8. Arthur Maass, *Congress and the Common Good* (New York: Basic Books, 1983), 69.

9. However, the process may lead to waste by distributing resources needed only in some districts to many other districts, which do not merit the benefits. The Model Cities program of the 1960s is often cited as an example.

10. Louis Fisher, *The Politics of Shared Power: Congress and the Executive*, 4th ed. (College Station: Texas A&M University Press), 105.

11. Paul E. Peterson, "The New Politics of Deficits," in John E. Chubb and Paul E. Peterson, *The New Direction in American Politics* (Washington, DC: The Brookings Institution, 1985), 365–398.

12. Carl N. Degler, *Out of Our Past: The Forces That Shaped Modern America* (New York: Harper Colophon Books, 1984), 97–98.

13. Cf. James L. Sundquist, *Dynamics of the Party System: Alignment and Realignment of Political Parties in the United States*, rev. ed. (Washington, DC: The Brookings Institution, 1983).

14. Samuel J. Eldersveld and Hanes Walton Jr., *Political Parties in American Society*, 2nd ed. (Boston: Bedford/St. Martins, 2000), 7–9, 32–35, 323–327.

15. This conclusion follows from inverting Stanley Greenberg's polling results cited above.

16. Strong parties do not require weak interest groups; both can be strong at the same time in a democracy. After campaign reform, interest groups would and should remain powerful in two ways. They would continue to educate and mobilize voters on issues, and they would continue to provide policy-relevant information to congressional committees. Legislators will always be eager to have information supplied by interest groups, because legislators need to anticipate the intense preferences of groups who can swing elections at the margin and because legislators want information provided by interest groups that would help them avoid backlashes arising from unintended consequences of legislating in ignorance. So interest groups will still be powerful after reform.

17. David R. Mayhew, *Divided We Govern* (New Haven: Yale University Press, 1991). Morris Fiorina, *Divided Government*, 2nd ed. (Boston: Allyn and Bacon, 1996).

18. Mayhew, op. cit. accepts a lesser standard by which to judge divided governments. His standard is what newspaper reporters, columnists, and policy experts concluded at the time were significant accomplishments, compared to no accomplishments. He thus implicitly claims that major change is not possible, that widely accepted collective goals simply cannot be achieved. Whence the hence?

19. See chapters seven and eight for a more complete treatment of this evidence.

20. Martin Neil Baily, Gary Burtless, and Robert E. Litan, *Growth with Equity: Economic Policymaking for the Next Century* (Washington, DC: The Brookings Institution, 1993), 1.

21. Pippa Norris (ed.), *Critical Citizens: Global Support for Democratic Governance* (New York: Oxford University Press, 1999), 5–6 ff.

22. See Paul C. Light, *Government's Greatest Achievements of the Past Half Century* (Washington, DC: The Brookings Institution, Center for Public Service, No. 2, November 2000).

23. Michael L. Dertouzos, Richard K. Lester, Robert M. Solow, and the MIT Commission on Industrial Productivity, *Made in America: Regaining the Productive Edge* (Cambridge, MA.: The MIT Press, 1989).

Chapter 6: Nine Party-Unifying Forces

1. (Senator) Dale Bumpers, "How the Sunshine Harmed Congress," *New York Times OP-ED*, January 3, 1999, 9. Senator Bumpers (D-Arkansas) wrote on the occasion of his retirement after 24 years in the Senate.

2. The period 1991 to 1992, during which these interviews were conducted, was the last time Democrats controlled Congress with a Republican in the White House. During this time, it was possible to observe the congressional Democratic majority without having to also understand Clinton's influences on and differences with them. So their own agenda, or lack thereof, was more clearly revealed then than was possible subsequently. The strong agenda put forward by congressional Democrats in the late 1950s during Eisenhower's presidency, which shaped the Kennedy and Johnson presidencies, is interesting to compare with the relatively weak agendas of the pre-Clinton period, as well as with the post-1968 agendas of the congressional Democrats. Cf. James L. Sundquist, *Politics and Policy: The Eisenhower, Kennedy, and Johnson Years* (Washington, DC: The Brookings Institution, 1968).

3. The studies that found these patterns are summarized in William J. Keefe and Morris S. Ogul, *The American Legislative Process*, 9th ed. (Englewood Cliffs, NJ: Prentice Hall, 1997), 104.

4. Ornstein et al., op. cit., 56.

5. Warren E. Miller and J. Merrill Shanks, *The New American Voter* (Cambridge: Harvard University Press, 1996), 117–149.

6. See chapter three.

7. Ornstein et al., op. cit., Table 2–19, 74. Their numbers include leaners. They point out that, though the extent to which local returns have diverged from national returns is greater in recent decades, "the resurgence of party-line voting in recent midterm elections suggests the electorate retains the capacity to respond to national political events in highly partisan ways." See page 50.

8. Gregory L. Giroux, "The Hidden Election: Day of the Mapmaker," *Congressional Quarterly Weekly Report*, Vol. 58, No. 8 (February 19, 2000): 345.

9. Paul S. Herrnson, *Congressional Elections: Campaigning at Home and in Washington* (Washington, DC: CQ Press, 1998), 72–102.

10. *National Journal*, December 1, 1990, No. 48.

11. Karen Foerstel, "Chairmen Worry Changes in Rules Will Erode Power," *ROLL CALL*, Thursday, September 17, 1972, 1; Karen Foerstel, "Chairmen Lose Power in DSG's Reform Plan," *ROLL CALL*, Monday, September 28, 1992, 1; Karen Foerstel, "Anxious over Reform Proposals, Committee Chairmen Meet with Foley, Get Assurances," *ROLL CALL*, Thursday, October 1, 1992, 1; Beth Donovan, "Leaders Set Caucus Docket: Agendas, Accountability," *Congressional Quarterly Weekly Report*, October 10, 1992, 3131.

12. Roger H. Davidson and Walter J. Oleszek, *Congress and Its Members*, 7th ed. (Washington, DC: CQ Press, 2000), 222–223.

13. Steven S. Smith and Eric D. Lawrence, "Party Control of Committees in the Republican Congress," in Lawrence C. Dodd and Bruce I. Oppenheimer, *Congress Reconsidered*, 6th ed. (Washington, DC: CQ Press, 1997), 186–187.

14. Ibid., 183.

15. Ibid.

16. Annenburg Public Policy Center, University of Pennsylvania, "Issue Advocacy Advertising during the 1997–1998 Election Cycle," http:\\www.appcepenn.org.

17. Herrnson, op. cit., passim.

18. Roger H. Davidson, "The New Centralization on Capitol Hill," *Review of Politics*, 10 (1988): 357. Cf. Davidson and Oleszek, op. cit., 163–195.

19. Cf. David W. Brady, Joseph Cooper, and Patricia A. Hurley, "The Decline of Party in the U.S. House of Representatives, 1887–1968," *Legislative Studies Quarterly*, 4, 1979: 381–407. Cf. John J. Coleman, *Party Decline in America: Policy, Politics, and the Fiscalist State* (Princeton: Princeton University Press, 1996), 73–111.

20. Nicol C. Rae, *Southern Democrats* (New York: Oxford University Press, 1994), 152–153.

21. Again, party unity among all House Democrats went down from the mid-1960s, and rose sharply from 1979 through 1996. The same pattern obtains among Senate Democrats across this period. Ornstein et al., op.cit., 211–212. Cf. Nolan M. McCarthy, Keith T. Poole, and Howard Rosenthal, *Income Distribution and the Realignment of American Politics* (Washington, DC: AEI Press, 1997), 9–10, 14–16.

22. James M. Glaser, *Race, Campaign Politics, and the Realignment in the South* (New Haven: Yale University Press, 1996). Cf. Earl Black and Merle Black, *Politics and Society in the South* (Cambridge: Harvard University Press, 1987).

23. Rohde, op. cit., 16.

24. Dodd and Oppenheimer, op. cit., 12.

25. Davidson, op. cit.

26. Barbara Sinclair, *Unorthodox Lawmaking: New Legislative Processes in the U.S. Congress* (Washington, DC: CQ Press, 1997), 84–88.

27. Gary W. Cox and Mathew D. McCubbins, *Legislative Leviathan: Party Government in the House* (Berkeley: University of California Press, 1993), 245–248. Cf. D. Roderick Kiewiet and Mathew D. McCubbins, *The Logic of Delegation: Congressional Parties and the Appropriations Process* (Chicago: University of Chicago Press, 1991); also Keith Krehbiel, *Information and Legislative Organization* (Ann Arbor: University of Michigan Press, 1991), 243. Krehbiel states, "Strong incentives for logrolling undoubtedly existed. However conference procedures seem not to have been effective vehicles for securing gains from trade. . . . Rather, postfloor procedures as a whole seem to come into play quite naturally as constraints on—not opportunities for—distributive excesses by conferees." Barbara Sinclair, *Legislators, Leaders, and Lawmaking: The U.S. House of Representatives in the Postreform Era* (Baltimore: Johns Hopkins University Press, 1998), passim.

28. Forrest Maltzman, *Competing Principals: Committees, Parties, and the Organization of Congress* (Ann Arbor: The University of Michigan Press, 1998). This study may well be the best analysis of the relationships between parties and committees in Congress.

29. Davidson and Oleszek, op. cit., 206–213.

30. Sometimes, though rarely, leaders go so far as to administer punishment to party members. Punishment in the form of taking away a member's committee assignment has been applied for gross disloyalty to the party. Recently, for example, Senator Charles S. Robb (D-Virginia) was

taken off of the Senate Budget Committee, and Congressman Romano L. Mazzoli (D-Kentucky), was removed from a Judiciary subcommittee chairmanship. Both men incurred the party's wrath for voting too often with the other party. Robb's displacement, however, became possible only because the Democrats lost a seat on the committee. Otherwise, he might have escaped sanctions. Mazzoli was disciplined, and he left Congress not long afterward, which he well may have wanted to do anyway. Interview with Congressman Romano L. Mazzoli, summer 1991. Such punishments are a warning to others, and thus have deterrence value even if they are extremely rare. What is not clear is whether such punishments are rare because a few well chosen warnings have a deterrent effect, or are rare because party control over its members is weak. In either case, punishment is far from being the only way parties can influence members' incentives.

31. Davidson and Oleszek, op. cit., 194

32. Thomas E. Mann, *Unsafe at Any Margin: Interpreting Congressional Elections* (Washington, DC: American Enterprise Institute, 1978).

33. Maltzman, op. cit., 24.

34. Jack L. Walker, *Mobilizing Interest Groups in America: Patrons, Professions, and Social Movements* (Ann Arbor: The University of Michigan Press, 1991), 156.

35. Robert H. Salisbury, "Parties and Pluralism," in Eric M. Uslander, *American Political Parties: A Reader* (Itasca, IL: F. E. Peacock Publishers, 1993), 30–54, esp. 47–48. Robert L. Nelson, John P. Heinz, Edward O. Laumann, and Robert H. Salisbury, "Inner Circles or Hollow Cores? Elite Networks in National Policy Systems," *Journal of Politics*, 52 (May 1990): 356–390. Compare Jerrold E. Schneider, *Ideological Coalitions in Congress* (Westport, CT: Greenwood Press, 1979).

36. Some of the literature treats ideology as a belief system of individual legislators and others. It is more useful to employ the concept as a coalition relationship among legislators, which may be driven by a member's ideas, by the demands of constituents, or both. See Aage Clausen, *How Congressmen Decide: A Policy Focus* (New York: St. Martin's Press, 1973); Jerrold E. Schneider, *Ideological Coalitions in Congress* (Westport, CT: Greenwood Press, 1979); Keith T. Poole and Howard Rosenthal, *Congress: A Political-Economic History of Roll Call Voting* (New York: Oxford University Press, 1997); Kenneth Koford, "Dimensions in Congressional Voting," *American Political Science Review*, 83 (1989): 949–962; Kenneth Koford, "On Dimensionalizing Roll Call Votes in the U.S. Congress, "*American Political Science Review*, 85 (1991): 955–975; Kenneth Koford, "What We Can Learn about Congressional Politics from Dimensional Studies of Roll Call Voting?" *Economics and Politics*, 6 (1994): 173–186.

37. David R. Mayhew, *Congress: The Electoral Connection* (New Haven: Yale University Press, 1974). Such uncommitted and entrepreneurial representatives are presumably loyal to almost no one. But if reducing the transaction costs of building support at all levels is crucial for politicians, then loyalty and ideology have cash value as coordinating mechanisms.

38. For several decades, the most influential empirical bulwark for the ever-shifting coalitions model was Clausen's "policy dimensional" model, which purported to prove empirically the structure of congressional coalitions shifts with the policy content. The 2000 Nobel Laureate in Economics James Heckman and James Snyder, who share Clausen's doubts about the competing

partisan/ideological model, state the principal objection to Clausen's "policy dimensional" model as follows:

> Rather, like Poole and Rosenthal (1991a) we find that [congressional] voting across several of these policy areas is so highly correlated—for example government management of the economy and social welfare policy—that it is not clear what is gained by treating them as distinct policy dimensions.

In other words, this evidence actually supports an ideological or unidimensional model because the correlations among supposedly plural dimensions are actually quite high.

Yet, Heckman and Snyder have reasons of their own for supporting a multidimensional model, and they compare their view with the views of Schneider and Poole and Rosenthal. However they note, "Our evidence challenges the unidimensional view [ideological model], *which has gained wide acceptance among congressional scholars* . . . [italics added]." James J. Heckman and James Snyder, "A Latent Linear Factor Model of Voting," prepared for the Quandtfest, Princeton University, May 17, 1995, 31, 35. See their "Linear Probability Models of the Demand for Attributes with an Empirical Application to Estimating the Preferences of Legislators," *The RAND Journal of Economics*, Vol. 28, No. 0 (Special Issue 1997): S142–S189.

39. Poole and Rosenthal, op. cit., 74.

40. A variety of studies show some coalitions form along some minor dimensions, which explain only very little of the variance in coalition structure, and whose theoretical significance is quite small to non-existent.

41. Steven D. Levitt, "How Do Senators Vote? Disentangling the Role of Voter Preferences, Party Affiliation, and Senator Ideology," *American Economic Review*, Vol. 86, No. 3 (June 1996): 425–441.

42. Jeffrey Levine, Edward G. Carmines, and Robert Huckfelt, "The Rise of Ideology in the Post-New Deal Party System, 1972–1992," *American Politics Quarterly*, Vol 25, No. 1 (January 1997): 19–34.

43. Cf. David King, "The Polarization of American Parties and Mistrust of Government," in Joseph Nye, Philip Zelikow, and David King, *Why People Don't Trust Government* (Cambridge: Harvard University Press, 1997), 172.

44. Michael Barone and Grant Ujifusa, *The Almanac of American Politics: 1998* (Washington, DC: National Journal/Times Mirror, 1997).

45. Similarly, a strong Democratic Party in Congress could be a conservative DLC-centered party, or it could be a more progressive party. The difference would have large implications. Cf. Jon F. Hale, "The Making of the New Democrats (Democratic Leadership Council)," *Political Science Quarterly*, Vol. 110, No. 2 (Summer 1995): 207–226.

46. Because of the above cited "wide acceptance" of the partisan/ideological model, and because of arguments presented here, I will proceed here on the assumption that coalitions in Congress are predominately partisan/ideological coalitions, at least until the two viewpoints and associated methodologies are more closely compared than they have been so far.

47. Cf. R. H. Coase, *The Firm, the Market, and the Law* (Chicago: University of Chicago Press, 1990), 174–179. Cf. Avinash K. Dixit, *The Making of Economic Policy: A Transaction-Cost Politics Perspective* (Cambridge, MA: The MIT Press, 1998), 31ff.

48. Cox and McCubbins, op. cit.; Glenn R. Carroll and David J. Terce (eds.), *Firms, Markets, and Hierarchies: The Transaction Cost Economic Perspective* (New York: Oxford University Press, 1999).

49. Gary W. Cox and Mathew D. McCubbins, "Bonding, Structure, and the Stability of Political Parties," in Kenneth A. Shepsle and Barry R. Weingast, *Positive Theories of Congressional Institutions* (Ann Arbor: University of Michigan Press, 1995), 103, 113.

50. Joseph A. Pechman (ed.), *Economics for Policymaking: Selected Essays of Arthur M. Okun* (Cambridge, MA: The MIT Press, 1983). For Okun's discussion of auction markets, customer markets, and implicit contracts, see pages 85–90, 106–107, 110–111, 120–130, and 139–141.

51. B. Douglas Bernheim and Michael D. Whinston, "Incomplete Contracts and Strategic Ambiguity," *American Economic Review*, Vol. 88, No. 4 (September 1998): 902–932.

52. Cf. The "Party Vote Model," in Jacobs and Shapiro, op. cit., 3–26.

53. Jeffrey M. Stonecash and Nicole R. Lindstrom, "Emerging Party Cleavages in the House of Representatives, 1962–1996," *American Politics Quarterly*, Vol. 27, No. 1 (January 1999): 58–88.

54. K. L. Schlozman and Sidney Verba, *Insult to Injury: Unemployment, Class, and Political Response* (Cambridge: Harvard University Press, 1979), 1.

55. Warren E. Miller and J. Merrill Shanks, *The New American Voter* (Cambridge: Harvard University Press, 1996), 532.

56. Cf. "John P. Holdren on Climate Change: Harvard Professor Urges Action on 'the Most Intractable Environmental Problem That Civilization Faces,'" http://www/preen.org/97sep23d.htm. But see the various studies of William Nordhaus in the *American Economic Review* and elsewhere.

57. Mancur Olson, *The Logic of Collective Action: Public Goods and the Theory of Groups* (Cambridge: Harvard University Press, 1965).

58. I am indebted to Ed Lorenzen of Congressman's Charles W. Stenholm's office for information about the Blue Dogs.

59. Nicol C. Rae, *Southern Democrats* (New York: Oxford University Press, 1994), viii.

60. Ibid., 75.

61. Ibid., 77–79. These findings were confirmed in the author's interviews.

62. Cf. Geoff Earle, "Conservative Southern Democrats Seek House Seats—and Credibility: Party Hopes to Regain Voters' Loyalty by Running Candidates with More Traditional Views on Social Issues in Key Districts," *Congressional Quarterly Weekly Report*, Vol. 56, No. 41, 2813–2815. Cf. Jon F. Hale, "The Making of the New Democrats," *Political Science Quarterly*, Vol. 110, No. 2 (Summer 1995): 207–226.

63. Some have argued Clinton was more progressive as a campaigner than he was as a legislative actor or regulator.

64. Cf. Stanley B. Greenberg, *Middle-Class Dreams: The Politics and Power of the New American Majority* (New Haven: Yale University Press, 1996) and his "The Popular Mandate of 1996," post-election national survey for the Campaign for America's Future (Washington, DC: Green-

berg Research, November 12, 1996). Byron E. Shafer and William J. M. Claggett, *The Two Majorities: The Issue Context of Modern American Politics* (Baltimore: The Johns Hopkins University Press, 1995). Cf. Ira Katznelson, "Reversing Southern Republicanism," in Stanley B. Greenberg and Theda Skocpol (eds.), *The New Majority: Toward a Popular Progressive Politics* (New Haven: Yale University Press, 1997), 238–263.

Chapter 7: Are the Democrats Big Spenders or Big Investors? Inequity and Productivity

1. Kirsten J. Forbes, "A Reassessment of the Relationship between Inequality and Growth," *The American Economic Review*, Vol. 90, No. 4 (September 2000): 869–887. Forbes establishes that better-quality public education is negatively correlated with inequality and positively related to growth. See page 885. She also demonstrates that higher levels of corruption tend to be positively related to inequality and negatively related to growth. Money that goes to corrupt interests is money unavailable for investment. These findings strongly support the thesis of this study.

2. Cf. Martin Neil Baily, Gary Burtless, and Robert E. Litan, *Growth with Equity: Economic Policymaking for the Next Century* (Washington, DC: The Brookings Institution, 1993), 1.

3. Ibid., 4.

4. Baumol et al., *Productivity and American Leadership: The Long View*, op. cit.

5. These figures represent after-tax income after adjusting for inflation. From the *Economic Report of the President, Transmitted to the Congress, February 1999, Together with the Annual Report of the Council of Economic Advisors* (Washington, DC: United States Government Printing Office, 1999), Table B-31, Total and per capita disposable personal income and personal consumption expenditures in current and real dollars, 1959–1998, 363. This was a period of unusually strong productivity growth, following depressed utilization of innovation and a build up of savings during the Depression and World War II.

6. Baily et al., op. cit., 24.

7. Cf. Joseph E. Stiglitz, *The Economics of the Public Sector, 3rd ed.* (New York: W. W. Norton, 2000).

8. Surprisingly the U.S. government lacks a human capital budget, indeed lacks a capital budget of any kind. Yet every corporation, every state government, and most foreign governments have a capital budget.

9. Chinhui Juhn, Kevin M. Murphy, and Brooks Pierce, "Wage Inequality and the Rise in the Returns to Skill," *Journal of Political Economy*, Vol 101, No. 3 (June 1993): 410–442, esp. 411.

10. Lawrence Mishel and Jared Bernstein, *The State of Working America, 1998–99* (Washington, DC Economic Policy Institute, 1999), Table 2.3, 95.

11. Frank Levy, *The New Dollars and Dreams: American Incomes and Economic Change* (New York: Russell Sage, 1998), Table 4.3, 72. Levy and Mishel show that including the value of fringe benefits, such as health and pension benefits, makes very little difference to the overall trends. Frank Levy and Richard C. Mishel, *The Economic Future of American Families: Income and Wealth Trends* (Washington, DC: The Urban Institute, 1991), 7. Bosworth and Perry show employer payments for health insurance have been rising for several decades, but were offset by a decline in

employer contributions to private pensions. Cf. Barry Bosworth and George L. Perry, "Productivity and Real Wages: Is There a Puzzle?" *Brookings Papers on Economic Activity*, 1994: 317–335, esp. 324: "Overall, fringe benefits increased from 8 percent of total compensation in 1960, to 16 percent in 1979, to 17 percent in 1993." Mishel and Bernstein show declines in both health and pension benefits of about seven percent for all workers between 1979 and 1989. Mishel and Bernstein, op. cit., 143.

12. James Heckman, "A Response to Richard Freeman's 'Solving the New Inequality,'" *Boston Review*, December–January 1996–97.

13. Levy, op. cit., 188–189.

14. Ibid., 16; Mishel and Bernstein, op. cit., 120–125.

15. Martin Neil Baily, Gary Burtless, and Robert E. Litan, *Growth with Equity: Economic Policymaking for the Next Century* (Washington, DC: The Brookings Institution, 1993), 67–68.

16. Levy and Mishel, op. cit., 12, 91–98; Mishel and Bernstein, op. cit., 111.

17. Levy, op. cit., 15. Cf. James K. Galbraith, *Created Unequal: The Crisis in American Pay*, (New York: Free Press, 1998), 23–36.

18. Lynn A. Karoly, "Anatomy of the US Income Distribution: Two Decades of Change," *Oxford Review of Economic Policy*, Vol. 12, No. 1 (Spring 1996): 92. Additional factors that may cause increased inequality include: (1) faster growth in capital income that goes primarily to the wealthy relative to earned income; (2) slightly reduced progressivity in federal taxation in recent decades; and (3) cutbacks in transfers to the poor from state and federal governments. The impact of these three factors on overall changes in income inequality is not known. Changes in tax policies in the 1980s do not account for most of the growth in inequality.

19. Peter Gottschalk and Timothy Smeeding, "Cross-National Comparisons of Earnings and Income Inequality," *Journal of Economic Literature*, XXXV (June 1997): 633–687, esp. 646–651. See the comments of Nobel Laureate Robert M. Solow and others in Janet L. Norwood (ed.), *Widening Earning Inequality: Why and Why Now?* (Washington, DC: The Urban Institute, 1994). Gary Burtless, "Interview: Why Wages Aren't Growing," *Challenge*, November–December 1995: 4–11.

20. See Levy, *The New Dollars and Dreams*, op. cit., 189.

21. Paul Krugman, *Peddling Prosperity: Economic Sense and Nonsense in the Age of Diminished Expectations* (New York: W. W. Norton, 1994), 146–148.

22. Steven Husted and Michael Melvin, *International Economics, 3rd ed.* (New York: Harper Collins College Publishers, 1995), 106.

23. Baily et al., op. cit., 51.

24. Ibid., 83. Blank has established that trends in family size are comparatively unimportant in accounting for higher inequality in the 1980s, but they were more important in the 1960s and 1970s. Rebecca Blank, "Why Are Poverty Rates So High in the 1980s?" in Dimitri B. Papadimitriou and Edward N. Wolff (eds.), *Poverty and Prosperity in the USA in the Late Twentieth Century* (New York: St. Martin's Press, 1993).

25. Karoly, "Anatomy of the US Income Distribution," op. cit., 91. Frank Levy and Richard J. Murname, "U.S. Earnings Levels and Earnings Inequality: A Review of Recent Trends and Proposed Explanations," *Journal of Economic Literature*, Vol. XXX, No. 3 (Sept. 1992): 1333–1381.

26. Lynn A. Karoly and Gary Burtless, "Demographic Change, Rising Earnings Inequality, and the Distribution of Personal Well-Being, 1959–1989," *Demography*, Vol. 32, No. 3 (August 1995): 379–405.

27. Ibid., 92. Consider total annual pre-tax money income divided by the official poverty line, or the adjusted family income (AFI). In 1973, the median individual in the highest educational group had 2.5 times the AFI as individuals in the lowest group. By 1993, this ratio had risen to over 4. Lynn A. Karoly, "The Trend in Inequality among Families, Individuals, and Workers in the United States: A Twenty-Five Year Perspective," in Sheldon Danziger and Peter Gottschalk (eds.), *Uneven Tides: Rising Inequality in America* (New York: Russell Sage Foundation, 1993), 29–37.

28. Lawrence Mishel, Jared Bernstein, and John Schmitt, *The State of Working America: 1996–97* (Washington, DC: Economic Policy Institute, 1996), 278. Individuals can fall back on borrowing against assets, if they have any, and can borrow against income. Yet any such loans would be as small as the income and wealth that could serve as collateral.

29. Financial wealth is defined as net worth minus net equity in owner occupied housing. Net worth is defined as "the current value of all marketable or fungible assets . . . less the current value of debts. Total assets are defined as the sum of: (1) the gross value of owner-occupied housing; (2) other real estate owned by the household; (3) cash and demand deposits; (4) time and savings deposits, certificates of deposit, and money market accounts; (5) government bonds, corporate bonds, and foreign bonds; (6) the cash surrender value of life insurance plans; (7) the cash surrender value of pension plans, including IRAs and Keogh plans; (8) corporate stock, including mutual funds; (9) net equity in unincorporated businesses; (10) equity in trust funds. Edward N. Wolff, *Top Heavy: A Study of the Increasing Inequality of Wealth in America, A Twentieth Century Fund Report* (New York: The Twentieth Century Fund Press, 1995), 59–60.

30. Ibid., 11. Compare Edward N. Wolff, "Trends in Household Wealth in the United States, 1962–83 and 1983–89," *Review of Income and Wealth*, Ser. 40, No. 2 (June 1994): 143–174. The share of wealth held by the top 1 percent increased over 5 percent from 1983, a gain just short of being equal to the total holdings of the bottom 80 percent.

31. Wolff, op. cit., 21.

32. Richard B. Freeman and Lawrence F. Katz (eds.), *Differences and Changes in Wage Structures* (Chicago: University of Chicago Press, 1995), 4.

33. Francine D. Blau and Lawrence M. Kahn, "International Differences in Male Wage Inequality: Institutions versus Market Forces," *Journal of Political Economy*, Vol. 104, No. 4 (August 1996): 791–837, esp. 794, 830.

34. Lawrence Mishel, Jared Bernstein, and John Schmitt, *The State of Working America, 1998–99* (Ithaca: ILR Press/Cornell University Press, 1999), 56–57.

35. Timothy Smeeding, "America's Income Inequality: Where Do We Stand," *Challenge*, September–October 1996, 45–53.

36. Cf. Clair Brown, *American Standards of Living, 1918–1988* (Cambridge, MA: Blackwell, 1994), 18.

37. Bruce P. Kennedy, Ichiro Kawachi, and Deborah Prothrow-Stith, "Income Distribution and Mortality: Cross Sectional Ecological Study of the Robin Hood Index in the United States," *British Medical Journal*, Vol. 312, 20 (April 1996): 1004–1007. Cf. Norman Daniels, Bruce

Kennedy, and Ichiro Kawachi, "New Democracy Forum: Justice Is Good for Our Health," and comments by other commentators, *Boston Review: 25th Anniversary Issue*, Vol. 25, No. 1 (February/March 2000): 4–52.

38. Kennedy, Kawachi, and Prothrow-Stith, ibid.

39. R. G. Wilkinson, *Unhealthy Societies: The Afflictions of Inequality* (London: Routledge, 1996); George A. Kaplan, Elsie R. Pamuk, John W. Lynch, Richard D. Cohen, and Jennifer L. Balfour, "Inequality in Income and Mortality in the United States: An Analysis of Mortality and Potential Pathways," *British Medical Journal*, Vol. 312, 20 (April 1996): 999–1003.

40. Kaplan et al., Ibid.

41. See references in the Kennedy and Kaplan studies cited above.

42. Robert M. Solow, "Should We Pay the Debt," *New York Review of Books*, Vol. XLVII, No. 15 (October 5, 2000): 8.

43. Ibid.

44. John H. Bishop, "Incentives to Study and the Organization of Secondary Instruction," in William E. Becker, and William J. Baumol (eds.), *Assessing Educational Practices: The Contribution of Economics* (Cambridge, MA: The MIT Press, 1996), 149–151. The increased cost nationally would be $34.4 billion for primary and secondary public schools, roughly three-fifths of the increase in spending that occurred between 1986 and 1991. An offset would come from reduced child care costs of working mothers, estimated at $8.45 billion.

45. F. M. Scherer, *New Perspectives on Economic Growth and Technological Innovation* (Washington, DC: The Brookings Institution, 1998), 1–2.

46. William J. Baumol, Sue Anne Batey Blackman, and Edward N. Wolff, *Productivity and American Leadership: The Long View* (Cambridge, MA: The MIT Press, 1989), 10–13, 52–56.

47. U.S. Department of Commerce, *Statistical Abstract of the United States, 1998* (U.S. Government Printing Office, 1998), Table 130, 95.

48. Baumol et al., op. cit., 52.

49. Baily et al., op. cit., 24. Since 1993, when this was written, and especially since 1995, the productivity numbers appear to have increased substantially. From the rate of growth in productivity evident between 1996 and 1999, something around two percent, it might appear the shortfall has disappeared, and that government policies to accelerate productivity are less needed and may be less able to make a difference. These issues are discussed below.

50. Ibid., 21.

51. Baumol et al., op. cit., 3; Krugman, op. cit., 274–277.

52. "Britain: The British Disease Revisited," *The Economist*, October 31, 1998, 61–62; "A British Miracle?" *The Economist*, March 25, 2000, 31–37; Bernard Elbaum and William Lazonick, "The Decline of the British Economy: An Institutional Perspective," *Journal of Economic History*, June 1984, 567–583. Richard E. Caves, "Productivity Differences among Industries," in Richard E. Caves and Lawrence B. Krause, *Britain's Economic Performance* (Washington, DC: The Brookings Institution, 1980).

53. Baumol et al., op. cit., 18–19. Angus Maddison, "Growth and Slowdown in Advanced Capitalist Economies: Techniques of Quantitative Assessment," *Journal of Economic Literature*, Vol. XXV (June 1987): 649–698.

54. Ibid., 649.

55. Baumol et al., op. cit., 69–71.

56. Robert J. Gordon, "Problems in the Measurement and Performance of Service-Sector Productivity in the United States," NBER Working Paper 4419, 1996, 4; Baumol et al., op. cit., 68–83. A particularly clear and authoritative discussion of the mismeasurement of productivity growth is found in *The Economic Report of the President* (Washington, DC: U.S. Government Printing Office, 1995), 108–116.

57. Compare *The Economic Report of the President* (Washington, DC: U.S. Government Printing Office, 1996), 48, 59. The revision of the government's National Income and Product Accounts, in particular the switch from a fixed to a chain weighted measurement of price changes, led to these results.

58. *The Economic Report of the President* (Washington DC: US Government Printing Office 2000), Table B–48, *Changes in productivity and related data, business sector, 1960–99,* 363.

59. "How Real Is the New Economy?" *The Economist,* July 24, 1999, 17–24. Robert J. Gordon, "Has the 'New Economy' Rendered the Productivity Slowdown Obsolete?" http://faculty-web.at.nwu.edu/economics/gordon. Cf. Gordon, "U.S. Economic Growth Since 1870: One Big Wave?" *The American Economic Review, Papers and Proceedings,* Vol. 89, No. 2 (May 1999), 123–132. Steve Lohr, "Computer Age Gains Respect of Economists," *New York Times,* April 14, 1999, A1.

60. Robert J. Gordon, "U.S. Economic Growth since 1870: One Big Wave," cit. 123–128, esp. 128.

61. Louis Uchitelle, "At the Desk, Off the Clock, and Below Statistical Radar," *New York Times,* July 18, 1999, BU 4.

62. The reason increased investment only temporarily leads to a higher rate of growth before leveling off at a new higher level is as follows: A larger capital stock depreciates (wears out or becomes obsolete) more than the older smaller capital stock. So, larger amounts of future investment are required to replace that larger stock, until depreciation rises to the point where it fully absorbs the higher investment. The higher investment rate at that point settles down to equal what the rate was before. There are diminishing returns to additional capital when other inputs, specifically technical change and labor supply, do not increase at the same rate and are exogenously determined by forces outside the control of government policy.

63. *The Economic Report of the President,* 1995, op. cit. 126–127.

64. *The Economic Report of the President,* 2000, op. cit. Table B–1, 306 Figure is for 1999, IV.

65. This assumes no major increase in savings going from the United States abroad. Schultze puts the percent of new savings from a higher saving rate that is likely to go abroad at 40 percent. Charles L. Schultze, "Is Faster Growth the Cure for Budget Deficits?" in Robert D. Reischauer (ed.), *Setting National Priorities: Budget Choices for the Next Century* (Washington, DC: Brookings Institution Press, 1997), 60.

66. Cf. Paul Romer, Gene Grossman, Elhanan Helpman, Robert M. Solow, and Howard Pack, "Symposium on New Growth Theory," *Journal of Economic Perspectives,* Vol. 8, No. 1 (Winter 1994): 3–112.

67. Schultze, op. cit., 60–61.

68. Ibid., 61.
69. Ibid., 53.

Chapter 8: Public Sector Investment

1. Herbert Kitschelt, Peter Lange, Gary Marks, and John D. Stephens (eds.), *Continuity and Change in Contemporary Capitalism* (Cambridge, UK: Cambridge University Press, 1999), 6–7.

2. The argument of this chapter requires that public sector investments be efficient, which they often are not. But it is assumed here (1) public investments would be much more efficient than at present if effective campaign finance reform removed the incentive of members of Congress to pass out pork to contributors; (2) contributor waste is much greater than the kinds of constituency waste that would survive enactment of campaign reform (see the argument at the beginning of chapter two); and (3) a third reason why post-reform public investments would be more efficient is that a post-reform Congress could be expected to alter the legislative process somewhat so as to support collective goals at the expense of narrow interest group goals.

3. The appropriability problem is discussed in F. M. Scherer, *New Perspectives on Economic Growth and Technological Innovation* (Washington, DC: The Brookings Institution Press, 1999), 54 ff. Edwin Mansfield, "Microeconomics of Technological Innovation," in Ralph Landau and Nathan Rosenberg (eds.), *The Positive Sum Strategy: Harnessing Technology for Economic Growth* (Washington, DC: National Academy Press, 1986), 307–325. Edwin Mansfield, John Rapoport, Anthony Romeo, Samuel Wagner, and George Beardsley, "Social and Private Rates of Return from Industrial Innovations," in Edwin Mansfield and Elizabeth Mansfield (eds.), *The Economics of Technical Change* (Brookfield, VT: Edward Elgar, 1993), 80–99.

4. Martin Neil Baily, Gary Burtless, and Robert E. Litan, *Growth with Equity: Economic Policymaking for the Next Century* (Washington, DC: The Brookings Institution, 1993), 204.

5. Michael L. Dertouzos, Richard K. Lester, Robert M. Solow, and the MIT Commission on Industrial Productivity, *Made in America: Regaining the Productive Edge* (Cambridge, MA: The MIT Press, 1989), 81. The commission brought together a large team of experts from among the MIT faculty, and was supported by a staff of 30. Participants were drawn from many different disciplines in MIT departments, including engineering, sciences, social sciences, and business. Working as interdisciplinary teams, they studied particular manufacturing industries, as well as government and education. They visited firms on three continents, and interviewed business and labor leaders. Their findings therefore have unusual authority. Cf. Lester Thurow, *Head to Head: The Coming Economic Battle among Japan, Europe, and America* (New York: William Morrow and Company, Inc., 1992). Since these books were written, Japanese economic problems have loomed larger, particularly in the Japanese banking industry. Some critics have been eager to take reassurance from the weaknesses of the Japanese and Europeans. But in failing to come to grip with sub par U.S. investments in human capital and other public investments other advanced nations have made, these critics fail to acknowledge suboptimal U.S. productivity performance. If and when the Japanese and Europeans resolve their current problems, American patterns of underinvestment may become more of a relative disadvantage as well as the absolute disadvantage they are now. Cf. Richard K. Lester, *The Productive Edge* (Cambridge, MA: The MIT Press, 1998).

6. *The Economic Report of the President,* February 1996 (Washington: United States Government Printing Office, 1996), 195.

7. Gary Burtless (ed.), *Does Money Matter? The Effect of School Resources on Student Achievement and Adult Successes* (Washington: DC: The Brookings Institution, 1996), 4.

8. Richard R. Nelson and Gavin Wright, "The Rise and Fall of American Technological Leadership," *Journal of Economic Literature,* Vol. XXX, No. 4 (December 1992): 1961–1962.

9. Robert Eisner, *The Misunderstood Economy: What Counts and How to Count It* (Boston: Harvard Business School Press, 1995), 66.

10. Symposium on Primary and Secondary Education, *Journal of Economic Perspectives,* Vol. 10, No. 4 (Fall 1996): 3–72. Contributions by Francine D. Blau, Eric Hanushek, David Card and Alan B. Krueger, and Carolyn Minter Hoxby.

11. OECD Education Data 96, OECD, Paris, 1996, 52–53.

12. Eric A. Hanushek, "School Resources and Student Performance," in Burtless, op. cit., 68–69.

13. John H. Bishop, "Incentives to Study and the Organization of Secondary Instruction," in William E. Becker and Willam J. Baumol (eds.), *Assessing Educational Practices: The Contribution of Economics* (Cambridge, MA: The MIT Press, 1996), 112–113.

14. Richard Rothstein, with Karen Hawley Miles, "Where's the Money Gone?" (Washington, DC: Economic Policy Institute 1999 [http://epn.org/epi/epwtmg.html]).

15. Frederich Flyer and Sherwin Rosen, "Some Economies of Precollege Teaching," in Becker and Baumol, op. cit., 39.

16. Larry V. Hedges and Rob Greenwald, "Have Times Changed? The Relation between School Resources and Student Performance," in Burtless, op. cit., 90.

17. Julian R. Betts, "Is There a Link between School Inputs and Earnings? Fresh Scrutiny of An Old Literature," in Burtless, op. cit., 178.

18. John H. Bishop, "Incentives to Study and the Organization of Secondary Instruction," in Becker and Baumol, op. cit., 149–151.

19. This and what follows comes from Bishop, op. cit., 114–118.

20. Ibid., 117.

21. Ibid.

22. Ibid., 104.

23. Richard J. Murnane and Frank Levy, *Teaching the New Basic Skills: Principles for Educating Children to Thrive in a Changing Economy* (New York: Martin Kessler Books/The Free Press, 1996), 9, 32.

24. Dertouzos, op. cit., 87–93.

25. Remarks of Alan Blinder in *President Clinton's New Beginning, Conducted by President Bill Clinton, The Complete Text, With Illustrations, of the Historic Clinton-Gore Economic Conference. Little Rock, Arkansas, December 14–15, 1992* (New York: Donald I. Fine, 1992), 27.

26. Baily et al., op. cit., 129

27. Dertouzos, op. cit.

28. Baily et al., op. cit., 110–111.

29. James J. Hechman, "What Should Be Our Human Capital Investment Policy?" in Garth

Magnum and Stephen Magnum (eds.), *Of Heart and Mind: Social Policy Essays in Honor of Sar A. Levitan* (Kalamazoo, MI: W. E. Upjohn Institute for Employment Research, 1996), 337.

30. See Gary S. Becker, *Human Capital: A Theoretical and Empirical Analysis, with Special Reference to Education*, 2nd ed. (Chicago: University of Chicago Press, 1975), 16–44.

31. Baily et al., op. cit., 132.

32. Bishop, op. cit., 129.

33. Ibid., 12.

34. Ibid., 63, 65.

35. Norton Grubb and Lorraine McDonnell, "Local Systems of Work Related Education and Training: Diversity Interdependence and Questions of Effectiveness," The RAND Corporation, October 1990. Cited in Rosemary Batt and Paul Osterman, *A National Policy for Workplace Training: Lessons from State and Local Experiments* (Washington, DC: Economic Policy Institute, 1993), 59.

36. Bishop, op. cit., 65.

37. Rochelle L. Stanfield, "Hire Learning," *National Journal*, May 1, 1993, 1042–1047. William Schneider, "Whatever Happened to Clintonomics," *National Journal*, June 16, 1993, 1680. Cf. *President Clinton's New Beginning*, op. cit.

38. Dertouzos, op. cit., 87–93.

39. Baily et al., op. cit., 204.

40. Murnane and Levy, op. cit., 3.

41. Rendigs Fels, "Making U.S. Schools Competitive," in Becker and Baumol, op. cit., 58.

42. Charles I. Jones, *Introduction to Economic Growth* (New York: W. W. Norton, 1998), 71–114.

43. Edwin Mansfield, "Microeconomics of Technological Innovation," in Ralph Landau and Nathan Rosenberg, (eds.), *The Positive Sum Strategy: Harnessing Technology for Economic Growth* op cit., 307–325. Edwin Mansfield, John Rapoport, Anthony Romeo, Samuel Wagner, and George Beardsley, "Social and Private Rates of Return from Industrial Innovations," in Mansfield and Mansfield *The Economics of Technical Change*, op. cit., 80–99.

44. Francis Nairn, Kimberly S. Hamilton, and Dominic Olivastro, CHI Research Inc. "The Increasing Linkage between U.S. Technology and Public Science," March 17, 1997. Submitted to *Research Policy*. See Nairn's book by the same title, published by CHI Research Inc., Haddon Heights, New Jersey, 1997.

45. Baily et al., op. cit., 82–89.

46. Ibid., 91–109.

47. Ibid., 89–91.

48. Linda R. Cohen and Roger G. Noll, *The Technology Pork Barrel* (Washington, DC: The Brookings Institution, 1991).

49. Baily et al., op. cit., 78, 81–84.

50. Catharine J. Morrison and Amy Ellen Schwartz, "State Infrastructure and Productive Performance," *American Economic Review*, Vol. 86, No. 5 (December 1996): 1095–1111.

51. Edward M. Gramlich, "Infrastructure Investment: A Review Essay," *Journal of Economic Literature*, XXII (September 1995), 1176–1196.

52. Ibid., 1177–1179.

53. Clifford Winston and Barry Bosworth, *Public Infrastructure* (Washington, DC: The Brookings Institution, 1992), 267–294.

54. Marilyn Werber Serafini, "Medicaid's Problem with Children," *National Journal*, Vol. 31, No. 36 (September 4, 1999): 2498–2499.

55. Ibid.

56. Uwe Reinhardt, "Reforming the Health Care System: The Universal Dilemma," in Gail E. Henderson, Nancy M. P. King, and others, *The Social Medicine Reader* (Durham: Duke University Press, 1997), 453. Linda J. Blumberg and David W. Liska, "The Uninsured in the United States: A Status Report," The Urban Institute, April 1996, http://www.urban.org/pubs/HINSURE/uninsure.htm.

57. Deborah J. Chollet, "Redefining Private Insurance in Changing Market Structure," in Stuart H. Altman and Uwe E. Reinhardt (eds.), *Strategic Choices for a Changing Health Care System* (Chicago: Health Administration Press, 1996), 37.

58. OECD Health Data 96, OECD, Paris, 1996.

59. Chollet, op. cit., 22.

60. While productivity growth is not a sufficient condition of raising living standards for all, it is a necessary condition, redistributionist policies aside. Most hopes for higher wages depend on productivity growth. If the rate of growth in productivity is poor, then there is that much less of a pie to divide up. Whether the gains from productivity gains get divided one way rather than another depends in part on political decisions.

61. Robert M. Solow, "Can a 'Third Way' Work? Five Responses to 'Equity with Employment,'" *Boston Review*, Vol. II, No. 3–4 (Summer 1997): 9.

62. John Karl Scholz, "In-Work Benefits in the United States: The Earned Income Tax Credit," *Economic Journal*, 106 (434) (January 1996): 156–169.

63. Edmund S. Phelps, *Rewarding Work* (Cambridge: Harvard University Press, 1997), esp. 132–134.

64. Robert H. Haveman, "Equity with Employment," *Boston Review*, Vol. XXXII, No. 3–4 (Summer 1997): 3–8.

65. David Card and Alan B. Krueger, *Myth and Measurement: The New Economics of the Minimum Wage* (Princeton: Princeton University Press, 1995). David Neumark and William L. Wascher, "The Effects of Minimum Wages on Teenage Employment and Enrollment: Evidence from Matched CPS Surveys," *National Bureau of Economic Research*, Working Paper 5092 (April 1995). Richard V. Burkhauser, Kenneth A. Couch, and David C. Wittenburg, "'Who Gets What' from Minimum Wage Hikes: A Reestimation of Card and Krueger's Distributional Analysis in Myth and Measurement: The New Economics of the Minimum Wage," *Industrial and Labor Relations Review*, 49 (3) (April 1996): 547–552. Richard B. Freeman, "The Minimum Wage as a Redistributive Tool," *Economic Journal*, 106 (436) (May 1996): 639–649. Gary Burtless, "Minimum Wages in the US," *New Economy*, 2 (4) (Winter 1995): 204–209.

66. Richard B. Freeman, "How Much Has De-unionization Contributed to the Rise in Male Earnings Inequality?" in Sheldon Danziger and Peter Gottschalk (eds.), *Uneven Tides: Rising Inequality in America* (New York: Russell Sage Foundation, 1993), 133–164. Henry S. Farber, "The

Decline of Unionization in the United States: What Can Be Learned From Recent Experience?" *Journal of Labor Economics*, 8: S75–S105. See Michael Goldfield, *The Decline of Organized Labor in the United States* (Chicago: University of Chicago Press, 1987).

67. Daniel J. B. Mitchell, *Unions, Wages, and Inflation* (Washington, DC: The Brookings Institution, 1980).

68. Richard B. Freeman and James L. Medoff, *What Do Unions Do?* (New York: Basic Books, 1984), 247.

69. Cf. The Milton S. Eisenhower Foundation and the Corporation for What Works, *The Millennium Breach: The American Dilemma, Richer and Poorer, Executive Summary*, 2nd ed. (Washington, DC: The Milton S. Eisenhower Foundation, 1998).

70. Baily, Burtless and Litan, ibid., 108–109.

71. Uwe Reinhardt, "Rationing Health Care: What It Is, What It Is Not, and Why We Can't Avoid It," in Altman and Reinhardt, op. cit., 63–100.

72. *Prosperity for American Families: The Gore Lieberman Economic Plan*, Addendum: The Gore-Lieberman Federal Budget and Surplus Plan; Table 3–Investments in Priorities ($billions), 182. See also http://a1604.gakamai.net/7/1604/1614/v 00000001 www.algore.com/pdf/gore-prosperity.pdf. This chart lists $170.2 billion total for "Investing in Education and Learning" over the ten-year period 2001 to 2010, or roughly $17 billion per year.

Chapter 9: Conclusions

1. Cf. Lawrence R. Jacobs and Robert Y. Schapiro, *Politicians Don't Pander: Political Manipulation and the Loss of Democratic Responsiveness* (Chicago: University of Chicago Press, 2000).

2. Stanley B. Greenberg's analysis of public opinion polls in his *Middle Class Dreams: The Politics and Power of the New American Majority* (New Haven: Yale University Press, 1996).

3. Robert M. Solow, "Should We Pay the Debt," *New York Review of Books*, Vol. XLVII, Number 15 (October 5, 2000): 7–9.

4. As the Baby Boom generation, those born between 1946 and 1964, enter their retirement years, outlays for Social Security, Medicare, and Medicaid benefits will increase sharply, while the number of working Americans whose taxes support these benefits will shrink in proportion to beneficiaries. The ratio of workers to retirees in 1960 was two to ten. Currently the ratio is three to ten, and will be five to ten by 2030. Over the next 35 years, the number of people over 65 will double, while those 20 to 64 will increase 20 percent in numbers. Hence, revenues from taxes dedicated to entitlement benefits will not keep up with the growing costs of providing benefits, and deficits will increase accordingly unless taxes are raised, benefits are cut, or new income is generated. U.S. Congress, Congressional Budget Office, *Long-Term Budgetary Pressures and Policy Options* (Washington, DC: U.S. Government Printing Office, 1998), 2–3.

Epilogue: Is Campaign Reform Politically Feasible?

1. See Robert Dreyfuss, "Reforming Reform," *The American Prospect*, Vol. 11, No. 26 (December 18, 2000): 26–30. Dreyfus offers a realistic appraisal of reform prospects.

2. Corrado et al., *Campaign Finance Reform: A Sourcebook*, op. cit., 337–338. David Broder, "Federal Lag, State Reform," *Washington Post*, July 18, 1999, B7.

3. Cf. Michael J. Malbin and Thomas L. Gais, *The Day after Reform: Sobering Campaign Finance Lessons from the American States* (Albany: The Rockefeller Institute Press, 1998).

4. For example, The Mellman Group for the Center for Responsive Politics, July, August, 1996.

5. Norris, *Critical Citizens*, 5–6ff.

6. Third, voters will be more likely to accept the costs of public financing if they are shown that the costs of the public financing of campaigns are small in comparison to other things government and business now willingly pay for. The annual advertising budgets of Proctor & Gamble and Philip Morris Company, the nation's two largest advertisers, added together are roughly equal to the amount spent by all federal and state political candidates and parties in a two-year election cycle. If public money matched private money, the amounts the taxpayers would be asked to provide would be quite modest compared to corporate advertising. Winning voter support would be somewhat easier if such comparisons were made, by helping the voter to ballpark the costs of reform. The entire cost of all federal elections, including primaries, in the 1996 election cycle was only $2.2 billion in a $10 trillion economy and a roughly $1 trillion 700 billion federal budget. Cf. Bradley Smith, "Faulty Assumptions and Undemocratic Consequences of Campaign Finance Reform," in Corrado et al., op. cit., 105.

7. Philip Converse's "The Nature of Belief Systems in Mass Publics" has been one of the most heavily cited articles in political science over several decades. Converse's analysis showed empirically the difference between elite and mass belief systems. What politically sophisticated elites could do, that ordinary voters could not, is link things up. They had "a functional interrelationship among attitudes." See Philip E. Converse, "The Nature of Belief Systems in Mass Publics," in David Apter (ed.), *Ideology and Discontent* (New York: Free Press, 1964).

8. Mellman, op. cit.

9. The choice is best presented as an all-or-nothing choice, where full reform means if a legislator voluntarily takes public money, he then would take no private money—"not one dime." Once legislators are allowed to take even some private money, the voter will lose confidence in reform, because she will lack any clear understanding of just how much private influence or corruption is left. All or nothing makes it probable that the people would see a clear choice, and would be more likely to choose reform.

10. Dreyfuss, op. cit.

11. At that time members did not want to vote for open recorded teller voting, since by informing voters, it would complicate members' need to satisfy interest groups and committee chairs at the same time. Opposition in Congress to recording votes was intense. But reformers in Congress reached out for and won the help of a national newspaper editorial campaign that denounced secrecy in government. Together, reformers and editors focused pressure on Congress as the vote neared. Interviews by the author at the time with the late Dick Conlon of the Democratic Study Group of the House; Judy Kurland, office of Congressman Thomas P. (Tip) O'Neill Jr.; and Congressman (later Speaker) O'Neill explained the inside-outside strategy that was used.

12. Norman J. Ornstein and David W. Rohde, "The Strategy of Reform: Recorded Teller

Voting in the U.S. House of Representatives," prepared for delivery at the 1974 Midwest Political Science Association Convention, Chicago, Illinois, April 23–27, 1974. Norman J. Ornstein, "Causes and Consequences of Congressional Change: Subcommittee Reforms in the House of Representatives 197–73," in Norman J. Ornstein (ed.), *Congress in Change: Evolution and Reform* (New York: Praeger, 1975), 111–112.

13. I'm indebted to my father-in-law, the late George Winchester Stone Jr. for this point.

14. Ordinarily the deliberations of the committee process should never be bypassed, lest unintended consequences of a piece of legislation remain hidden. But the process inevitably will be unusual when the rules of the game are themselves at issue.

Appendix: Two Prominent Reform Plans

1. Anthony Corrado, "Money and Politics: a History of Federal Campaign Finance Law," in Corrado, *Sourcebook* . . . op. cit., 25–59.

2. These are what the campaign laws identify as 501(c) 4 and 527 groups.

Cf. Congressional Research Service, "Report for Congress: RS20346: Campaign Finance Bills in the 106th Congress: Comparison of Shays-Meehan, as passed, with McCain-Feingold, as considered," Joseph E. Cantor, updated January 12, 2000. See http://www.cnie.org/nle/rsk-9.html.

Common Cause, "The Bipartisan Campaign Reform Act of 2001 (McCain-Feingold-Cochran)," http://www.commoncause.org/issue_agenda/secsum012401.htm.

The Public Citizen, "Key Provisions of the McCain-Feingold-Cochrane Bill (S.27)," http://www.citizen.org/congress/reform/mcfinkeyprovisions,htm.

Ray LaRaga, Institute of Governmental Studies, University of California, Berkeley, "McCain-Feingold Will Give Us the Wylys," http:/www.igs.Berkeley.edu:8880/publications/par/May 2000/LaRaga.html.

3. David Donnelly, Janice Fine, and Ellen S. Miller, "Going Public," *Boston Review*, Vol. 22, No. 2 (April/May 1997): 3–7; reprinted in Corrado et al., op. cit., 365–370.

4. Gebe Martinez and Carroll J. Doherty, "Narrower Campaign Finance Bill Still a Long Shot in Senate," *Congressional Quarterly Weekly Report*, Vol. 57, No. 36 (September 18, 1999): 2157–2159.

5. Ellen S. Miller, "The Hard Truth about McCain's Soft Money Ban," op. cit., 12. And Miller and Micah Sifry, "The Hard and the Soft of It," *The American Prospect*, Vol. 11, No. 25 (December 4, 2000), 8.

6. See the analysis by Public Citizen at http:/www.publiccampaign.org./reformtes.html.

7. Donnelly, Fine, and Miller, op.cit., 367–368.

8. Ornstein, Mann, et al., in Corrado, op. cit., 379–380.

9. Compare chapter two.

10. They would also permit national parties to share their added funds with state and local parties, but with tightened disclosure.

11. Donnelly et al., *Money and Politics: Financing Our Elections Democratically*, op. cit., 7. Cf. Ellen Miller, remarks at the Brookings Working Group on Campaign Finance Reform, Round 6

of Discussion: Topic: House Republican and House Democratic alternatives to McCain-Feingold, 5. Also see http://www.brook.edu/GS/CAMPAIGN/round6.htm. Federal candidates do not have to report contributions of less than $200, and so the incomes of those who contribute less than $200 are not known. But smaller contributions are also made disproportionately by wealthier people.

12. Pippa Norris (ed.), *Critical Citizens: Global Support for Democratic Governance* (New York: Oxford University Press, 1999), 5–6 ff.

13. Ibid. Public Campaign, The Power of Public Opinion, http://www.peoplefirst.org.pubop.html#CRP.

References

Aaron, Henry J. and William G. Gale (eds.). *Economic Effects of Fundamental Tax Reform* (Washington, D.C.: The Brookings Institution, 1996).

Aaron, Henry J. and Robert D. Reischauer (eds.). *Setting National Priorities: The 2000 Election and Beyond* (Washington, D.C.: The Brookings Institution, 1999).

Ackerman, Bruce and Anne Alstott. *The Stakeholder Society* (New Haven: Yale Univeristy Press, 1999).

Aldrich, John H. *Why Parties? The Origins and Transformation of Party Politics in America* (Chicago: The University of Chicago Press, 1995).

Alesina, Alberto, and Howard Rosenthal. *Partisan Politics, Divided Government, and the Economy* (Cambridge, UK and New York: Cambridge University Press, 1995).

Alexander, Herbert. *Financing Politics*, 4th ed. (Washington, D.C.: Congressional Quarterly Press, 1992).

Arnold, R. Douglas. *The Logic of Congressional Action*, (New Haven: Yale University Press, 1990).

Auerbach, Alan J. (ed.). *Fiscal Policy : Lessons from Economic Research* (Cambridge: M.I.T. Press, 1997).

Baily, Martin Neil, Gary Burtless, and Robert E. Litan. *Growth with Equity: Economic Policymaking for the Next Century* (Washington, D.C.: The Brookings Institution, 1993).

Baker, Edwin. *Advertising and a Democratic Press* (Princeton: Princeton University Press, 1994).

Baker, Ross K. *House and Senate*, 2nd ed. (New York: Norton, 1995).

Bartels, Larry M. and Lynn Vavreck (eds.) *Campaign Reform: Insight and Evidence* (Ann Arbor: The University of Michigan Press, 2000).

Baumol, William J., Sue Anne Batey Blackman, and Edward N. Wolff. *Productivity and American Leadership: The Long View* (Cambridge, Mass.: The MIT Press, 1992).

Becker, William E., and Wilam J. Baumol (eds). *Assessing Educational Practices: The Contribution of Economics* (Cambridge, Mass: The MIT Press, 1996).

Birch, Anthony H. *Concepts and Theories of Modern Democracy*, 2nd ed. (London and New York: Routledge, 2001).

Black, Earl, and Merle Black. *Politics and Society in the South* (Cambridge: Harvard University Press, 1987).

Bok, Derek. *The State of the Nation: Government and the Quest for a Better Society* (Cambridge, Mass.: Harvard University Press, 1996).

Burtless, Gary (ed.). *Does Money Matter? The Effect of School Resources on Student Achievement and Adult Successes* (Washington: D.C.: The Brookings Institution, 1996).

Cain, Bruce, John Ferejohn, and Morris Fiorina. *The Personal Vote: Constituency Service and Electoral Independence* (Cambridge, Mass.: Harvard University Press, 1987).

Campbell, Colin and Bert A. Rockman (eds.). *The Clinton Presidency: First Appraisals* (New York: Chatham House, 1995).

Carmines, G. Edward, and James A. Stimson. *Issue Evolution, Race and the Transformation of American Politics* (Princeton: Princeton University Press, 1989).

Clausen, Aage. *How Congressmen Decide: A Policy Focus* (New York: St. Martin's Press, 1973).

Clawson, Dan, Alan Neustadtl, and Mark Weller. *Dollars and Votes: How Business Campaign Contributions Subvert Democracy* (Philadelphia: Temple University Press, 1998).

President Clinton's New Beginning, Conducted by President Bill Clinton, The Complete Text, With Illustrations, of the Historic Clinton-Gore Economic Conference. Little Rock, Arkansas, December 14–15, 1992, (New York: Donald I. Fine, 1992).

Coase, R. H. *The Firm, The Market, and the Law* (Chicago: University of Chicago Press, 1990).

Cohen, Linda R. and Roger G. Noll. *The Technology Pork Barrel* (Washington, D.C.: The Brookings Institution, 1991).

Coleman, John J. *Party Decline in America: Policy, Politics, and the Fiscal State* (Princeton: Princeton University Press, 1996).

Commission on Campaign Finance Reform. The Association of the Bar of the City of New York, Richard Briffault, Executive Director, *Dollars and Democracy: A Blueprint for Campaign Finance Reform* (New York: Fordham University Press, 2000).

Committee on Political Parties, American Political Science Association, 1950. "Toward a More Responsible Two Party System," *American Political Science Review* 44: supplement to the March issue.

Connelly, William E. (ed.), *The Bias of Pluralism* (New York: Lieber-Atherton, 1973).

Corrado, Anthony, Thomas E. Mann, Daniel R. Ortiz, Trevor Potter, and Frank J. Sorauf (eds.). *Campaign Finance Reform: A Sourcebook* (Washington, D.C.: Brookings Institution Press, 1997).

Corrado, Anthony. *Campaign Finance Reform: Beyond the Basics* (New York: The Century Foundation Press, 2000).

Cox, Gary W., and Mathew D. McCubbins. *Legislative Leviathan* (Berkeley: University of California Press, 1993).

Cutler, Daivd M. "Review of John M. Quigley and Eugene Smolensky (eds.). *Modern Public Finance* (Cambridge, MA: Harvard University Press, 1996)," *Journal of Economic Literature* Vol. XXXIV (June 1996): 778–779.

Dahl, Robert A. *Who Governs* (New Haven: Yale University Press, 1961).

Dahl, Robert A. *Dilemmas of Pluralist Democracy* (New Haven: Yale University Press, 1982).

Danziger, Sheldon and Peter Gottschalk (eds.). *Uneven Tides: Rising Inequality in America* (New York: Russell Sage Foundation, 1993).

Davidson, Roger H. "The New Centralization on Capitol Hill," *Review of Politics* (10: 1988): 357.

Davidson, Roger H., and Walter J. Oleszek. *Congress and Its Members, 7th ed.* (Washington, D.C.: CQ Press, 2000).

Dertouzos, Michael L., Richard K. Lester, Robert M. Solow, and the MIT Commission on Industrial Productivity. *Made in America: Regaining the Productive Edge* (Cambridge, Mass.: The MIT Press, 1989.

Dixit, Avinash K. *The Making of Economic Policy: a Transaction-Cost Politics Perspective* (Cambridge, Massachusetts: The MIT Press, 1998).

Donnelly, David, Janice Fine, and Ellen S. Miller. *Money and Politics: Financing Our Elections Democratically* (Boston: Beacon Press, 1999).

Dodd, Lawrence C., and Calvin Jillson (eds.). *The Dynamics of American Politics: Approaches and Interpretations* (Boulder, Westview Press, 1994).

Dodd, Lawrence C., and Bruce I. Oppenheimer. *Congress Reconsidered, 6th ed.* (Washington, D.C.: CQ Press, 1997).

Drew, Elizabeth. *The Corruption of American Politics: What Went Wrong and Why* (Woodstock and New York: The Overlook Press, 1999).

Dwyre, Diana, and Victoria A. Farrar-Myers. *Legislative Labryrinth: Congress and Campaign Finance Reform* (Washington, D.C.: CQ Press, 2001).

Eldersveld, Samuel J., and Hanes Walton Jr. *Political Parties in American Society, 2nd ed.* (Boston: Bedford / St. Martins, 2000).

Ericson, David F., and Louisa Bertch Green (eds.). *The Liberal Tradition in American Politics: Reassessing the Legacy of American Liberalism* (New York and London: Routledge, 1999).

Ferguson, Thomas. *Golden Rule: The Investment Theory of Party Competition and the Logic of Money-Driven Political Systems* (Chicago: University of Chicago Press, 1995).

Fiorina, Morris P. *Congress: Keystone of the Washington Establishment, Second ed.* (New Haven: Yale University Press, 1989).

_____. *Divided Government, 2nd ed.* (Boston: Allyn and Bacon, 1996).

Fisher, Louis. *The Politics of Shared Power: Congress and the Executive, Fourth ed.* (College Station: Texas A&M University Press).

Frank, Robert H. *Choosing the Right Pond: Human Behavior and the Quest For Status* (New York: Oxford University Press, 1985).

_____. *Luxury Fever: Why Money Fails to Satisfy in an Era of Excess* (New York: Free Press, 1999).

Freeman, Richard B., and Lawrence F. Katz (eds.). *Differences and Changes in Wage Structures* (Chicago: University of Chicago Press, 1995).

Freeman, Richard B. and James L. Medoff. *What Do Unions Do?* (New York: Basic Books, 1984).

Galbraith, James K. *Created Unequal: The Crisis in American Pay* (Chicago: University of Chicago Press and the Century Foundation, 1998).

Gierzynski, Anthony. *Money Rules: Financing Elections in America* (Boulder, Colorado: Westview Press, 2000).

Glaser, James M. *Race, Campaign Politics, and the Realignment in the South* (New Haven: Yale University Press, 1996).

Glasser, Theodore L., (ed.). *The Idea of Public Journalism* (New York: The Guilford Press, 2000).

Goidel, Robert K., Donald A. Gross, and Todd G. Shields. *Money Matters: Consequences of Campaign Finance Reform in House Elections* (Lanham, Maryland: Rowman & Littlefield, 1999).

Gordon, Robert J. "Problems in the Measurement and Performance of Service-Sector Productivity in the United States." NBER Working Paper 4419. 1996.

Gramlich, Edward M. "Infrastructure Investment: A Review Essay," *Journal of Economic Literature* (Vol. XXII. September 1995): 1176–1196.

Gravelle, Jane G. *The Economic Effects of Taxing Capital Income* (Cambridge, Mass.: The MIT Press, 1994).

Green, John C., and Daniel M. Shea (eds.). *The State of the Parties: The Changing Role of Contemporary American Parties, 3rd ed.* (Lanham, Maryland: Rowman & Littlefield, 1999).

Greenberg, Stanley B. *Middle-Class Dreams: The Politics and Power of the New American Majority* (New Haven: Yale University Press, 1996).

Greenberg, Stanley B., and Theda Skocpol (eds.). *The New Majority: Toward Popular Progressive Politics* (New Haven: Yale University Press, 1997).

Guttman, Amy, and Dennis Thompson. *Democracy and Disagreement* (Cambridge, Mass: The Belknap Press of Harvard University Press, 1996).

Hacker, Jacob S. *The Road to Nowhere: The Genesis of President Clinton's Plan For Health Security* (Princeton: Princeton University Press, 1997).

Herrnson, Paul S. *Congressional Elections: Campaigning at Home and in Washington* (Washington, D.C.: CQ Press, 1998).

Jackson, Brooks. *Honest Graft: Big Money and the American Political Process* (Washington, D.C.: Farragut Publishing Company, 1990).

Jacobs, Lawrence R., and Robert Y. Shapiro. *Politicians Don't Pander: Political Manipulation and the Loss of Democratic Responsiveness* (Chicago: University of Chicago Press, 2000).

Jacobson, Gary C. *The Electoral Origins of Divided Government: Competition in U.S. House Elections 1946-1988* (Boulder: Westview Press, 1960).

Johnson, Dennis W. *No Place for Amateurs: How Political Consultants Are Reshaping American Democracy* (New York and London: Routledge, 2001).

Johnson, Haynes, and David S. Broder. *The System: The American Way of Politics at the Breaking Point* (Boston: Little, Brown and Company, 1996).

Kaplan, George A., Elsie R. Pamuk, John W. Lynch, Richard D. Cohen, and Jennifer L. Balfoour. "Inequality in Income and Morality in the United States: An Analysis of Morality and Potential Pathways," *British Medical Journal.* Vol. 312, 20 Vol. 312, 20 (April 1996): 999–1003.

Kennedy, Bruce P., Ichiro Kawachi, and Deborah Prothow-Stith. "Income Distribution and Morality: Cross Sectional Ecological Study of the Robin Hood Index in the United States," *British Medical Journal* Vol. 312, 20 (April 1996): 1004–1007.

Kiewiet, D. Roderick, and Mathew D. McCubbins. *The Logic of Delegation: Congressional Parties and the Appropriations Process* (Chicago: University of Chicago Press, 1991).

Krehbiel, Keith. *Information and Legislative Organization* (Ann Arbor: University of Michigan Press, 1991).

Keith, Bruce E., David B. Maglby, Candice J. Nelson, Elizabeth Orr, Mark Westlye, and Raymond E. Wolfinger. *The Myth of the Independent Voter* (Berkeley: University of California Press, 1992).

Key, V. O., Jr. *Politics, Parties, and Pressure Groups, 5th ed.* (New York: Thomas Y. Crowell, 1964).

Krugman, Paul. *Peddling Prosperity: Economic Sense and Nonsense in the Age of Diminished Expectations* (New York: W. W. Norton, 1994).

Kuttner, Robert Robert. *Everything for Sale: The Virtues and Limits of Markets* (Chicago: University of Chicago Press and the Century Foundation, 1999).

Ledbetter, James. *Made Possible By. . . . : The Death of Public Broadcasting in the United States* (New York: Verso Press, 1997).

Lester, Richard K. *The Productive Edge* (Cambridge, Mass.: The MIT Press, 1998).

Levine, Peter. *The New Progressive Era: Toward a Fair and Deliberative Democracy* (Lanham, Maryland: Rowman & Littlefield, 2000).

Levy, Frank. *The New Dollars and Dreams: American Incomes and Economic Change* (New York: Russell Sage, 1998).

Lewis, Charles, and the Center for Public Integrity. *The Buying of Congress: How Special Interests Have Stolen Your Right to Life, Liberty, and the Pursuit of Happiness* (New York: Avon Books, 1998).

Light, Paul C. *Government's Greatest Achievements of the Past Half Century* (Washington, D.C.: The Brookings Institution, Center for Public Service, No. 2 (November 2000).

Maass, Arthur. *Congress and the Common Good* (New York: Basic Books, 1983).

Maddison, Angus. "Growth and Slowdown in Advanced Capitalist Economics: Techniques of Quantitative Assessment," *Journal of Economic Literature*. Vol. XXV (June 1987): 649–698.

Magelby, David. *Outside Money: Soft Money and Issue Advocacy in the 1998 Elections* (Lanham, Maryland: Rowman & Littlefield, 1999).

Maisel, L. Sandy. *The Parties Respond: Changes in American Parties and Campaigns, Third ed.* (Boulder, Colorado: Westview Press, 1998).

———. *Parties and Elections in America: The Electoral Process* (Lanham, Maryland: Rowman & Littlefield, 1999).

Malbin, Michael J., and Thomas L. Gais. *The Day after Reform: Sobering Campaign Finance Lessons from the American States* (Albany, New York: The Rockefeller Institute Press, distributed by the Brookings Institution, 1998).

Maltzman, Forrest. *Competing Principals: Committees, Parties, and the Organization of Congress* (Ann Arbor: The University of Michigan Press, 1998).

Marcus, George E., and Russell L. Hanson (eds.). *Reconsidering the Democratic Public* (University Park, Pennsylvania: The Pennsylvania State University Press, 1993).

Mayer, William G. *The Divided Democrats: Ideological Unity, Party Reform, and Presidential Elections* (Boulder, Colorado: Westview Press/HarperCollins, 1996).

Mayhew, David R. *Divided We Govern* (New Haven: Yale University Press, 1991).

McCarthy, Nolan M., Keith T. Poole, and Howard Rosenthal. *Income Distribution and the Realignment of American Politics* (Washington, D.C.: AEI Press, 1997).

McConnell, Grant. Private Power and American Democracy (New York: Alfred A. Knopf, 1967).

Mill, John Stuart. *On Liberty, and Other Essays,* edited with an introduction by John Gray (New York: Oxford University Press, 1991).

Miller, Ellen. "The Hard Truth about McCain's Soft Money Band," *The American Prospect*. Vol. 11, No. 9 (March 13, 2000):12.

Miller, Warren E., and J. Merrill Shanks. *The New American Voter* (Cambridge: Harvard University Press, 1996).

Mishel, Lawrence, and Jared Bernstein. *The State of Working America 1998–99,* (Washington, D.C. Economic Policy Institute, 1999).

Murnane, Richard J., and Frank Levy. *Teaching the New Basic Skills: Principles for Educating Children to Thrive in a Changing Economy* (New York: Martin Kessler Books/The Free Press, 1996).

Neimi, Richard G., and Herbert F. Weisberg. *Controversies in Voting Behavior*, 3rd ed. (Washington, D.C.: CQ Press, 1993).

Nordhaus, William D. "Budget Deficits and National Savings," Challenge. (March–April 1996): 48.

Ornstein, Norman J. Thomas E. Mann, and Michael J. Malbin, *Vital Statistics on Congress, 1999–2000* (Washington, D.C.: AEI Press, 2000).

Okun, Arthur M. *Equality and Efficiency: The Big Tradeoff* (Washington, D.C.: The Brookings Institution, 1975).

Olson, Mancur. *The Rise and Decline of Nations* (New Haven: Yale University Press, 1982).

Olson, Mancur. *The Logic of Collective Action: Public Goods and the Theory of Groups* (Cambridge: Harvard, 1965).

Pechman, Joseph A. *Federal Tax Policy*, 5th ed. (Washington, D.C.: The Brookings Institution, 1987).

Poole, Keith T., and Howard Rosenthal. *Congress: a Political-Economic History of Roll Call Voting* (New York: Oxford University Press, 1997).

Rae, Nicol C. *Southern Democrats* (New York: Oxford University Press, 1994).

Rose-Ackerman, Susan. *Corruption and Government: Causes, Consequences, and Reform* (Cambridge, UK and New York: Cambridge University Press, 1999).

Rosencranz, E. Joshua, and the Brennan Center of the New York University School of Law. Report of the Twentieth Century Fund Working Group on Campaign Finance Litigation, *Buckley Stops Here: Loosening the Judicial Stranglehold on Campaign Finance Reform*, 1998.

Rosencranz, E. Joshua (ed.). *If Buckley Fell: a First Amendment Blueprint for Regulating Money in Politics* (New York: The Century Foundation Press, 1999).

Schram, Martin. *Speaking Freely: Former Members of Congress Talk about Money in Politics* (Washington, D.C.: Center for Reponsible Politics, 1995).

Schattschneider, E. E. *The Semisovereign People: A Realist's View of Democracy in America*, Reissued with an Introduction by David Adamany (Hinsdale, Illinois: The Dryden Press, 1975).

Schneider, Jerrold E. *Ideological Coalitions in Congress* (Westport, Conn: Greenwood Press, 1979)

Schieber, Sylvester J., and John B. Shoven (eds.). *Public Policy Toward Pensions*—a Twentieth Century Fund Book (Cambridge: MIT Press, 1997).

Scherer, F. M. *New Perspectives on Economic Growth and Technological Innovation* (Washington, D.C.: The Brookings Institution, 1998).

Schozman, K. L. and Sidney Verba. *Insult to Injury: Unemployment, Class, and Political Response* (Cambridge, MA: Harvard University Press, 1996).

Shafer, Byron E., and William J. M. Claggett. *The Two Majorities: The Issue Context of Modern American Politics* (Baltimore: The Johns Hopkins University Press, 1995).

Shapiro, Robert J. *Cut-and-Invest: A Budget of the United States Government: Progressive Policy Institute Policy Report No. 23.*

Sinclair, Barbara. *Unorthodox Lawmaking: New Legislative Processes in the U.S. Congress* (Washington, D.C.: CQ Press, 1997).

Sinclair, Barbara. *Legislators, Leaders, and Lawmaking: The U.S. House of Representatives in the Postreform Era* (Baltimore: Johns Hopkins University Press, 1998).

Skocpol, Theda. *Boomerang: Health Care Reform and the Turn Against Government* (New York: W. W. Norton, 1997).

Slemrod, Joel, and Jon Bakija. *Taxing Ourselves: A Citizen's Guide to the Great Debate over Tax Reform* (Cambridge, Mass.: The MIT Press, 1996).

Slemrod, Joel (ed.). *Tax Policy in the Real World* (Cambridge, UK and New York: Cambridge University Press, 1999).

Smeeding, Timothy. "America's Income Inequality: Where Do We Stand?" *Challenge* (September–October 1996): 45–53.

Solow, Robert. "Can a 'Third Way' Work? Five Responses to 'Equity with Employment,'" *Boston Review.* Vol. II, No. 3–4 (September 1997): 9.

_____. "Should We Pay the Debt?" *New York Review of Books.* Vol. XLVII, No. 15 (October 5, 2000): 8.

Sorauf, Frank. *Inside Campaign Finance Reform* (New Haven: Yale University Press, 1992).

Stiglitz, Joseph E. *The Economics of the Public Sector, Third ed.* (New York: W. W. Norton, 2000).

Sundquist, James L. *Dynamics of the Party System: Alignment and Realignment of Political Parties in the United States, Revised ed.* (Washington, D.C.: The Brookings Institution, 1983.

_____. *Politics and Policy: The Eisenhower, Kennedy, and Johnson Years* (Washington, D.C.: The Brookings Institution, 1968).

Teixeira, Ruy A. *The Disappearing American Voter*, (Washington, D.C.: The Brookings Institution, 1992), 58–105.

Teixeira, Ruy A., and Joel Rogers. *America's Forgotten Majority: Why the White Working Class Still Matters* (New York: Basic Books/Perseus Books Group, 2000).

Tobin, James. *Full Employment and Growth* (Brookfield: Edward Elgar 1996).

Truman, David B. *The Governmental Process* (New York: A. A. Knopf, 1951).

Uslander, Eric M. *American Political Parties: A Reader.* (Itasca, IL: F. E. Peacock Publishers, 1993).

Walker, Jack L. *Mobilizing Interest Groups in America: Patrons, Professions, and Social Movements* (Ann Arbor: The University of Michigan Press, 1991).

Wattenberg, Martin P. *The Decline of American Political Parties 1952–1992* (Cambridge: Harvard University Press, 1994).

West, Darrell M. and Burdett A. Loomis, *The Sound of Money: How Political Interests Get What They Want* (New York: W. W. Norton, 1998).

West, Darrell M. *Checkbook Democracy: How Money Corrupts Political Campaigns* (Boston: Northeastern University Press, 2000).

Wolff, Edward N. *Top Heavy: A Study of the Increasing Inequality of Wealth in America, A Twentieth Century Fund Report* (New York: The Twentieth Century Fund Press, 1995).

Name Index

Abramowitz, Alan I., 170n. 7
Aldrich, John H., 170n.4

Baily, Martin Neal, 76, 107, 126, 130
Bakija, Jon, 57
Barthelmas, Wes, 1, 2, 3
Baumol, William J., 56, 108, 110, 178n. 44
Beck, Paul Allen, 172n. 33
Bernheim, 62–63
Biden, Joseph, 1
Biggs, Jeffrey, 83
Bishop, John, 106, 123
Blank, Rebecca, 188n. 24
Bok, Derek, 49, 174n. 1
Bonifaz, John, 166n. 24
Bosworth, Barry P., 187n. 11
Bradley, Bill, 1, 17
Brady, David W., 183n. 19
Broder, David, 17, 46, 174n. 60
Bumpers, Dale, 79, 182n. 1
Burnham, Walter Dean, 37, 42
Burtless, Gary, 76, 107, 120, 163n. 23
Bush, George H. W., 40, 45
Bush, George W., 29, 161n. 3, 164n. 26
Byrd, Robert C., 86

Carmines, Edward G., 170n. 7
Carter, Jimmy, 74, 75
Clawson, Dan, 168n. 35
Clinton, Bill, 45, 74, 95, 164n. 26, 172n. 19, 174n. 54, 182n. 2, 186n. 63
Coase, R. H., 186n. 47
Cohen, Linda R., 130–31
Coleman, John J., 183n. 19
Converse, Philip, 197n. 7
Corrado, Anthony, 22, 155, 156, 157, 158–59, 161n. 2

Cox, Gary W., 91
Cranston, Alan, 165n. 7
Cressman, Derek, 29
Cutler, David, 66

Dahl, Robert A., 162n. 9, 180n. 7
Daschle, Tom, 83, 87
Davidson, Roger H., 85, 87–88
DeConcini, Dennis, 165n. 7
Dionne, E. J., Jr., 164n. 26
Donnelly, David, 164n. 1, 167n. 32
Drew, Elizabeth, 165n. 3, 169n. 52
Dreyfuss, Robert, 174n. 56, 196n. 1

Eisner, Robert, 121, 177n. 43

Ferguson, Thomas, 164n. 3
Fine, Janice, 164n. 1, 167n. 32
Fiorina, Morris, 71–72
Fisher, Louis, 72
Foley, Tom, 83–84, 86
Frank, Robert H., 163n. 17
Frankel, Max, 25
Freeman, Richard B., 102, 135

Gale, William G., 66
Gephardt, Richard, 20, 81, 84
Gingrich, Newt, 46, 84, 153
Glenn, John, 16, 165n. 7
Gordon, Robert H., 110–11, 112, 116
Gore, Al, 10, 45–46, 82, 161n. 3
Gramlich, Edward M., 132
Greenberg, Stanley B., 42, 144, 181n. 15

Hanushek, Eric, 122
Hart, Gary, 2
Hastert, Dennis, 84

Hatch, Orrin, 40
Haveman, Robert H., 135
Hechman, James, 99, 126, 184n. 38, 185n. 38
Herrnson, Paul, 182n. 9, 183n. 17
Humphrey, Hubert H., 2, 166n. 26

Jackson, Brooks, 165n. 7
Jacobs, Lawrence R., 162n. 14, 169n. 3
Jacobson, Gary C., 38
Johnson, Dennis W., 174n. 51
Johnson, Haynes, 17, 46, 174n. 60

Kaplan, George A., 104
Katz, Lawrence, 102
Keating, Charles, 72, 165n. 7
Kennedy, Bruce P., 103
Kennedy, Robert F., 1
Kennedy, Ted, 75
Key, V. O., Jr., 8, 77
Koford, Kenneth, 184n. 36
Krugman, Paul, 100

Lawrence, Robert, 130
Levy, Frank, 99, 187n. 11
Lewis, Charles, 165n. 5
Lieberman, Joe, 10, 137, 164n. 26
Litan, Robert E., 76, 107
Lott, Trent, 87, 90

Maass, Arthur, 180n. 8
Maddison, Angus, 110, 178n. 44
Magleby, David B., 165n. 10, 171n. 9
Malbin, Michael J., 22, 155
Maltzman, Forrest, 183n. 28
Mann, Thomas E., 22, 155, 156, 157, 158–59, 161n. 2
Mansfield, Edwin, 119, 129–30
Mayhew, David R., 181n. 18
Mazzoli, Roman L., 184n. 30
McCain, John, 16, 165n. 7
McConnell, Grant, 8, 77
McConnell, Mitch, 69, 180n. 1

McCubbins, Mathew D., 91
Medoff, James L., 135
Mill, John Stuart, 168n. 42, 169n. 60
Miller, Ellen S., 29, 156, 164n. 1, 167n. 32
Miller, Warren E., 92
Mirrless, James, 66
Mishel, Lawrence, 187n. 11
Mitchell, George, 83, 87
Mondale, Walter, 65

Nelson, Candice J., 165n. 10, 171n. 9
Nelson, Richard R., 121
Nichols, Jim, 87
Niskanen, William, 55
Noll, Roger G., 130–31
Nordhaus, William, 58, 66

O'Donnell, Lawrence, 84
O'Neill, Tip, 2, 85, 197n. 11
Okun, Arthur M., 2, 31–32
Oleszek, Walter, 88
Oppenheimer, Bruce I., 182n. 13
Ornstein, Norman J., 22, 155, 156, 157, 182n. 7
Ortiz, Daniel R., 161n. 2

Patterson, Thomas E., 163n. 23
Pechman, Joseph A., 51
Peterson, Paul E., 72
Phelps, Edmund S., 135
Poole, Keith T., 185n. 38
Potter, Trevor, 161n. 2

Rae, Nicol C., 183n. 20
Raskin, Jamin, 166n. 24
Rayburn, Sam, 85
Reagan, Ronald, 40, 83
Rehnquist, William, 165n. 15
Reigle, Donald, 165n. 7
Reischauer, Robert D., 50
Robb, Charles S., 183n. 30
Rogers, Joel, 161n. 5, 172n. 17

Rose-Ackerman, Susan, 161n. 6
Rosencranz, E. Joshua, 167n. 26, 168n. 37
Rosenthal, Howard, 162n. 15, 174n. 55
Russakoff, Dale, 45–46

Salisbury, Robert H., 89
Scalia, Antonin, 21, 165n. 15
Schattschneider, E. E., 8, 77
Scherer, F. M., 190n. 45, 192n. 3
Schlozman, K. L., 92
Shanks, J. Merrill, 92
Shapiro, Robert J., 54–55
Shapiro, Robert Y., 162n. 14, 169n. 3
Shea, Daniel M., 174n. 57
Silvert, Kalman H., 169n. 61
Sinclair, Barbara, 183n. 26
Skocpol, Theda, 187n. 64
Slaughter, Louise, 84
Slemrod, Joel, 57, 66, 179n. 58
Smeeding, Timothy, 103
Smith, Bradley A., 162n. 9, 197n. 6
Smith, Steven S., 182n. 13
Sniderman, Paul M., 170n. 5
Solow, Robert M., 2, 105, 134, 142

Sorauf, Frank J., 161n. 2, 165n. 6
Stiglitz, Joseph E., 2, 177n. 43
Stimson, James A., 170n. 7
Stonecash, Jeffrey, 93
Sundquist, James L., 181n. 13, 182n. 2

Taylor, Paul, 22, 155, 156, 157
Teixeira, Ruy A., 45–46
Thomas, Clarence, 31, 165n. 15
Thurow, Lester, 2
Tobin, James, 2, 60, 177n. 44, 178n. 44
Truman, Harry S., 9
Tsongas, Paul, 2

Verba, Sidney, 92

Walker, Jack L., 88–89
Wattenberg, Martin P., 172n. 19
Wilkinson, R. G., 104
Wirth, Tim, 2
Wise, Bob, 83
Wolff, Edward N., 179n. 61
Wright, Gavin, 121

Subject Index

advertising: attack, 18, 20–23, 31, 43, 50, 85, 140, 150, 155, 157, 167n. 32; campaign (*see* campaign, advertising); issue, 18, 28, 30, 70, 75, 85, 140, 155, 157; political, 18, 19, 20–23, 25, 27, 31, 43, 139–40, 150, 156–57, 166n. 26, 197n. 6
advocacy: expenditures, 21–22, 155; express, 22, 27, 157; issue, 21–22, 27, 28, 156, 157
Alaska, 28
allocation of resources, 2, 3, 4, 5, 7–8, 16–17, 69, 71–72, 105, 109, 114, 117, 139–41, 142–43, 144, 150 (*see also* campaign finance reform, reallocation of wasted funds and)
American political system, 1–3, 9, 75, 93, 139, 143, 159, 162n. 7, 164n. 26; anomalies in theories of, 8–10; distrust of, 17, 76; money in the, 1, 3, 5, 13, 20, 24, 32, 45, 148
Arizona, 22, 28, 40
Arkansas, 28
Atari Democrats. *See* Democrats, Atari
Austin v. Michigan State Chamber of Commerce, 14, 16, 20–21

ballot: access, 95; initiatives, 144
British Disease, 108–109, 116, 143
Buckley v. Valeo, 14, 16, 18–19, 20, 21, 22, 24, 26, 140
business subsidies, 2 (*see also* federal waste, business subsidies; tax, subsidies)

California, 28, 40, 147
campaign: advertising, 2, 4, 8, 17, 19, 20–23, 25, 27–28, 30, 85, 157; money, 70, 131, 155

campaign contributions, 4, 5, 13–19, 29–30, 33, 35, 47, 50, 52, 56, 61, 69–70, 72, 77, 96, 97, 140–41, 148, 151, 155, 157–59, 165n. 7, 166n. 21, 167n. 32; direct, 22; out-of-state, 27–28; private, 3–5, 13, 16, 19, 20–23, 31, 75, 148, 151, 154, 155, 156, 168n. 32
campaign contributors, 1, 2, 3, 6–7, 9–10, 14–15, 24, 31, 43–44, 47, 50, 60, 68, 72, 82, 85, 96, 132, 137, 139, 141, 148–49, 151, 153, 155, 157; corporate, 28, 72, 155; corrupting, 6, 14, 16, 19, 26–27, 155, 166n. 26; influence of, 13, 17, 174n. 2, 192n. 2; labor union, 28, 155; large, 29, 155; private, 16, 155; small, 27, 30; wealthy, 5, 14
campaign finance, 3, 8, 27, 72, 80, 89, 150
campaign finance law, 1, 3, 27, 33, 145, 147–48, 155; loopholes in, 1, 17, 28, 32, 145, 151, 153, 154, 155
campaign finance reform: aggregations of wealth and, 14, 21, 24; Bush Pioneers, 29; contribution limits (*see* contribution limits); costs of, 23, 149–50; democratic representation and, 5, 24, 32; economic output and, 60–61; effects of, 5, 17–18, 24, 76, 105; elements of, 26–31; enacting into law, 26, 32, 139, 151–53; expenditure limits and (*see* expenditure limits); feasibility of, 13–33, 147–54; in the states (*see also* individual states), 19, 22, 28–29, 147, 167n. 31; incentives of congresspersons and, 27–28, 155–56; incomes and, 14, 60–61, 62–65; independent expenditures and, 16, 20–23, 27; issue advocacy *vs.* express advocacy (*see also* advocacy, express and issue); loopholes of, 3, 17, 28, 32;

matching funds and, 18–19, 20–25, 28, 30–31; McCain-Feingold (*see* McCain-Feingold bill); movement, 145; Okun's theory, 31–32; Ornstein, Mann, Taylor, Malbin, & Corrado plan, 22, 155, 156, 157, 158–59, 182n. 7; party systems and programs and, 75–76; political action committees and (*see also* PACs), 14, 27; political debts to contributors (*see also* contributors; corruption; quids pro quo), 13, 16–17, 20, 29; pork, 14–15, 131, 132, 192n. 2; post reform money chase, 49–68; public financing of campaigns and (*see also* public financing of campaigns), 4, 5–6, 18, 20–23, 26, 28–31; quids pro quo and, 13–14, 20, 29 (*see also* quids pro quo); reallocation of wasted funds and, 15–16, 51–58, 60–67, 142–43, 150 (*see also* allocation of resources); soft money and (*see* soft money), 1, 22, 28; waste and, 14–16, 44, 49–68; weaknesses in current proposals of, 30, 156–59
campaign spending, 1, 16, 21, 155, 166n. 22
campaigns: privately financed, 3–5, 13, 16, 27; tv-centered, 2, 8, 43, 139
candidates, 32, 155, 158, 164n. 26; congressional, 42; presidential, 27, 50, 70
capitalism, 32, 105
child care, 9, 45, 67, 94, 105, 123, 136, 143, 144, 190n. 44
Citizens for Tax Justice (CTJ), 55–56
Clinton: administration, 40, 128; health plan, 17
coalitions: congressional, 7, 8, 87, 89, 91, 184n. 38, 185n. 46; interest group, 8; partisan, 6, 8, 73–74, 80; transaction costs of, 6, 91–92, 141; voter, 8, 74
congressional districts, 15, 40, 44–45, 70–71, 80, 81, 91, 92
congressional members, 6, 50, 68, 69, 71–73, 77, 80, 82–83, 93, 131, 141, 148, 151, 152, 154, 157–58, 192n. 2; Democrat, 2, 7, 10, 42–43, 44, 71, 79, 82, 85–86, 97, 129, 143, 145, 148, 171n. 15, 182n. 2, 183n. 21, 185n. 45; incumbent, 7, 42–44, 70, 71, 81, 148, 152; independence of, 70, 94, 184n. 30; leaders, 87–88; partisanship of, 82–83, 87, 88–89, 90, 92; party vote of, 70, 71, 80–81; personal vote of, 70, 71, 80, 81; Republican, 42–43, 87, 97, 148, 171n. 15
consumption, 8, 113, 116, 187n. 5
contribution limits, 22, 27–31, 32, 140, 157
corporations, 22, 23, 28, 45, 54–56, 130–31, 136
corruption, 13, 19, 20–21, 26–28, 31–32, 50, 144, 161n. 6, 187n. 1; magnitude of, 13–17; of candidates, 24, 32, 157–58, 197n. 9; of officeholders, 6, 18–19, 20, 32, 157–58, 197n. 9; remedies for, 31–32
Council of Economic Advisors (CEA), 113–14
Crisis School, the, 109–10

Day v. Holahan, 21, 166n. 26
democracy, 3, 4, 5–6, 18, 21, 24, 25–27, 32, 93, 98, 144, 167n. 26, 181n. 16, 182n. 2; capitalist, 32 (*see also* capitalism); representative, 14, 21; social, 120, 122
democratic: leadership, 46, 82; programs, 74–75; representation, 4, 5–7, 30, 32, 155; system, 14, 21, 26
Democratic Party, 1, 3, 5, 10, 68, 72, 75, 76–77, 86, 95, 139–40, 143, 185n. 45; and campaign reform, 49–68, 76–77; collective interests of, 74–75, 93; decline of, 3, 7, 9–10, 35–47, 49, 139, 143; identification, 36–38, 41, 80; ideology of, 74–75, 90–91; partisan interests groups of, 80–81, 94–95, 170n. 7; party messages of, 41–42, 46, 49, 81–85; party services to candidates, 85; party vote of, 80–81; sources of party strength, 76, 79; theories of cohesion of, 79–96, 141, 144–45; theories of party weakness, 74–76, 94–96; transaction costs

of coalitions of, 91–92, 96, 141; unifying forces of, 79–96, 141, 145, 183n. 21; voter base of the, 1, 3, 7, 9–10, 35, 36, 37, 41, 43, 45, 49, 74, 79, 95, 100, 139, 143, 144, 171n. 15

Democrats, 7, 9–10, 36–47, 67, 69, 74–75, 83, 89, 90, 91–92, 94, 96, 137, 145, 161n. 3, 164n. 26, 169n. 2, 175n. 2, 184n. 30; Atari, 2; Blue Dog, 94; congressional, 2, 7, 37, 40, 84; conservative, 44, 86, 94–95; liberal, 86, 89; northern, 2; politicians, 35, 41, 42, 45, 49, 65, 81, 139; progressive, 44, 95; southern, 43, 44, 79, 81, 86, 94; young, 2

disclosure requirements, 22, 157

distribution of wealth and income, 14, 76, 102, 103–106, 134, 179n. 61, 189n. 27; mortality rates and, 104–106, 163n. 23

education, 7, 9, 37, 46, 49, 50, 67, 75, 76, 90, 101, 104, 116, 119, 120–26, 134, 136, 137, 143, 144, 151, 161n. 3, 164n. 26; investments in, 121–26, 187n. 1; national, 9, 120–21; programs, 10, 98; public, 123, 187n. 1, 190n. 44; spending, 10, 106, 122, 137; teacher training and, 124; test scores, 121–22, 124–25, 129, 136, 161n. 4

elections, 7, 21, 38, 82, 144, 150, 156, 159, 161n. 3, 167n. 31, 168n. 36, 170n. 7, 182n. 7; 1980, 41; 1988 presidential, 10; 1992, 41–42, 139; 1994, 35, 41–42, 139; 1996, 13, 28, 42, 90, 139, 156, 158, 169n. 1, 197n. 6; 1998, 42, 45, 85, 139, 152, 169n. 1; 2000, 10, 29, 42, 44–45, 50, 75, 82, 137, 139, 152, 169n. 2; congressional, 29, 82, 156, 171n. 15; law, 21–22, 28; resources for, 21, 23

environmental issues, 2, 50, 72, 76, 93, 132, 151, 152

equal protection, 21, 32

Europe, 37, 102, 108, 110, 122, 124, 127, 129, 178n. 44, 192n. 5

expenditure limits: campaign finance reform and, 18–19, 22–23, 30, 150, 166n. 22; democracy and, 24; *versus* matching funds, 23–25; voluntary, 23, 156

federal: bureaucracies, 71; debt, 50, 60, 62, 73; funds, 47, 49, 57, 70; government, 134, 137; programs, 2, 51, 58, 70–71, 130, 134; spending, 16, 52, 66, 74; subsidies, 15, 55, 131

Federal Election Commission (FEC), 27, 28, 156, 166n. 22

Federal Election Commission v. Furgatch, 22

federal waste, 3, 5, 15–16, 23, 44, 49, 50, 51, 59, 65, 67, 69, 95, 130–31, 137, 139–40, 144, 149, 152, 168n. 36, 181n. 16; business tax and non-tax subsidies and, 54–57, 59, 130, 139; direct program waste, 51, 58, 59–60, 71; individual tax expenditures and, 51, 52–54, 57, 59; reducing, 51–58, 60, 65, 67–68, 116; rent seeking as, 51, 56–57, 139; total of, 51; uncollected revenue as, 51, 57, 59, 139

First Amendment, 21–22, 24, 27–28, 32, 140, 166n. 22, 167nn. 26

Florida, 40

Fourteenth Amendment, 21

free: speech, 18–19, 20–22, 166n. 22; trade, 121

fundraising, 18, 26, 29, 43, 44–45, 69, 158

globalization, 45–46, 99, 116, 123, 143

Gore-Lieberman campaign, 10, 137, 164n. 26

government: divided, 75–76; local, 132; spending, 16, 52, 66, 74; state, 132

grassroots reform, 151, 152, 153

Gross: Domestic Product (GDP), 113–15, 122, 133, 142; National Product (GNP), 73

hard money, 28, 29, 156

Head Start Program, 125

health care, 45–46, 104, 105, 133–34, 136–37, 151, 161n. 3, 163n. 23, 164n. 26, 169n. 3, 170n. 3; long-term, 37, 49
health insurance, 7, 9, 15, 52, 67, 132–35, 136–37, 143, 170n. 3, 187n. 11; companies, 133–34; universal, 9, 15, 35, 37, 46, 66, 74, 79, 134, 139, 144, 163n. 23

incumbents, 26, 30, 41, 42–43, 70, 71, 82, 148, 156–57, 169n. 2
inequality, 8, 24, 68, 76, 93, 97–117, 120, 126, 135, 155, 163n. 23, 187n. 1, 188nn. 11; cross-national comparisons of, 102–103; declining wages (*see also* wages), 100–101, 103, 116; Democrats in context of, 143–44; growth of, 1, 99–101, 143–44, 179n. 61; harm to individuals of, 15, 103–106; harm to the economy, 105–106; income, 99, 101, 102–103, 188n. 11, 189n. 27; politics of, 97–117; remedies for, 133–35, 137, 140, 143; sources of, 98–100; weakening of democratic legitimacy and, 21, 97–117; wealth, 101–102
inflation, 110–12
infrastructure, 119, 132, 136; spending, 132
interest groups, 4, 6, 8, 16–17, 70–74, 77, 85, 93, 94, 95–96, 140, 155, 164n. 26, 181n. 16, 197n. 11; campaign contributions of, 5, 14, 30; coalitions of (*see* coalitions); democracy and, 4, 5–6; local, 7, 14, 70, 141; partisan, 6, 88–89; powerful, 16; system of, 5; wealthy, 5, 20, 21, 23, 24, 31–32, 73, 155, 157
Internet, the, 25–26
investment: domestic business, 115; government, 97–98, 112, 115–16, 119; human capital, 101, 104, 116, 121, 126, 192n. 5; in education (*see* education, investments in); infrastructure, 132; national, 65; private, 8, 9, 51, 67–68, 97–99, 105, 109, 113, 115–16, 119, 137, 142, 143, 177n. 42; private return on, 119, 129–30; productive, 119; public (*see* public investments); rate of, 114–15, 142; social return on, 119, 130; spending, 128; technological, 129

Japan, 110, 122, 124, 177n. 42, 178n. 44, 192n. 5

Keating Five, 16, 18

labor: abroad, 101; cheap, 108; force, 134; movement, 135
legislation, 8, 91, 93; buying, 1; pork barrel, 14–15
legislators, 1, 4, 5, 70, 71, 80–81, 85, 95, 139, 181n. 16, 184n. 36; conflicts of interest of, 6; contributions influencing, 5, 13, 18–19, 70, 197n. 9; corruption of, 6, 31, 197n. 9
lobbyists, 3, 14, 17, 29, 50, 72, 89, 131; business, 17, 72; grassroots, 4, 70, 75, 152
local interests, 4, 6

Maine, 22
Massachusetts, 22
matching funds, 20–23, 26, 28, 30, 150, 166nn. 20, 168n. 32; public financing of, 18–19, 36, 149–50, 157, 167n. 32, 168nn. 32, 197n. 6; to counter attack ads, 31, 140; *versus* expenditure limits, 23
McCain-Feingold bill, 23, 28, 155, 156, 157, 159
media, 4, 16–17, 25, 31, 43, 45, 82, 85, 150, 151, 156; public, 18, 25–26, 31 (*see also* public broadcasting)
Medicaid, 76, 132, 196n. 4
Medicare, 50, 76, 161n. 3, 196n. 4
Minnesota, 19
mortality rates and income distribution, 103–106, 163n. 23

national priorities, 3, 4, 5, 16, 50, 51, 54, 66–67, 69, 137, 140
national savings, 43, 44, 60, 67, 113, 177nn. 42, 178n. 48, 187n. 5, 191n. 65; costs of no plan; elements of, 61–65; opposition to, 60–61; plan, 60, 67, 68, 97, 109, 137; voluntary, 61–65, 116, 137, 188n. 11
New Growth Theory, 114–15
New York, 147
Nixon v. Shrink Missouri Government PAC, 29
No Crisis School, the, 110

OECD systems, 133
Okun's countervailing resources theory of reform, 31–32

PACs, 14, 27, 31, 155, 156
parties, 4, 6, 8, 22, 32, 69, 73, 77, 85, 94, 98, 141, 155, 158; cohesion of, 95–96, 141; contributors to, 155; cross-cutting cleavages in, 4–5, 7–8; goals of, 80; identification, 38; incumbency return rates of, 7, 71; independent, 75; interest groups and, 85, 88–89, 93, 95–96; leaders of, 4, 6, 70, 83, 85, 91, 92; minor, 31; need for, 75–76; public funding of, 31; relative issues and, 69–71, 92–93; strong, 70, 71, 74, 75; system of, 5, 75; unifying forces in, 6, 7, 79–96, 141; voter base of, 5, 6, 72, 85; voter partisanship (*see* voter, partisanship of); weak, 69–77, 94, 95–96
partisanship, 7, 79–80
Pennsylvania, 45
Pluralism, 3–4, 7–8, 69–71, 73
pluralist theory, 3–5, 8, 43, 69–70, 73–75, 77, 89; ever shifting coalitions theory, 8, 95–96; political pluralism, 7–8; social pluralism, 7, 70, 73, 80
political: debts, 27, 31, 140; equality, 32; leaders, 66, 152
popular programs, 4, 7, 35, 37, 44, 47, 49, 68, 69, 71, 77, 79, 97, 139, 141

pork, 14–15, 131, 132, 192n. 2
poverty, 102, 111, 135, 189n. 27
private investment. *See* investment, private
productivity, 132, 134, 178n. 44, 190n. 49; health care and, 132–34, 136–37; remedies, 135–37; U.S., 126–29, 133, 142, 192n. 5
productivity growth, 1, 9, 63, 66, 68, 76, 93, 97–117, 119, 126, 129, 132, 134, 140, 142, 187n. 5, 195n. 60; benefits of, 107, 121; British Disease and, 108–109, 116, 143; education and, 98, 99, 101, 121; effects on aging U.S. population, 63; gains from faster, 111, 113–15, 117; growth in, 98, 114–15; levels and rates of, 107–111, 112–17, 143, 178n. 44; new economy and, 98, 111–12; politics of, 97–117; public investment and, 97–99, 106, 109, 112; slowdown controversy and, 109–111, 115–16; sources of, 97–98, 106–107, 110–12, 113–15
public: capital, 106, 116; goods, 8, 94, 104, 105, 107–108, 119; investment (*see* investment, public); money, 3, 14–15, 72, 148; policy, 7, 18, 71, 77, 112; subsidies, 23
public broadcasting (*see also* media, public): deliberative democracy and, 31; expanding, 18, 25–26, 31, 32
public financing of campaigns, 4, 5–6, 18, 20–23, 26, 28–32, 35, 36, 114, 140, 147, 148–49, 150, 155–59, 166n. 26, 168nn. 32, 197n. 6; congressional, 97; voluntary, 18–20
public investments, 5, 8, 9, 10, 42, 51, 65, 67–68, 69, 94, 96, 97–99, 105–106, 109, 112, 113, 115–17, 119–37, 139–40, 142–43, 144, 150, 192nn. 2; health insurance as, 132–34, 136–37; in education, 120–26, 136, 187n. 1; infrastructure and, 119, 132, 136; job training subsidies as, 119, 126–29, 136 (*see also* training, job); technology policy and, 119, 129–31, 136

quids pro quo, 14, 19, 20–21, 29, 31, 60, 89, 139, 157, 174n. 2 (*see also* campaign finance reform, quids pro quo)

race, 10, 86, 170n. 7
Reagan administration, 36
Regan v. Taxation Without Representation, 21
rent seeking, 51, 56–57
Republican Party, 38, 72, 74, 84, 144
Republicans, 7, 35, 36–37, 40, 41–43, 44, 45, 67, 73–74, 86, 89, 90, 91–92, 94, 96–97, 139, 144, 145, 148, 169n. 2, 171n. 15; moderate, 90
research, 121, 136; and development, 129, 131, 136, 161n. 4; investment in, 129–30; tax credits for, 130, 136
Robin Hood Index, 104

saving. *See* national saving
securities industry, 56, 61
social: insurance, 42, 51, 94, 96, 123, 144, 150; issues, 10, 95, 126, 163n. 23; security, 52, 61–62, 80, 134–35, 150, 161n. 3, 196n. 4; wages, 135, 137; welfare, 67, 164n. 26, 185n. 38
soft money, 1, 22, 28, 155, 157, 167n. 27
South, the, 40, 86
standard of living. *See* U.S., standard of living
status quo, 4, 24, 50
Strong Parties Theory, 3, 5–8, 44, 45, 74, 75–76, 80, 89, 92, 141, 144, 181n. 16; campaign finance reform and, 5–8, 141; unifying forces of, 75–76, 89

tax: avoidance, 55, 57; breaks, 56; business, 51, 54–57, 130; code, 66, 188n. 11; credit for contributions, 158–59; cuts, 50, 74, 97, 105, 137, 139–40, 161n. 3; earned income credit, 52, 134–35, 137; evasion, 57; expenditures, 2, 13, 51–54, 55, 59, 139, 175n. 7; incentives, 10, 130; increases, 23,
49, 65–67, 90, 142, 179n. 61; laws, 57, 74; liability, 55; progressive, 53, 65–67, 137, 188n. 11; rates, 66–67; reductions, 105; revenues, 51, 65–67, 107; subsidies, 54–56, 59, 131, 139, 175n. 7
Tax Reform Act of 1986
taxation: economic growth and, 105, 107
taxes: capital gains, 53–54, 94; corporate, 51, 52, 54–57, 59, 130; home mortgage deduction, 52–53; individual, 51, 52–53, 57, 59; on social security income, 52; on wages, 134; property, 53
taxpayers, 60, 134, 150, 168n. 36, 179n. 61, 197n. 6
teachers: pay rates of, 124, 136; training of, 124
technological innovation, 100, 113, 129–30, 143
technologies, 110, 116, 119; information, 111; new, 107, 111, 115, 121, 129; policy, 129–31, 136
term limits, 24, 84, 144
Texas, 40
ticket-splitting, 41, 45
training, 116, 120–21, 135, 137; community-college, 127–28; job, 9, 37, 49, 50, 67, 98, 101, 119, 126–29, 136, 143, 144, 161n. 4, 164n. 26; policies, 134
transfer pricing, 55–56

U.S.: economy, 1, 2, 3, 9, 10, 45, 98, 100, 102, 109–10, 111–15, 137, 139, 143, 145, 161n. 4, 177n. 42; government, 3, 130, 134, 137, 187n. 8; House of Representatives, 4, 94, 139, 155, 171n. 15; industry, 130; Senate, 44, 89, 94, 139, 153, 155, 156, 171n. 15, 183n. 21; standard of living, 104, 106–108, 111, 113, 115, 116, 119, 126, 135, 178n. 44, 195n. 60; Supreme Court, 6, 14, 18, 20, 22, 24, 29, 42, 157, 166n. 26, 167n. 32

U.S. Congress, 1, 2, 3, 4, 6, 9, 14, 16, 17–19, 22, 24, 26, 29, 35, 36, 37, 43, 44–45, 47, 49, 52, 70–71, 73–75, 76, 79, 90, 93, 96, 105, 106, 114, 128, 131, 135, 140, 143, 145, 147, 148–49, 151, 153–54, 155, 197n. 11; coalitions in, 6, 7, 8, 87, 89, 91, 184n. 38, 185n. 46; control of, 45, 79; incumbents in, 27, 41, 42, 44; majority party in, 7, 10, 37, 44; minority party in, 7

underinsured, the, 133, 136, 170n. 3

unemployment, 108, 111

uninsured, the, 52, 132, 136, 170n. 3

unions, 2, 7, 22, 27, 28, 30, 45, 72, 94, 103, 129, 135, 137, 144, 156

voter: registration, 36; turnout, 37, 44, 45, 149; volatility, 37–40

voters, 4–5, 6, 7–8, 9, 14, 15–16, 18–19, 21, 23, 26, 28, 30–31, 32, 37–41, 43, 45–46, 51, 69–70, 71, 76, 80, 93, 94, 139, 141, 145, 147, 148–50, 152–53, 156, 159, 168n. 35, 170nn. 8, 179n. 61, 181n. 16, 197n. 6, 197n. 11; African-American, 86; base, 82, 85, 97; choices, 25; coalitions of (*see* coalitions); Democratic, 36–37, 41, 45–47, 74, 94, 171n. 15; issues, 45–46, 65–66, 76, 140–41; loyalty of, 10, 36, 44–45, 81; partisanship of, 6, 36–38, 41, 45, 71, 80–81, 82, 182n. 7; preferences of, 9, 18, 77; Republican, 36, 37, 46, 74; southern, 95; swing, 85

wages: declining real, 100, 116, 143; growing, 107, 195n. 60; minimum, 100, 103, 134–35, 137; offsets to declining, 100, 103, 105, 107; real, 100, 102, 116, 143; U.S., 100–101, 128

waste: constituency, 14–16; contributor, 14–16, 35, 192n. 2; direct, 51; federal (*see* federal waste); in the health system, 15, 133–34, 136; indirect, 51; reduction, 116; resource, 99

Weak Parties Theory, 69–77, 96; arguments against, 71–75

workers: educated, 101; immigrant, 100; low-skilled, 134–35, 161n. 4; reskilled, 116; rights of, 135; skilled, 100, 120, 128, 161n. 4; unskilled, 99–101, 103, 116

Working Group on Electoral Democracy, 23

World War II, 2, 40, 113